MILESTONES IN CINEMA

50 Visionary Films & Filmmakers

© DAVID WORTH / 2014

Contact: davidworthfilm@gmail.com

Table of Contents:

Forward By: Professor Richard Walter, UCLA

Preface By: The Author

I. The Silent Masters

Chapter 1: 1916 / **INTOLERANCE**

DW Griffith / Master Of Cinema

Chapter 2: 1925 / **POTEMKIN**

Sergei Eisenstein / Master Of Montage

Chapter 3: 1927 / **NAPOLEON**

Abel Gance / Master Of Innovation

II. The Studio Mavericks

Chapter 4: 1939 / **THE GRAPES OF WRATH**

John Ford / New Deal Docudrama

Chapter 5: 1940 / FANTASIA
Walt Disney / Visualizing Music

Chapter 6: 1941 / CITIZEN KANE
Orson Welles / The Best Film Ever Made

III. The International New Wave

Chapter 7: 1947 / THE BICYCLE THIEF
Vittorio De Sica / A New Realism

Chapter 8: 1950 / RASHOMON
Akira Kurosawa / Reflections Of Truth

Chapter 9: 1958 / HIROSHIMA MON AMOUR
Alain Resnais / Reimagining The Unimaginable

IV. The Vanishing Traditions

Chapter 10: 1959 / SHADOWS
John Cassavetes / Improvising Independent

Chapter 11: 1960 / BREATHLESS
Jean-Luc Godard / Breaking All The Rules

Chapter 12: 1960 / PSYCHO
Alfred Hitchcock / An Ice Cold Shower

V. The Confusion, The Bomb, & MTV

Chapter 13: 1963 / 8 1/2
Federico Fellini / A Director's Vision

Chapter 14: 1964 / DR. STRANGELOVE...
Stanley Kubrick / The Unimaginable As Satire

Chapter 15: 1964 / A HARD DAYS NIGHT
Richard Lester / The Fab Four

VI. Global & Personal Conflicts

Chapter 16: 1965 / WARGAME

Peter Watkins / The Unimaginable As Documentary

Chapter 17: 1966 / PERSONA
Ingmar Bergman / Cinematic De-con-struc-tion

Chapter 18: 1966 / THE BATTLE OF ALGIERS
Gillo Pontecorvo / Occupation & Insurrection

VII. In A Class By Itself

Chapter 19: 1969 / 2001, A SPACE ODYSSEY
Stanley Kubrick / Beyond The Infinite

VIII. The Year Of Dubious Bad Taste

Chapter 20: 1971 / SWEET SWEETBACK'S BAADASSS SONG
Melvin Van Peebles / In Your Face

Chapter 21: 1971 / THE DEVILS
Ken Russell / The Politics Of Religion

Chapter 22: 1971 / A CLOCKWORK ORANGE

Stanley Kubrick / Ultra Violence

IX. Four International Visions

Chapter 23: 1974 THE CONVERSATION

Francis Ford Coppola / A Matter Of Privacy

Chapter 24: 1974 / SWEPT AWAY...

Lina Wertmuller / The Bare Essentials

Chapter 25: 1975 / AND NOW MY LOVE

Claude Lelouch / Amazingly Hand Held

Chapter 26: 1975 / BARRY LYNDON

Stanley Kubrick / Candlelight By NASA

X. Words & Music

Chapter 27: 1976 / NETWORK

Sidney Lumet / The Boob Tube

Chapter 28: 1980 / STARDUST MEMORIES
Woody Alan / The Loyal Opposition

Chapter 29: 1980 / RAGING BULL
Martin Scorsese / Cinematic Redemption

Chapter 30: 1981 / CHARIOTS OF FIRE
Hugh Hudson / A Triumphant Score

XI. Film Of The Century

Chapter 31: 1991 / JFK
Oliver Stone / The Assassination Of Democracy

XII. New Guerrilla Filmmakers

Chapter 32: 1992 / El MARIACHI
Robert Rodriguez / Brilliant Simplicity

Chapter 33: 1997 / IN THE COMPANY OF MEN
Neil LaBute / Barbed Wit

Chapter 34: 1998 / THE CELEBRATION
Thomas Vinterberg / Digital Dogma

XIII. World War II Revisited

Chapter 35: 1993 / SHINDLER'S LIST
Steven Spielberg / Honoring The Six Million

Chapter 36: 1998 / SAVING PRIVATE RYAN
Steven Spielberg / The Price Of War

XIV. An Entirely New Paradigm

Chapter 37: 1999 / THE BLAIR WITCH PROJECT
D. Myrick & E. Sanchez / No Director No Crew

Chapter 38: 2000 / TIMECODE
Mike Figgis / No Film No Editing

Chapter 39: 2003 / **28 DAYS LATER**
Danny Boyle / Big Budget Home Video

Chapter 40: 2003 / **ZERO DAY**
Ben Coccio / No Budget Home Video

XV. Big Films Bold Visions

Chapter 41: 2003 / **CHICAGO**
Rob Marshall / Redefining Mise-en-scène

Chapter 42: 2004 / **THE BOURNE SUPREMACY**
Paul Greengrass / State-Of-The-Art Action

Chapter 43: 2004 / **COLLATERAL**
Michael Mann / The HD Revolution

Chapter 44: 2005 / **KING KONG**
Peter Jackson / The CGI Revolution

XVI. Today's Studio: Anywhere...

Chapter 45: 2005 / **GRIZZLY MAN**

Warner Herzog / Home Video: Alaska

Chapter 46: 2007 / **ONCE**

John Carney / Digital Film: Ireland

Chapter 47: 2007 / **THE DIVINGBELL & THE BUTERFLY**

Julian Schnabel / 35mm POV: France

Chapter 48: 2008 / **SLUMDOG MILLIONAIRE**

Danny Boyle / HD Home Run: India

XVII. Microcosm & Macrocosm

Chapter 49: 2009 / **PARANORMAL ACTIVITY**

Oren Peli / Right Film Right Place Right Time

Chapter 50: 2009 / **AVATAR**

XVIII. Epilogue

Summing Up

Appendix: Acknowledgements & Suggested Reading:

Special Thanks:

About The Author:

Forward By: Professor Richard Walter, UCLA

The films selected for analysis in David Worth's worthy book: MILESTONES IN CINEMA, represent a splendidly eclectic array focusing on nearly every aspect of the art, craft, and business of film and filmmaking.

What do Intolerance, *Potemkin, Fantasia, Rashomon, Psycho, A Hard Days Night, A Clockwork Orange, Barry Lyndon, Network, Stardust Memories, Schindler's List, The Blair Witch Project, King Kong, Slumdog Millionaire,* and *Avatar* have in common? The reader will have to read this engaging book to discover the answer, however all of these films are among the 50 that the author considers to be "Visionary Films created by Visionary Filmmakers."

There is much useful information here concerning the various movies, ranging from raw data about the artists and craftspeople responsible for each film and then moving on to truly profound insights into the nature of these visionary films and filmmakers. There's precisely the right mix, in my view, of the historical record behind each movie, as well as the way the selected films constitute part of the broad fabric that is film, film history, and film theory.

There is also evidence here that film scholarship that is rigorously academic does not have to be boring. That's why this book is appropriate not only for serious students of film but also for folks who love film as well as for those who are interested more broadly in the nature of creative expression across all forms, formats, and platforms.

The writing is warm, witty and engaging so kindly remember, just because you're enjoying yourself reading this book, that does not mean that you are not at the same time expanding your horizons as an artist and as an observer of art.

Professor Richard Walter is a celebrated storytelling educator, movie industry expert and longtime co-chairman of UCLA's legendary graduate program in screenwriting. He has written numerous feature assignments for the major studios and has sold material to all three networks. He has also written many informational, educational and corporate films. He lectures on screenwriting and storytelling throughout North America and the world.

He has conducted master classes in London, Paris, Jerusalem, Madrid, Rio de Janeiro, Mexico City, Beijing, Sydney and Hong Kong.

Students from Walter's screenwriting program at UCLA have written more than ten projects for Steven Spielberg alone.

Plus dozens of other Hollywood blockbusters and prestigious indie productions, including three recent Oscar™ winners for best screenplay: "The Descendants," "Milk," and "Sideways."

Preface By: The Author

The venerated Hollywood director Henry Hathaway once told one of his minions, "Son, every producer in Hollywood has two things: an asshole and an opinion; and my job is to see that the one fits neatly into the other!" This old school filmmaker may not have been politically correct by today's standards, but he was absolutely right. No craftsman or artist is able to do their best work "by committee." Instead they must pursue their vision with passion and persistence in order to see it through to its logical and sometimes illogical conclusion.

Today, with the overabundance of bloggers eagerly expelling their viewpoints and convictions on every imaginable subject, one might have to update Mr. Hathaway's statement to read: "Son, everyone with a computer and a keyboard has two things - an asshole and an opinion..." Or, that in today's media savvy world, everyone is going to have their own list of films that they believe to be, "The top one hundred" or "The ten best" or possibly "The top 1000 films that you must observe, & discuss before your demise."

I acknowledge that there are literally tens of thousands of outstanding and meaningful films that can be viewed, studied, written about and categorized, depending upon whatever your personal genre preferences might be. However, for this book, MILESTONES... I have attempted to select only those productions that have been, among the most influential, revolutionary and groundbreaking when it comes to the Language, Art, Craft & Technique of Filmmaking.

It is simply my attempt to draw attention to those films that have pushed the envelope, that have gone beyond what the norm or the accepted ways of film production happened to be at the time.

Films that, out of artistic choice or sheer necessity, were able to elevate, expand and finally democratize the Art & Craft of Filmmaking. Many of these films were blockbusters, others were small heartfelt productions, and each of them was willed into existence by extraordinary, independent filmmakers whose vision, persistence and passion made them happen.

I've had the privilege and good fortune of spending many years of my life working as an independent filmmaker on many exotic locations in the far corners of the world. After transitioning into academia, I discovered that many of my students, knew little or nothing about the films that I considered MILESTONES... Films that I believed were essential and that had been pivotal in the History, Language and Art of the Cinema...

Many of today's "next generation" have never actually touched a piece of celluloid film, nor have they taken the time to screen and study the films of the masters, giants, innovators and visionaries of the past. Instead, they have gained their knowledge from cable television, video games, DVD's, the ever-present Internet, their favorite contemporary super hero comic book 3D films, TV series, and streaming videos, usually by binge watching while multitasking.

The poet E. E. Cummings once wrote: "...progress is a comfortable disease..." and that may well be what we are witnessing today. If so, then MILESTONES... is finally, my attempt at giving future generations an easily accessible "Crash Course" in the truly visionary motion pictures that have shaped, influenced and ultimately democratized today's filmmaking.

My hope is that each of you might come to realize and appreciate these filmmakers upon whose shoulders we are all standing whenever we capture images using our palm-sized HD or digital cameras, edit on our laptop's latest non-linear editing software and upload our creations to the Internet.

I trust that my efforts will send you in search of some of these visionary films and filmmakers. You will not be disappointed.

Agree. Disagree. Enjoy.

DW

I. The Silent Masters

Chapter 1

1916
INTOLERANCE

DW Griffith
Master Of Cinema

SPOILER ALERT!
This film is nearly 100 years old and viewing it today can be difficult for any modern audience and especially for anyone from the MTV, YouTube, Facebook, instant-gratification generation. Many of the film's production and acting styles are quite dated by today's standards and of course being a silent film, there is no spoken dialog, only music and title cards.

To appreciate the experience, you must be able to listen and read. You must be able to let yourself go, to "take a trip," and ease back into another time, another age, one where there was no Internet, no mass communication, no television, and no cell phones. If you do, you will discover a film filled with staggering cinematic accomplishments. Sets that stood over ten stories high, extended for nearly half a mile in length and were filled elephants, camels and thousands of costumed extras. Battle scenes, love scenes, semi-nudity, violence, as well as a never-seen-before-or-since storytelling structure that encompassed four separate narratives and four different epochs of time.

THE CREATIVE TEAM:
Writers: D.W. Griffith, Anita Loos
Director: D. W. Griffith
Cinematographer: G. W. "Billy" Bitzer, Karl Brown
Editors: D. W. Griffith, James Smith & Rose Smith

WHY IS THIS FILM VISIONARY:
Even though it was produced in 1916, D.W. Griffith's astonishing cinematic vision propelled the language of film decades into the future. His use of huge master shots, extreme close ups, masking the frame horizontally and vertically, the iris in and the iris out, massive dolly and crane work, not to mention laying out for the audience four separate stories of humanity's Intolerance, told in four different colors through four different times in history: This film is truly an unparalleled cinematic achievement and one

that has never been attempted again, even with today's amazing technology

THE BASICS:
In his extraordinary Masterwork, D.W. Griffith had each story hand tinted a different color, to help the audience follow along as the film progressed, covering nearly 2,500 years of human history and Intolerance. A lot has transpired since 1916 and much of the original hand tinting has been lost, or re-printed incorrectly. Basically from what I have been able to discover:

The Modern Story was Black & White (Sepia). The Fall of Babylon was Purple (& Blue for Night, & Orange for Fire). The Crucifixion of Christ was Violet and the French Huguenots was Green.

First: 1914 AD. <u>The Modern Story:</u> That opens and closes the film, the tale of a mother losing her child to those who felt morally superior and of her husband about to be hanged for a crime that he did not commit.

Second: 539 BC. <u>The Fall Of Babylon:</u> The excesses, intrigues and deceptions that lead to its destruction visualized with immense sets, racing chariots and thousands of costumed extras.

Third: 27 AD. The Crucifixion of Christ: The Judean story of the trial and eventual death of Jesus of Nazareth.

Fourth: 1572 AD. The Slaughter Of The French Huguenots: The political intrigues and plots that led to the Catholic majority murdering the Protestant minority.

All of these stories were linked visually by the shot of a mother, Lillian Gish, rocking a cradle that symbolized both the cradle of civilization as well as humanity's ongoing promise of a fresh beginning with every new birth. In the words of Walt Whitman, "...out of the cradle endlessly rocking..."

Then during the final reels, as all of these separate stories are simultaneously being edited toward their conclusion, Mr. Griffith often did away with the shot of the mother rocking the cradle and was freely intercutting between all four (4) epochs of time! Showing the audience that the evils of *Intolerance* have always been with us.

Sergei Eisenstein later called this "Intellectual Montage" by intercutting separate epochs of time

D.W. Griffith was utilizing: Thesis + Antithesis = Synthesis and was cinematically decades ahead of his time.

As a grace note in the final reel, Mr. Griffith envisioned all of the warring factions on earth throwing down their weapons and embracing as the heavens opened... When I finally caught up to this monumental film it was during the late 1960's, the Age of Aquarius... the Summer of Love... and it seemed to me as if, fifty years earlier, Mr. Griffith had already envisioned it.

BIOGRAPH STUDIOS:
During the early 1900's, along with his extraordinary and possibly "The Original" Cinematographer, G. W. "Billy" Bitzer, Mr. Griffith had invented the language of motion pictures and he did so while serving a very long apprenticeship at Biograph Studios in New York. It was there that he discovered the art and craft of telling stories visually. Experimenting with the use of: Establishing Shots, Medium Shots, The Close Up, Cropping The Frame, The Iris In and Out, The Moving Camera and Cross Cutting between those in peril and those rushing to the rescue.

Mr. Griffith got his "chops" by directing not one hundred, not two hundred, not three hundred, but over 450 one and two-reel films before ever attempting a longer feature.

THE BIRTH OF A NATION:
In 1915 Mr. Griffith virtually invented the Hollywood Blockbuster with the breathtaking, *The Birth Of A Nation*. The film played to both Presidential praise and vile criticism for its portrayal of the KKK and racial stereotypes. However let's do Mr. Griffith the courtesy of putting this all into its correct historical perspective. In 1915 there were no civil rights, women were second-class citizens who couldn't vote and the President of the United States himself, was given to making racial slurs.

Mr. Griffith did not invent the ignorance or the lack of tolerance of that time. Nor was he the originator of either the KKK or racial stereotypes. What he did, was to bring a popular Southern Novel and Stage Play to the Motion Picture Screen. To brand Mr. Griffith as a "racist" during a time when there were no civil rights is as ridiculous as it is patently unfair. To hold a Hollywood Director to a higher moral standard than the President of the United States is not only ignorant, it is ludicrous!

In our present age of political correctness, many have resorted to "blaming the messenger" by laying

America's racial sins at Mr. Griffith's feet and labeling him a "racist" for making *The Birth Of A Nation*. That allegation is as absurd as branding the brilliant filmmakers, Richard Brooks as a "murderer" for making *In Cold Blood*, or William Friedkin a "homosexual" for making *The Boys In The Band* or *Cruising*!

THE PRODUCTION:

By 1916, after being the brunt of so much vile backlash and critical abuse, Mr. Griffith decided to make a film that he hoped would be an answer to his critics. That film was *Intolerance*. Unfortunately, his vision was far too advanced for its time and even though it received critical acclaim, the film never achieved the kind of acceptance or distribution to make it profitable. Eventually, Mr. Griffith had to destroy his Masterpiece, cutting it up and releasing it as separate films.

What makes this epic film all the more phenomenal is that it was shot entirely with available sunlight or firelight, by one of "The Original" Cinematographers, G.W. "Billy" Bitzer. In fact the original subtitle of the Film was: "A Sun Play For The Ages." In an article for the American Cinematographer Magazine in October, 1934 Mr. Bitzer stated: "... every bit of this photography was taken in sunlight, except the night fire scenes of the Babylon towers and walls. These were taken at dusk and with flares. No 24's, 36's, sun arcs or electric lights of any kind were used and, if you remember the picture, you can imagine the original figuring on the placing of sets, all of which had to be shot in sunlight."

For the Feast of Belshazzar scene which took place in the Babylonian period, the set itself was nearly half a mile long and in order to accomplish an establishing shot, that he envisioned Mr. Griffith had a huge dolly / crane invented and built. This stupendous piece of equipment stood 140 feet high, six feet square at the top and sixty feet square at the base. It was mounted on six sets of railroad car wheels and was pushed forward or backwards on railroad tracks by a team of 25 men. Another team of men operated the elevator that moved up or down as the dolly was pushed into or out of the scene.

All of Mr. Griffith's assistant directors, Alan Dwan, Erich von Stroheim, Tod Browning, Jack Conway, Victor Fleming and W.S. Van Dyke became major Hollywood directors. Why? They all had learned the art and craft of filmmaking from observing the masterful Mr. Griffith at work. To show the careful detail and planning that was involved, the marriage scenes set during the time of Christ were all done in accordance with Jewish tradition and supervised by Rabbi Myers, the father of Carmel Myers who played "The Favorite of the Harem one of dancers in the Babylonian sequence. The execution scenes in The Modern Story was supervised by the former warden of Sing Sing Prison Martin Aguerre who also made sure that the gallows being used were historically accurate.

FINALLY:
Through the unique vision of the Inventor of The Language and The Art of American Filmmaking D.W. Griffith, the sideshow novelty of the Motion Pictures had been transported nearly into the next century, transforming them forever into an entirely New Art Form and leaving the legacy of his masterpiece *Intolerance* as one of the most visionary films of all time.

ONLINE RESOURCES:
Use Google Images & Google Videos for dozens of links...

Screen: Intolerance: Love's Struggle Throughout the Ages
Watch It: at www.InternetArchive

Buy it on Amazon, Google Play, or iTunes.

The Beatles & Intolerance:

Help:
http://www.youtube.com/watch?v=Em1uxAYZrm8

Revolution:
http://www.youtube.com/watch?v=vvTuv0Zemnk

Day In The Life:
http://www.youtube.com/watch?v=zb_3gqQUmac

THINKING OUTSIDE THE BOX:
Class Exercises:

1. Putting the Beatles music to the visuals of Intolerance is a brilliant way of getting a young audience interested in this classic silent film. Each student should experiment with Intolerance or another silent film and find a piece of contemporary music that helps them enjoy watching it.

2. For many of us, political correctness is an ongoing blessing and a curse. Each student should think about the pros and cons of being "PC," and come up with a list of both the good and bad aspects of it.

3. Many filmmakers will tell you that the best way to study a film is to turn off the sound. The dialog and especially the music tend to cover a multitude of otherwise glaring errors. Each student should take a favorite film and turn off the sound. Then write an essay about what new aspects, good or bad that they discover by viewing it in this way.

4. D.W. Griffith made over 450 one and two reel short films, many of which have been lost, before he made his first feature. Each student should calculate how long it took to accomplish this astounding number of films if he completed one film each week. Then they should write an essay about what Mr. Griffith might have learned over this extraordinary apprenticeship.

5. In Intolerance, D.W. Griffith told four different stories from four epochs of time. Each student should write a treatment using a similar template to highlight an aspect of human nature or an injustice they would like to point out.

Chapter 2

1925
POTEMKIN

Sergei Eisenstein
Master Of Montage

SPOILER ALERT!
The Battleship Potemkin is another black and white silent film classic, whose acting and production styles may seem outdated by today's standards. However, to dismiss this film or any works of art from years past, simply because they do not have today's thrills, pace or technique, is to overlook a vast amount of important, imaginative and creative work from many artists and artistic disciplines.

We must always do our best to be open-minded in our appreciation of the extraordinary work that has been accomplished by previous generations. We should train ourselves to appreciate this type of viewing experience, which is similar to being able to appreciate Greek Tragedies, Grand Opera, or Shakespeare. Yes, it is definitely an acquired taste; it is one, however, that will inform and enlighten the viewer regardless of their age.

Potemkin. Black and white film, theatrical acting, heavy music, title cards, no dialog, no CGI, no hit songs, no teenage vampires; just amazing Cinematography, Editing, and Directing.

THE CREATIVE TEAM:
Writer: Nina Agadzhanova
Director: Sergei Eisenstein
Cinematographers: Vladimir Popov & Edward Tisse
Editors: Grigori Aleksandrov & Sergei M. Eisenstein

WHY IS THIS FILM VISIONARY:
Potemkin represents the culmination of Eisenstein's advanced theories of Montage and Editing, which he saw as a "Kino Fist" or Film Fist that a Director could use to smash home his visionary ideas to an audience. Sergei Eisenstein and his Russian contemporaries, Vertov, Kuleshov, and Pudovkin were early film theorists who developed important concepts and techniques, especially when it came to editing and montage.

Kuleshov believed that the experience of viewing a film was predominately a matter of the editing and the juxtaposition of images one with the other. For one of his most famous experiments on film acting and editing, he used the close up of an important Russian actor, who was told to register no emotion. Then he intercut that close up with the shots of a child, a bowl of soup and a coffin. When the edited footage was shown to an audience, they marveled at the actors range of emotions showing first his love for the child, then his hunger for the soup and finally his fear of death for the coffin.

THE BASICS:
Eisenstein went even further theorizing that editing was dialectic between two opposites: Thesis and Antithesis that gave rise to an entirely new idea or Synthesis. His inter-cutting of the slaughter of a bull with workers being attacked by the police, gave rise to the idea that the workers were being treated like cattle and furthered his concept of the "Kino Fist."

Eisenstein's various Theories of Montage can be broken down into five separate categories:

<u>Metric</u>: In which the Editing Style follows a certain number of frames, such as making each succeeding shot shorter and shorter when you are building

tension, suspense, or to a climax.

Alfred Hitchcock was a master of this technique and most chase scenes today utilize this style of editing.

Rhythmic: Used composition and movement as well as the number of frames to determine the Editing pace and style. Once there was sound, the Rhythmic style was used when cutting to the beat of the music.

Examples of this can be seen in any Bob Fosse musical number, the musical films *Jesus Christ Superstar* and *Chicago*, or many of today's music videos.

Tonal: Where the Editing Style elicits an emotion from the audience by the content of the shot.

For example, the shot of a baby can elicit joy and happiness or when it is shockingly used as with the runaway baby carriage on the Odessa Steps, in *Potemkin*, it elicits fear and terror.

Associational: Is an accumulation of the Metric, Rhythmic and Tonal Editing Styles, that give the audience a new idea or revelation at the end of the scene or the end of the film.

Intellectual: Is an Editing Style that elicits an entirely new meaning from a montage of separate events and shots.

Like inter-cutting the bull being slaughtered and the workers being beaten by police which gives rise to the entirely new meaning that the workers are being treated like cattle.

Mr. Eisenstein admitted to being very much influenced by the work of D.W. Griffith, especially his masterpiece, Intolerance. But he took Mr. Griffith's cross cutting and melodrama a step further. He did not want to show the seamless story telling techniques that the Hollywood Master had developed, instead Eisenstein used his theories about dialectic and the juxtaposition of opposing images to give rise to an even greater and more startling cinematic idea: Thesis + Antithesis = Synthesis

THE PRODUCTION:
The Battleship Potemkin tells an authentic story about the beginning of the Russian Revolution. It occurred when the sailors onboard this historic ship were forced to eat maggot-infested meat and eventually mutinied. After the citizens of Odessa rallied on the steps of the city to show support for the sailor's cause, the Russian Militia and Cossacks mercilessly

slaughtered them.

All of Eisenstein's theories came together in the still rousing Odessa Steps sequence in *Potemkin*. The merciless Russian Militia is often shown as only a line of shadows, a faceless row of soldiers, of rifles, or advancing boots that kill unarmed civilians or crush a child as they descend the stairs, firing and murdering the defenseless, fleeing citizens.

The murdering militiamen are inter-cut with many simultaneous stories; the surge of the panicked crowd, the mother looking for her lost child, the mother who is shot and as she falls, loses her baby carriage down the Odessa Steps, the old lady wanting to reason with the soldiers and "talk them out of it…"

This is an important piece of Cinematic Theory that was put into Practice in order to arouse in the viewing audience the will to rise up against the slaughterers of innocents and the oppressors of the proletariat. It worked then and it still works today standing as a testament to the power of filmmaking.

HOLLYWOOD'S ATTITUDE:
To show you how ignorant and insensitive Hollywood executives were to Mr. Eisenstein's films, when he was in America in the 1930's to study film

production, especially sound recording, he had a meeting with the eminent producer, Samuel Goldwyn.

Mr. Goldwyn told the Russian director through an associate, since Mr. Eisenstein did not speak English. "Please tell Mr. Eisenstein that I have seen his film Potemkin and admire it very much. What we should like, would be for him to do something of the same kind, but cheaper, for Ronald Coleman."

ONLINE RESOURCES:
Use Google Images & Google Videos for dozens of links...

Buy it on Amazon, Google Play, or iTunes.

THINKING OUTSIDE THE BOX:
Class Exercises:

1. Eisenstein stated that his Theories of Editing were very influenced by the work of DW Griffith, especially his film, *Intolerance.* Each student should write an essay listing as many examples as possible of what these influences might have been.

2. Eisenstein's theories of montage are: Metric, Rhythmic, Tonal, Associational and Intellectual. Each student should write an essay listing as many

examples as possible that they see in today's films, television or on the Internet that put these theories into practice.

3. Putting the Beatles Music over parts of Intolerance, may have provided today's young audience an easier way to view an old classic. Each student should see if they are able to discover a piece of contemporary music that would fit over parts of Potemkin.

4. The Odessa Steps is one of the most famous scenes in film history. Each student should write an essay about how viewing it affected them and on the various editing techniques that were used.

5. Each student should select one of Eisenstein's theories of montage: Metric, Rhythmic, Tonal, Associational or Intellectual and do a short film, treatment, outline or storyboards, showing how they would use it to tell a story, sell a product or shoot a music video.

Chapter 3:

1927
NAPOLEON

Abel Gance
Master Of Innovation

SPOILER ALERT!
If you get motion sickness you may have to turn away from parts of this film. Abel Gance could be called, the MTV music video director, or Tony Scott of his day. He was bold, daring, and prided himself in being able to do things his own way and that way was very, very far ahead of his time in the 1920's.

He was always finding another new, inventive way to use the camera. He used it hand held long before anyone else was doing so but that was only the beginning, read on to discover his amazing invention called "Polyvision."

THE CREATIVE TEAM:
Writer: Able Gance
Director: Able Gance
Cinematographers: Leonce-Henri Burel, Jules Kruger, Jean-Paul Mundviller & Nikolai Toporkoff
Editor: Abel Gance

WHY IS THIS FILM VISIONARY:
This is an epic production about an historic figure that incorporates black and white and color film as well as a host of other innovative, revolutionary and experimental techniques that include: Cameras swinging on pendulums, hand held and on horseback, multiple superimpositions, 8, 6, 4, 2, and single frame fast cutting, as well as the cinema's first three camera, three projector, wide screen phenomenon, which Mr. Gance called "Polyvision."

THE BASICS:
Abel Gance might also be called the D.W. Griffith of France, because with his production of Napoleon, he created a Monumental Historical and Cinematic Epic that was many years ahead of its time, and for his grand finale, the screen opened up to three times its width as he used three cameras and three projectors to create his infamous triptych that predated the thrills of three camera Cinerama by some thirty years!

Gance thought that this process, which he called "Polyvision" would revolutionize the Cinema, and said, "...The theme, the story one is telling, is on the central screen. The center screen is story is the prose; the wings, the side screens, are the poetry. That is what I call Cinema. I must admit that from the first moment I saw Polyvision, the normal cinema had no further interest for me. I was convinced that Polyvision would be the cinema's new language..."

That might well have happened, but unfortunately within six months of Napoleon's release, Al Jolson sang "Mammy," and a new fad called "Sound" appeared in the form of the Hollywood hit, *The Jazz Singer.* That invention quickly became the new favorite with the viewing public and soon, like Mr. Griffiths monumental achievement, *Intolerance*, the innovations of Napoleon and Polyvision had been set aside. The film was eventually re-edited, then shelved and finally, totally forgotten.

Many butchered versions of this cinematic milestone were in circulation over the years until finally in 1981 silent film historian Kevin Brownlow after twenty years of work, managed to assemble the original 4-hour restored version. For this restoration, there were two different musical scores produced: For the

"Francis Ford Coppola Presents..." version, Francis's father Carmine Coppola, of The Godfather fame, created the score. For the other version shown in the United Kingdom, Carl Davis created the score.

COPPOLA'S COPYRIGHT:
Later in 2004 when Mr. Brownlow wanted to show the now newly restored 5-hour plus version of Able Gance's Napoleon with a score by Mr. Davis, Zoetrope Studios attempted to prevent the screening by stating that the Coppola family now owned the copyright to the film.

Unfortunately, this dispute is still going on, so if you are interested in seeing the newest version of this remarkable cinematic epic, you may want to first call your travel agent and attempt to schedule a screening along with your next trip to England or Europe.

FINALLY:
Abel Gance, like Mr. Griffith and Mr. Eisenstein, was a cinematic genius. He was pioneering techniques in the 1920's that would finally be embraced decades later by the Italian Neo-Realists, The French New Wave, Experimental Filmmakers, even advertising and MTV. Natural Locations, Available Light, Hand Held Cameras, Fast Cutting, Superimpositions, Abstract Imagery... We can only look back on this

man's masterpiece today and marvel at his astounding style, creativity, and imagination.

ONLINE RESOURCES:
Use Google Images and Google Videos for dozens of links...

Buy it on Amazon, Google Play, or iTunes.

THINKING OUTSIDE THE BOX:
Class Exercises:

1. Each student should write an essay listing many of the revolutionary cinematic innovations used in *Napoleon* that have now found their way into today's storytelling, advertising and music videos.

2. Abel Gance was far ahead of his time. Each student should write an essay about what it might be like to see ways of doing things that your contemporaries do not as yet comprehend or understand.

3. One apocryphal story was told, that in the 1950's Abel Gance was discovered, forgotten and selling pencils in front of a train station in Paris. Each student should write an essay about what it might be like to be a visionary that causes a huge sensation and then is totally forgotten.

4. Each student should write an essay discussing how Polyvision was used in Napoleon and how the same basic technique was later used in Cinerama.

5. The singing of The Marseillaise is a very important sequence in Napoleon. Each student should write an essay about the various techniques Mr. Gance used in this scene.

II. The Studio Mavericks

Chapter 4:

1939
THE GRAPES OF WRATH

John Ford
New Deal Docudrama

SPOILER ALERT!
No more silent films. Now we are into the era of sound and the actor's voice. The Grapes Of Wrath is a classic Academy Award winning John Ford film that features rich emotion filled performances from its ensemble cast.

Even though this was a Big Studio Hollywood film, it has the look and feel of a documentary. This is largely due to the Director John Ford's insistence that the Director of Photography Gregg Toland and the entire production carefully following the details in the still photographs from the dust bowl and the Great Depression that were done by the extraordinary Dorothea Lange. The tone was set by Mr. Ford who also banned all make up and perfume from the set because he felt that it was not in keeping with the somber mood of the film. The film's look was carried out by the amazingly stark black and white photography of the masterful Gregg Toland.

THE CREATIVE TEAM:
Writers: John Steinbeck / Nunnally Johnson
Director: John Ford
Cinematographer: Gregg Toland
Editor: Robert Simpson

WHY IS THIS FILM VISIONARY:
Based on the bestselling novel by John Steinbeck, *The Grapes Of Wrath* is about the desperate plight of American migrant workers after the great depression. President Franklin D. Roosevelt had come to office in 1933 by stating, "... I pledge myself to a new deal for the American people..." That "New Deal" included Relief, Reform, and Recovery during those awful

times. This film is a tribute to both the America's migrant workers and to the bold and visionary filmmakers.

THE BASICS:
When Orson Welles was doing his research on American Film Directors, while preparing to direct his first feature film *Citizen Kane*, he screened *Stagecoach* over forty times and told anyone who would listen that he had come to the conclusion that there were only three great American directors: "John Ford, John Ford, and John Ford!"

Like D.W. Griffith, John Ford spent a long apprenticeship before emerging as one of Hollywood's Great Directors. He directed over 50 ten-day westerns before his first major feature film, *The Iron Horse*, was released in 1924. He went on to amass over 150 directing credits and collected four Academy Awards as Best Director, more than any other director thus far, and along the way he guided a total of 10 different actors to Best Actor Academy Award nominations.

He was known as a tough disciplinarian who would often belittle his actors during production. In his later years, he even embarrassed then-film-critic Jean-Luc Godard, when he asked Mr. Ford, "What brought you to Hollywood?" Ford tersely replied, "...the train."

MR. FORD SAID:
"I love making pictures but I don't like talking about them..."

"Directing is not a mystery, it's not an art. The main thing about directing is: photograph the people's eyes..."

"It's no use talking to me about art, I make pictures to pay the rent..."

BY 1939:
Mr. Ford, also known to his band of stock players and cohorts as "Pappy," "Coach," or "The Admiral" was paying the rent just fine. Over the next 18 months he would deliver four feature films: *Stagecoach, Young Mr. Lincoln, Drums Along The Mohawk* and *The Grapes of Wrath*.

The year that I worked with Clint Eastwood as his DP (Director of Photography) on *Bronco Billy* and *Any Which Way You Can*, I came across a bit of film trivia that both Clint and I found to be absolutely astounding. How much film had Mr. Ford printed for the Academy Award winning feature, starring Henry Fonda, *The Grapes Of Wrath*?

The answer was the remarkably low figure of 37,000 feet of film. Back in the day the length of a normal 100-minute feature was around 9,000 feet of 35mm film. What Mr. Ford had printed was still a ratio of over 4 to 1, which was well over his average of usually only doing one or two takes per shot and moving on.

By the way, Mr. Eastwood had also studied the masterful, John Ford and that was exactly the number of takes that Mr. Eastwood liked to do, one or two per set up. He would usually print the rehearsal or the first take and after checking to see that we "got it" he would nod and quietly state, "…moving on."

DARRELL F. ZANUCK:
Prior to production of The Grapes Of Wrath, Darrel F. Zanuck sent investigators into California's produce fields to see if John Steinbeck had exaggerated the situation of the migrant workers; when he discovered that if anything, Mr. Steinbeck had played it down, he proceeded with the film.

Mr. Zanuck also paid $100,000 for the rights to the novel and was so exceedingly meticulous in his preparation and in managing every detail of the production, that he not only drew praise from the screenwriter, Nunnally Johnson, Mr. Ford also permitted him to oversee the editing of the picture, a privilege that the cantankerous Director seldom if ever doled out, and especially not to a Producer.

THE PRODUCTION:
In typical Ford style, *The Grapes Of Wrath* was done quickly, needing only seven weeks of principal photography from October 4th to November 16th, 1939 and at the surprisingly low cost of only $750,000. As has been pointed out, Mr. Ford even banned all make up and perfume from the set, because he felt that it was not in keeping with the stark, semi-documentary tone of the subject matter.

The brilliant Director of Photography, Gregg Toland who would go on to photograph "The Best Movie Ever Made" *Citizen Kane* the very next year, was amazingly not nominated for an Academy Award for his work in this Award winning film, which contains some of the most stark and daring Cinematography that had ever been put up on the big screen.

In one unparalleled sequence, he had a small intense light placed in the back of a hollowed out candle, with an extension cord running up Henry Fonda's arm and down his pants leg, in order to simulate the effect of candlelight lighting the entire scene. This bold, dramatic, daring and innovative technique of using what appeared to be a "practical candlelight" was absolutely unheard of at that time!

THE AWARDS:
The Grapes Of Wrath, was nominated for seven Academy Awards and both The New York Film Critics Circle and the Academy Awards selected John Ford as Best Director.

A LESSON FROM THE MASTER:
When a fledgling director approached the aging Mr. Ford one day in his office for advice, Mr. Ford pointed to a landscape painting on the wall and ask the young man why the horizon was near the bottom of the frame. When he couldn't come up with an answer, Mr. Ford told him that when he knew why the horizon belonged at the bottom of the frame, he would have become a film director. Then, Mr. Ford proceeded to throw the young man out of his office. That young man's name was Steven Spielberg and I believe that since that meeting, he has accomplished the task of becoming a film director quite successfully!

ONLINE RESOURCES:
Use Google Images & Google Videos for dozens of links...

Buy it on Amazon, Google Play, or iTunes.

Trailer Video URL:
http://www.imdb.com/video/screenplay/vi1686962457/

John Steinbeck & The Grapes of Wrath
http://www.youtube.com/watch?v=xqaTv8cCWeg

THINKING OUTSIDE THE BOX:
Class Exercises:

1. Like many classic filmmakers, John Ford served a long apprenticeship and directed over 50 ten-day westerns before making his first major film; each student should write an essay about what Mr. Ford might have learned about film production during that time.

2. *The Grapes Of Wrath* was shot in seven weeks at a cost of under a million dollars, exposed only 37,000 feet of film and was nominated for seven Academy Awards, each student should write an essay comparing and contrasting John Ford and a contemporary director like McG, who spends tens of millions of dollars, exposes over 1,500,000 feet of film and delivers an inane product like, *Charlie's Angels II.*

3. John Ford was known for only doing one or two takes for each setup. Each student should write an essay comparing and contrasting that way of working, with directors like Stanley Kubrick, William Wyler or David Fincher, who usually require fifty takes for each setup. What are the advantages and or disadvantages?

4. Each student should write an essay describing how the great Cinematographer, Gregg Toland did the scene in the abandoned Joad house that appears to be lit by candlelight, then compare that to shooting the same scene today on HD.

5. *The Grapes Of Wrath,* both the novel and the film pointed out the immense social problems in 1930's America. Each student should write an essay or a film treatment about a contemporary social issue that needs to be addressed.

Chapter: 5

1940
FANTASIA

Walt Disney
Visualizing Music

SPOILER ALERT!
The one and only, the original, the all hand-drawn animation masterpiece, abstract, visionary, risqué, spellbinding, stereophonic, timeless, trippy, thrilling, classic, outside of the box and far, far ahead of its time. By the way, what exactly was its time? 1940! That's right. Way, way back before the middle of the last century! Fasten your seat belts.

THE CEATIVE TEAM:
Writers: Joe Grant, Dick Huemer
Directors: See Below
Cinematographer: James Wong Howe (Live action, un-credited)
Editor: John Carnochan (1990 restoration)

WHY IS THIS FILM VISIONARY:

Fantasia is the film that singlehandedly elevated cartoons and the craft of animation into the realm of Art. That's Art with a capital "A." It broke animation free from being thought of as only a short additional piece of entertainment on the program and turned it into a top of the bill, main, road show, hard ticket feature attraction. In so doing, it also became the first feature film to surround the movie going audiences of the 1940's with a stereophonic musical sound track.

This film contains totally abstract sequences, others that feature topless female characters all presented with glorious classical music accompaniment. The Rite of Spring sequence depicts in near scientific and graphic detail the "evolution" of the planet earth, the emerging of the first living creatures and the millions of years of volcanoes and earthquakes leading up to the cataclysm that caused the extinction of the dinosaurs. This alone was, and still is, an astounding, groundbreaking and enlightening accomplishment given the American public's allegiance to the King James Bible and the Christian Fundamentalist view of everything including "creation."

THE BASICS:

The production started out simply enough. Due to

waning box office figures, Mr. Disney wanted to make a special all musical cartoon for the hopeful reemergence of his favorite character, Mickey Mouse. By 1938 work was underway on The Sorcerer's Apprentice, and a chance meeting of Mr. Disney and Leopold Stokowski over dinner resulted in the world famous conductor volunteering his services to record the music for the cartoon.

The animation department was driven by Mr. Disney's insistence that their work must be the most ambitious to date and the increased attention to detail in color, layout, character and effects animation led to a cartoon that was nine minutes long and when completed, cost a whopping $125,000. The normal Disney cartoons during that time were seven minutes long, cost around $40,000, and even their best ones only made back about $60,000 at the box office.

Mr. Disney was already in way over his head. With his business partner and brother Roy behind him, Mr. Disney decided to expand the production to a feature length film containing several animated musical sequences including The Sorcerer's Apprentice. As the project developed, Mr. Stokowski regularly referred to it as *"Fantasia"* which means, "a medley of familiar themes, with variations and interludes." Mr. Disney liked the sound of it and the name stuck.

THE PRODUCTION:

By 1939, all of the additional sequences that were about to be added needed to be as exceptionally done as The Sorcerer's Apprentice. Each of the sequences are credited as follows:

Toccata and Fugue in D Minor: J.S Bach
Story by: Lee Blair, Elmer Plummer, Phil Dike
Directed by: Samuel Armstrong

Nutcracker Suite: Tchaikovsky
Story by: Sylvia Moberly-Holland, Norman Wright, Albert Heath, Bianca Majolie, Graham Heid.
Directed by: Samuel Armstrong

The Sorcerer's Apprentice: Paul Dukas
Story by: Perce Pearce, Carl Fallberg
Directed by: James Agar

The Rite of Spring: Igor Stravinsky
Story by: William Martin, Leo Thiele, Robert Sterneer, John Fraser McLeish
Directed by: Bill Roberts, Paul Satterfield

Intermission /Meet The Soundtrack:
Directed by: Ben Sharpsteen, David D. Hand

The Pastoral Symphony: Beethoven
Story by: Otto Englender, Webb Smith, Erdman Penner, Joseph Sabo, Bill Peet, George Stallings
Directed by: Hamilton Luske, Jim Handley, Ford Beebe

Dance of the Hours: Ponchielli
Directed by: T. Hee, Norm Ferguson

Night on Bald Mountain: Mussorgsky
Ave Maria: Schubert
Story by: Campbell Grant, Arthur Heinemann, Phil Dike
Directed by: Wilfred Jackson

Of course there were also countless Art Directors, Animators, Character Designers, Background painters, etc. etc. etc. As a result the final cost of the film was an astounding $2,280,000 and nearly $400,000 of it had been spent on developing and implementing new groundbreaking and extraordinary musical recording techniques.

Unhappy when the mono recorded soundtrack for The Sorcerer's Apprentice was played back to him, Mr. Disney insisted that his sound department do their best to develop a better sound system. Under the leadership of William E. Garity, they invented a multi-channel system that they called "Fantasound" which was used to present the worlds first stereophonic recorded feature film, Fantasia.

On November 13, 1940, *Fantasia* was premiered in New York City in full stereophonic sound with 30 speakers surrounding the audience. It was a special event black tie screening, presented like a road show concert with reserved seating and programs given to everyone containing all of the credits, since only the title of the film, *Fantasia* was presented on the screen.

Because of all the logistics necessary, only 12 theaters were ever fully equipped with Fantasound, and only 16 Fantasound prints were ever made. The final Ave Maria sequence was rushed to New York and spliced into the print just hours prior to its premier due to a series of nearly fatal errors.

First, the sequence had been filmed using the wrong lens and technicians could be seen in the background. Next, an earthquake destroyed a take and finally the scene was completed correctly, then processed, printed and rushed by plane to New York, to be cut into the film for the premier.

Over the past seventy plus years, *Fantasia* has had nine different releases, the most significant however, was during 1969 when the youth audience, the hippies and the drug counter-culture discovered how cool it was to get high on grass or LSD and trip out to the mind-bending production. They are the audience that made Mr. Disney's dream project the huge hit that it always should have been.

The animators on The Sorcerer's Apprentice named the Sorcerer Yen Sid, which is Disney backwards and modeled him after their boss, who was a stern taskmaster. Watch for the Sorcerer's raised eyebrow the next time you see this classic film. Yes, Mr. Disney was tough on his crew, but he was also thinking so far outside the box that he even envisioned a 3D version of the film, with new animated sequences being added every few years.

Well, Mr. Cameron or Mr. Jackson, now that the technology is here, how about a 3D version of *Fantasia*?

THE AWARDS:
In 1942 Walt Disney, William E. Garity, and J. N. A. Hawkins shared an Honorary Academy Award "For their outstanding contribution to the advancement of the use of sound in motion pictures through the production of *Fantasia*." Leopold Stokowski (and his associates) also received an Honorary Academy

Award "For their unique achievement in the creation of a new form of visualized music in Walt Disney's production *Fantasia*, thereby widening the scope of the motion picture as entertainment and as an art form."

ONLINE RESOURCES:
Use Google Images & Google Videos for dozens of links...

Buy it on Amazon, Google Play, or iTunes.

THINKING OUTSIDE THE BOX:
Class Exercises:

1. Each student should write an essay discussing what they liked best about the production and what if anything they did not like as well as what worked best in *Fantasia* and what did not work for them.

2. Each student should write an essay comparing and contrasting Disney's hand-drawn animation with today's Pixar computerized 3D style of animation.

3. Each student should write an essay comparing and contrasting Disney's hand-drawn animation with today's South Park Cut Out style animation.

4. The Creationists say, "God created the world in six days..." Each student should write an essay comparing and contrasting that with the scientific view of creation that was presented in The Rite of Spring sequence in *Fantasia,* way back in 1940.

5. The students should team up and make a short animated film using their computers and a piece of evocative classical music.

Chapter: 6

1941
CITIZEN KANE

Orson Welles
The Best Film Ever Made

SPOILER ALERT!
I know, you're tired of hearing about *Citizen Kane*. The greatest this, the greatest that; but you still find it boring and tedious. I've got three words for you: "Get Over It!" Sit down and appreciate this film. This film was the *JFK* of its day. It was controversial. It was banned. It was under attack by one of the most powerful men in America at the time, William Randolph Hearst.

The brilliant wunderkind, Orson Welles was in his early twenties and actually knew nothing about filmmaking. Nothing, except to hire the best team in the business, ask those people the right questions and push them to their limits to make a film: "THE Film," that in the end expanded not only the language of Cinema, but also the perception of what filmmaking could accomplish and become.

He was young, he was daring, he was brash and he was often so full of himself that some around him would muse, "There but for the grace of God, goes God!" He was also a visionary and the Tony Scott and James Cameron of his time.

Come on, you can do it. Learn to love this film!

THE CREATIVE TEAM:
Writers: Herman J. Mankiewicz / Orson Welles
Director: Orson Welles
Cinematographer: Gregg Toland
Editor: Robert Wise

WHY IS THIS FILM VISIONARY:
Citizen Kane has managed to stand the test of time and if anything, like a vintage wine, it has gotten better and even more appreciated as the years go by. It's impossible to find any other film that has used so many groundbreaking filmmaking techniques or has encapsulated a man's life in such an experimental, fragmented, multifaceted and ultimately cinematic manner. All of the sound and fury of his existence,

from childhood to old age, signifying nothing as it goes up in smoke, with the final burning of all of his worldly possessions. It is truly a mind-expanding film experience.

THE BASICS:
This monumental production from the 25 year-old Orson Welles was and still is a huge Milestone In Cinema... and the second most important film behind Mr. Griffiths *Intolerance.* Although it was unsuccessful at the time of its release in 1941, by the late 1940's and early 1950's it would eventually become the standard by which all other films would be measured and judged. It contained so many new and startling innovations that are now commonplace in the language of Cinema that it becomes difficult when viewing this film today to realize that back when it was made, all of these innovations were being seen for the very first time.

So much fact and fiction has been written and fantasized about Mr. Welles and the making of this amazing production that it's virtually impossible to find anything new to say and, as is so often the case when it comes to Mr. Welles, it has also become impossible to separate the fact from the fiction, the myth from the legend, and legend from the man.

After his Mercury Theater of the Air, Radio production of H.G. Wells, The War Of The Worlds, panicked most of the American listening audience, Mr. Welles name became a household word and of course, he was wooed by Hollywood. They wanted him to leave the confines of the Theater and Radio in cold New York City and come out to Hollywood, to the shores of sunny southern California and direct a motion picture. The Studios hoped that the same public that had been so frightened by Mr. Welles Radio Play would soon flock to their local theaters to see The Boy Wonder's first Hollywood movie.

THE CRASH COURSE IN CINEMATOGRAPHY:
As has been mentioned, in preparation for directing his first feature film, Mr. Welles watched the John Ford film *Stagecoach*, over 40 times. Then after several projects failed to materialize, he finally began to work on a script called "American" with the screenwriter Herman J. Mankiewicz. The RKO Studio boss George Schaefer, just prior to the film going into production, eventually changed the title to Citizen Kane.

The story goes that Mr. Welles was approached by the Academy Award winning Cinematographer, Gregg Toland who wanted to work with him based mainly on the fact that he knew little or nothing about the process of making movies and Gregg thought that that was the best way to make new discoveries. Plus, he had also offered to give Orson a crash course in cinematography and film production and that sealed the deal.

Later, Mr. Welles told his many admirers as well as anyone who would listen, that he had learned "Everything about the Art of Cinematography in half an hour from the great cameraman Gregg Toland!"

PERSONALLY:
I first saw this ground breaking film on television, complete with commercials, one afternoon while I was still in high school, and it immediately created within me the epiphany that started me on the lifelong journey of becoming a filmmaker. If you would like to read my rather graphic, irreverent and "Wildly Fictional" account, of what may have happened during the wild Hollywood weekend when Mr. Toland taught Mr. Welles all the basics of Cinematography and Filmmaking you may purchase a copy of my book:

The Citizen Kane Crash Course In Cinematography...
ISBN: 9781932907469
It is available at www.amazon.com.

I will also be more than happy to personally sign your copy whenever we happen to meet...

RKO 281:
That was the production number of *Citizen Kane* when it began production in late June of 1940 and finished on October 23rd. The cast and crew under the leadership of Mr. Welles and Mr. Toland, began by telling the Studio that they were only "shooting tests," and before the Studio caught on they already had several days of work in the can.

THE INNOVATIONS:
Starting with the News On The March "mocumentary" about the life of Charles Foster Kane, we are in totally uncharted waters compared to what was the norm for the Cinema of the 1940's. Robert Wise, the Editor, on the insistence of Mr. Welles often dragged the film across the cement floor of the editing room and ran it numerous times though a projector that would scratch it before repeatedly duping it in order to make it look like and match authentic archival documentary footage. If you look carefully you can even see a Freeze Frame, Flash Frames, and Jump Cuts - techniques that wouldn't be used again until the French New Wave of the 1950's! There are even several Hand Held shots that appear to be "stolen footage" spying on an elderly Mr. Kane being pushed

in a wheel chair. All of these techniques were absolutely unheard of during that time!

Then we come to one of the first major "Time Cuts" in Cinema history as the young Kane's guardian, Mr. Thatcher wishes him a "Merry Christmas..." The young Kane answers him with a scornful, "Merry Christmas..." of his own. Then as we once again cut back to a now gray-haired Mr. Thatcher, it is fifteen years later as he answers with the words, "...and a Happy New Year..." Groundbreaking, to say the least and it anticipated Stanley Kubrick's famous Time Cut in *2001: A Space Odyssey* from the bone to the space satellite by nearly thirty years.

We have scenes in a projection room played in nearly total silhouette, and shots that, with the help of the Optical Printer, seem to travel up walls, through neon signs and down through skylights. Then we are treated to Mr. Kane's marriage to Emily that seems to fall apart before our eyes, over a series of breakfasts. All of the transitions linking these breakfast scenes are known as "Swish Pans as the technique became referred to decades later in the 1960's when it finally became popular.

Then we have the "Flash Backs" that tell the story of Charles Foster Kane from the POV of each of the people who knew him and who all seem have a very different version of the man. It wouldn't be until ten years later that the Masterful Japanese Filmmaker, Akira Kurosawa would more or less use this same template to show the audience, various versions of "The Truth" in his 1950, ground breaking film, *Rashomon.*

The meticulous aging and un-aging of the cast of characters, most of whom were first time film performers from Mr. Welles Mercury Theater troupe, Kane breaking up Susan's bedroom in one take with two cameras capturing it, the McGuffin of "What is Rosebud?" only being revealed to the audience, in one of the final shots of the film. Absolutely revolutionary filmmaking for that time!

GREGG TOLAND:
Mr. Toland was the cinematic genius behind much of Citizen Kane. Mr. Welles had admitted to him that he basically knew "nothing" about filmmaking and Mr. Toland had taken the time to give him a "crash course" on the basics. Then those two creative giants conspired on the visuals of this masterpiece. Mr. Toland had already pioneered the use of "deep focus" but Mr. Welles took it to the limit. He would often play entire scenes in one shot with one character hovering in a close up in the foreground, another in

the middle ground and the main character of Kane, in the background. Without the technical and artistic contributions of Mr. Toland, this film might never have achieved its greatness.

THE OPTICAL PRINTER:
Linwood Dunn and Vernon Walker achieved much of the magic of this production on the Optical Printer. When recalling the experience, Mr. Dunn stated: "Orson used an optical printer the way an artist uses a certain kind of paint brush. He would want to do certain things and I would say... it would take too much time and money. But he would get an OK form the front office, we'd go ahead and I learned so very much from the experience."

THE AWARDS:
Citizen Kane, won the National Board of Review and The New York Film Critics Circle Award as Best Film and went on to be nominated for a total of nine Academy Awards, winning for Best Original Screenplay.

ONLINE RESOURCES:
Use Google Images & Google Videos for dozens of links...

Buy it on Amazon, Google Play, or iTunes.

Trailer Video URL:
http://www.imdb.com/video/screenplay/vi2612920601/

Watch the movie:
http://www.dailymotion.com/video/x613pl_watch-citizen-kane-free_shortfilms

THINKING OUTSIDE THE BOX:
Class Exercises:

1. *Citizen Kane* is now going on eighty years old. Each student should write an essay, listing all of the cinematic innovations that were new and startling when this film was made.

2. Orson Welles was already a star of the theater and radio, whose radio show "*The War of the Worlds*" had frightened the listening audience and caused a sensation. Each student should write an essay discussing the innovative "Sound Design" used by Mr. Welles in *Citizen Kane.*

3. The behind the scenes genius on *Citizen Ka*ne was the great Director of Photography, Gregg Toland. Each student should Google and IMDb Mr. Toland, then write an essay about his contributions to this

film.

4. Although he had a long career as a Director and Actor, Orson Welles never again reached the level of acclaim that he achieved after *Citizen Kane,* each student should write an essay about what Mr. Welles meant when he said, "I started at the top and worked my way down."

5. Each student should write an essay about why this film has achieved the vast acclaim that it has and do they think that it is deserved? How long do they think that it will last?

III. The International New Wave

Chapter: 7

1947
THE BICYCLE THIEF

Vittorio De Sica
New Realism

SPOILER ALERT!
In the dictionary "realism" is defined as: "The quality or fact of representing a person, thing, or situation accurately or in a way that is." That is exactly what Vittorio De Sica was doing in *The Bicycle Thief*. He was showing us the reality of 1947 post-war Italy, the unemployment, the desperation, and the hopelessness.

In many scenes he was using real people – not trained actors. Real locations and available light, not studio sets and traditional lighting. Real true to life episodic stories not contrived predictable scripts. These were many of the key elements of the Italian Neo Realist movement that happened after World War II.

Although many of these techniques had been used before, the Italian Neo-Realists are the ones who forged them into a template for independent production and set the stage for the French New Wave, The American Independents and eventually the total democratization of the Cinema that we have today.

THE CREATIVE TEAM:
Writers: Luigi Bartolini / Cesare Zavattii / Suso d'Amico / Vittorio De Sica / Oreste Biancoli / Adolfo Franci / Gerardo Guerrieri
Director: Vittorio De Sica
Cinematographer: Carlo Montuori
Editor: Eraldo Da Roma

WHY IS THIS FILM VISIONARY:
As a result of the devastation caused by WWII, the Italian Neo-Realists were forced to strip away nearly all of the artifice from the process of film production and distill it down to its very essence.

Of course, they would use whatever equipment and

crewmembers they could scrape together, but often their team only consisted of a handful of collaborators. They had a director, a cinematographer, a script advisor taking down what the actors said (because there was no direct sound) and an assortment of assistants and technicians. The actors were often non-actors, who were cast for their look, or, as Mr. De Sica has stated in the case of the man and his son in *The Bicycle Thief*, for their distinctive walks.

THE BASICS:
After World War II, Europe and many parts of Italy lay in ruins. The young critics and filmmakers in Italy led by Luchino Visconti with *Ossessione* and Roberto Rossellini with *Rome, Open City*, simply got into the streets and began to make their post-war films using whatever they had. They were rebelling against the sophisticated studio-made "white telephone" films of pre-war Italy and wanting to reveal the plight of the ordinary citizens who were now facing a staggering, 25% unemployment.

These visionary Directors often utilized the bold innovations of natural locations, available light, and non-professional actors to tell their stories; by doing so, discovered a fresh and vibrant way of filmmaking.

They became known as, the Italian Neo-Realists and the repercussions of their pioneering efforts are still being felt today. The French New Wave of the 1950's, The American Independents of the 1960's through the 1990's, even the pretentious Dogme 95 movement in Denmark as well as the innovative *The Blair Witch Project,* the recent Academy Award winning film *Once* and even *Paranormal Activity* and *Tangerine* can all trace their lineage back to the Italian Neo-Realists of the mid 1940's.

ORDINARY PEOPLE:
These films were truly the first to begin to democratize filmmaking by focusing on the lives of ordinary, everyday people. They told stories that were not so much plotted, as they were organic and episodic, often using the slang, dialog and language of the streets.

Most importantly, they left the stale confines of the film studio and began to make use of natural locations, available light and non-actors, which made these films both revolutionary and a revelation to the world of film production. So much so, that *The Bicycle Thief* was awarded an honorary Academy Award in 1949 and was named as the "Greatest Film Of All Time" in 1952 by the prestigious film magazine, Sight and Sound.

THE BIRTH OF INDEPENDENT FILMS:

The Bicycle Thief can be a devastating film to watch as it recounts he plight of an ordinary man, who must have a bicycle in order to hold onto his job. When it is stolen he and his young son search endlessly through the side streets and alleys of Rome, culminating with the desperate man attempting to steal a bicycle himself and being humiliated in front of his boy. For the most part, this film feels like an authentic slice of life and looks like a documentary. By the time that we reach the end of the journey, the anguish and the hopelessness of the finale are all too palpable.

This is a film that should be seen over and over again, generation after generation, if for no other reason than to remind the filmmakers of today where the alternative to big name, big budget, big studio films and truly independent cinema actually had its origins.

Their Template:
1. Natural Locations
2. Available Light
3. Non-Actors
4. Very Little Money
5. Inexpensive Equipment
6. Organic Episodic Stories

ONLINE RESOURCES:
Use Google Images & Google video for dozens of links...

Buy it on Amazon, Google Play, or iTunes.

Trailer Video URL:
http://www.imdb.com/video/screenplay/vi4035510553/

THINKING OUTSIDE THE BOX:
Class Exercises:

1. Each student should write an essay discussing what led to the birth of Italian Neo-Realism, the directors who created it and the revolutionary elements that they used.

2. Each student should write an essay listing the various film movements, from 1950's to the present, which can be traced back to the Italian Neo Realists.

3. Each student should make a list of contemporary TV Shows and Films that they have seen, that use elements initiated by the Italian Neo Realists.

4. The Italian Neo Realist were pointing out problems in Post World War II Italy. Each student should write

an essay or treatment pointing out several contemporary problems that could be addressed using their technique.

5. Each student should go on line, Google and IMDb the Italian Neo Realists as well as several of their directors and find a film that they were not aware of, to rent or purchase and view.

Chapter: 8

1950

RASHOMON

Akira Kurosawa
Reflections of Truth

SPOILER ALERT!
Whether by Fate, design, or necessity, this very small production became one of the Cinema's truly great Art Films. A film that not only dares to conjecture about the nature of "Truth" but also leaves the audience wondering what exactly that truth is and if in fact, it can ever be known.

A brilliantly complex film that a decade later, used a similar flashback technique like *Citizen Kane*. Also, like the Orson Welles classic, it uses each episode to tell a different version of what the facts of its seemingly simple story might be…

In ancient Japan, a Thief takes captures a Samurai, rapes his wife, and then murders him. Or, did the Wife enjoy the encounter and afterward beg the Thief take her with him and to kill her husband? Or, did both the Thief and the Samurai fight honorably over the prize of the Wife's affection? Or, did the Wife kill her husband after he scorned her for her behavior? Or, were both men cowards who did not deserve her affection? The participants and witnesses to this tragic event present each version of the truth as fact, and we are left to wonder: what exactly is the truth of this violent encounter?

THE CREATIVE TEAM:
Writers: Ryunosuke Akutagawa / Akira Kurosawa
Director: Akira Kurosawa
Cinematographer: Kazuo Miyagawa
Editor: Akira Kurosawa

WHY IS THIS FILM VISIONARY:
It asks some very important questions concerning the nature of truth and the human condition, while utilizing a fresh, bold, and very cinematic style. *Rashomon* also fought a huge uphill battle, since it was a very small production made by a handful of cinematic artists half a world away in 1950's Japan. It was also universally unappreciated there and

disowned by the studio that made it. In fact, it might never have reached a worldwide audience, if not for a helping hand from someone totally unexpected.

THE BASICS:
Rashomon was adapted from two stories by the Japanese author Ryunosuku Akutagawa. The first story, "*Rashomon*" provides the setting of the gate where the story is being recounted, while the second "In A Grove" provides the basic characters and plot for the story itself. However, this Milestone In Cinema... might never have seen the light of day were not for the assistance of those twin Asian icons, Fate and Destiny.

The studio, Daiei, did not understand the script and gave the production only the sum of $5000 US to make the film. Even if you multiply that budget by 100 times to reach today's equivalent, a half a million dollars for a film as extraordinary as *Rashomon* is still an astounding bargain. Having to use their creativity in place of money forced the Director, his Cinematographer, and the entire production team to use their imaginations.

They shot the entire film on only three exterior locations and because Mr. Kurosawa liked to keep the camera away from the actors to improve their performances, they often used long lenses. His nickname on the set was literally "the emperor" because he was so exacting in getting the result that he wanted.

He also gave the cast their wardrobe weeks in advance of shooting so that they would get used to it and grow into it. This production was so small that the Cinematographer, Mr. Miyagawa, had to "borrow" full-length mirrors from the wardrobe department in place of using expensive electric lights, cables and generators, in order to shine sunlight into the dark regions of their forest location.

FATE AND DESTINY:
After the film was completed, the Japanese critics called the film a failure for the reasons that tt was too complicated, didn't properly visualize the original stories, and had too much swearing. This extraordinary film might have simply languished in obscurity were it not for the intervention of Fate and Destiny in the person of an Italian, Ms. Giuliana Stramigioli.

Ms. Stramigioli happened to be teaching the Italian language and literature at Tokyo University and had been assigned by the Italian film promotion agency to select a Japanese film for the 1951 Venice Film

Festival. She happened to see *Rashomon* at a screening, liked it and selected it to be shown at Venice over the objections of the Japanese government, who thought that the film was not, "representative of the Japanese Film Industry."

THREE SETS:
It's been said that Kurosawa's admiration of Silent Films led to his infusing this production with long passages of pure visual storytelling. The film was also designed around only three basic exterior sets, The Gate, The Forest, and The Court. During filming, in order to save money, the entire cast and crew lived together. This also enabled them to address, talk over, and solve many production problems on a round-the-clock basis.

This sparse and eloquent film tells several versions of a tragic rape and murder one summer afternoon in ancient Japan, and then asks the audience to question and ponder, "What actually is the truth?" The films obscurity and ambivalence has led to many film scholars writing volumes about the films "symbolism," calling it: An allegory for the defeat of Japan at the end of WWII, or an allegory for the atomic bomb, or that the dappled light symbolizes all of the character's ambiguity...

KAZUO MIYAGAMA:
The film's masterful Cinematographer Kazuo Miyagawa, has been a hero of mine for years and I always use one of his quotes in all of my cinema courses, telling my students his insightful and Zen-like words: "Forget the expensive equipment, only a beautiful person can take beautiful pictures…" However, he also added to the "symbolism" controversy by saying in an interview that, "…the forest setting was symbolic of the mystery shrouding the actual details of the dramatic events…"

However you interpret the story, *Rashomon* is a masterpiece and one that managed to find its way out of an unappreciative Japan and into the hearts of the cinematic world. It also introduced a young Toshiro Mifune and Akira Kurosawa to an international audience and they soon took their place among the major stars and filmmakers of the last century.

AWARDS:
Rashomon won the 1951 National Board of Review - Best Director Award, the 1951, Venice Film Festival – Golden Lion, the 1953, 25th Annual Academy Awards – Honorary Academy Award, and the 1953, Directors Guild of America – Outstanding Achievement in Motion Pictures.

ONLINE RESOURCES:

Use Google images & Google videos for dozens of links...

Buy it on Amazon, Google Play, or iTunes.

THINKING OUTSIDE THE BOX:
Class Exercises:

1. *Rashomon* is a complex and intriguing film. Each student should write an essay on his or her personal interpretation of the story.

2. This is a film about discovering "the truth" concerning a rape and murder in ancient Japan. It is told in flashbacks and every character seems to have their own version of the "truth." Each student should write an essay about which character's version of the story that they believe and why.

3. Each student should write an essay about how they interpret the great Cinematographer Kazuo Miyagawa's statement that: "...only a beautiful person can take beautiful pictures."

4. *Rashomon* was made on only $5000 US dollars, the equivalent of around $500,000 dollars today. Each student should write an essay describing the pros and

cons of working on a very small budget and having to use your imagination instead of a big budget to tell your story.

5. Each student should use Google and IMDb to find out more about Akira Kurosawa and select a film of his that they have not seen, that they can rent, buy or view online.

Chapter: 9

1958
HIROSHIMA, MON AMOUR

Alain Resnais
Remembering the Unimaginable

SPOILER ALERT!
This is a major film by a major filmmaker and it is not for the faint of heart. It's a tone poem of images, thoughts and emotions that intertwines a modern love story with many of the documentary horrors of Hiroshima, Japan as well as World War II Europe.

Hiroshima, Mon Amour is a film that asks a lot of an audience and at times it can be difficult to watch. It is, however, a masterpiece and an important Milestone In Cinema of the last century. Dazzling, Brilliant, Stunning, Bold, Horrific...

Give this film your complete and undivided attention.

THE CREATIVE TEAM:
Writer: Marguerite Duras
Director: Alain Resnais
Cinematographers: Michio Takajashi & Sacha Vierny
Editors: Jasmine Chasney, Henri Colpi & Anne Sarraute

WHY IS THIS FILM VISIONARY:
It is the boldest, most shocking, creative, and controversial use of the Art of Editing since D.W. Griffith's masterpiece, Intolerance. The Director, Alain Resnais, had already made a successful documentary on the Holocaust, *Night and Fog*, when he was approached to do another documentary on the subject of the atomic bomb.

He felt that a short documentary wouldn't work and instead he decided to do a feature film that had a love story in the foreground and the subject of the atomic bomb in the background. He recruited a contemporary young writer, Marguerite Duras, to write what he thought would be, "... a sort of poem in which the images would act as a counterpoint to the text." But he ended up with a stunning and classic film.

THE BASICS:
Even though Jean-Luc Godard's groundbreaking film *Breathless* has been credited with inventing the Jump Cut, it actually happened first in *Hiroshima Mon Amour*. No doubt the fact that the subject matter of this film, dealing with the horrors of nuclear war and with Hiroshima in particular, barely fifteen years after that tragedy, made this film easy to overlook in favor of the fresh and trendy young-tough-on-the-lam film from Mr. Godard that followed barely two years later.

THE FRENCH NEW WAVE:
Paris in the late 1950's was ripe and ready for a cinematic revolution. Influenced by the Italian Neo-Realists and led by the theorist and co-founder of the magazine "Cahiers du Cinema" Andre Bazin, the writers and critics who became the directors, Jean-Luc Godard, Francois Truffaut, Eric Rohmer, Claude Chabrol and Jacques Rivette led the way, as the French New Wave stormed the ivory towers of old fashioned glossy studio productions and international cinematic complacency. Their films were fresh, inventive, done with little or no budgets and often with family and friends in front of and behind the cameras. They dealt with the themes of existentialism, nihilism, and the meaninglessness of life, and they soon became the darlings of the

International Cinema.

THE LEFT BANK:
Their co-conspirators were the older and some say wiser members of what was then called The Left Bank. A group of writers, artists and filmmakers made up of Alain Resnais, Agnes Varda, Chris Marker, Marguerite Duras, and Alain Robbe-Grillet. These older young people were heavily influenced by austerity and formalism on the one hand, and the New Roman School of literature on the other, which de-emphasized plot and action while replacing it with an emphasis on language, memory, and subjectivity.

(You may Google, research, rent, and screen Alain Resnais's controversial feature *Last Year At Marienbad* to see a classic example of this kind of highly stylized, subjective art film, carried to its audience-confusing, absurdly illogical, story defying conclusion.)

The Left Bank proved to be an ideal setting for *Hiroshima, Mon Amour,* a production that would boldly set new standards in cinematic language. This film was destined to take filmmaking into the realm of pure poetry while at the same time, demonstrating the possibilities of cinematic memory and undertaking the deadly serious subject of the horrors of nuclear war.

THE INFAMOUS JUMP CUT:
Mr. Resnais ended up creating a landmark film that broke all kinds of new ground in its modern Jump Cut editing style, its use of language, and especially in its almost free associational cutting between the 1950's present and World War II Japan, as well as the 1950's present and World War II France.

If you look carefully, you can see in scenes that are supposed to contain "continuous dialogue" that the actor is "Jump Cut" to a different position with nearly each and every phrase; to my knowledge that had never been done prior to this film.

THE PRODUCTION:
The film was also shot in a revolutionary way, with Mr. Resnais shooting the film in two different parts of the world for a very practical reason: the producers had "blocked funds" in Japan. Mr. Resnais also used a different crew and film stock in each location; he completed the scenes in Japan first, using Cinematographer Michio Takahashi in August and September of 1958, and then completed scenes in France in December of that year with renowned French Cinematographer Sacha Vierny.

Emmanuelle Riva played the French woman, and Eiji Okada played the Japanese man. Okada spoke no French and had to literally learn each syllable of his dialogue phonetically.

Hiroshima, Mon Amour certainly stands alone as a modern day Milestone In Cinema... with its flamboyant avant-garde editing style, its images, its dialogue and its memories associated with the horrors of World War II. When I first saw this stunning film in the mid 1960's I thought that it was light years ahead of everything else in the cinema.

It was only slightly diminished several years later, when I discovered the gargantuan task that Mr. Griffith had given himself with *Intolerance*, inter-cutting four epochs of time that spanned nearly 2500 years of human history. That visionary production was basically *Hiroshima, Mon Amour* squared, and was done over forty years earlier in 1916!

Today, aside from a few Cinema Purists and scholars, *Intolerance* and the remarkable work of Mr. Griffith, has been politicized, forgotten, set aside and goes mostly unremembered. However, *Hiroshima, Mon Amour* still lives on. It is modern enough to speak to each new generation as it continues to stand as a testament to the ever-evolving language of Cinema and to the unspeakable horrors of nuclear war.

ONLINE RESOURCES:
Use Google images & Google videos for dozens of links...

Buy it on Amazon, Google Play, or iTunes.

THINKING OUTSIDE THE BOX:
Class Exercises:

1. Each student should write an essay describing why they think that this film has been called "...the boldest, most shocking, creative and controversial use of the Art of Editing since D.W. Griffith's masterpiece, Intolerance."

2. It was very controversial to intercut the horrors of Hiroshima with intimate love scenes. Each student should write an essay or a treatment that describes another horrific event or worldwide concern that might be brought to light in a similar manner.

3. Shooting in two different countries, with two different crews, DP's and film stocks, a leading man who had to learn each line phonetically... Each student should write an essay describing, what they imagine the daily production concerns might have

been.

4. Each student should write an essay comparing and contrasting Italian Neo Realism and the French New Wave. How are they similar and how do they differ.

5. The students should team up and make a small HD film in the style of Hiroshima Mon Amour.

IV. The Vanishing Traditions

Chapter 10

1959
SHADOWS

John Cassavetes
Improvising Independent

SPOILER ALERT!
You are probably not going to like this film. I don't like this film. It is tedious, boring, unstructured, and full of amateur actors whose performances are over-the-top and mannered. Its production values are minimal and amateurish. It was shot on 16mm in the streets of New York in 1957, and then much of it was re-shot in 1959.

However, I do respect this film, enormously. Why?

Because it is an important landmark in American Independent filmmaking, that was exactly the right film in exactly the right place at exactly the right time. Most importantly it is a film that helped to set the template for how to make an Independent film for many years to come.

For some of you this may be similar to having to go through a prolonged dental procedure. It may not be fun or even remotely close to a good time, but in the end, it is beneficial and very good for you.

THE CREATIVE TEAM:
Writer: John Cassavetes
Director: John Cassavetes
Cinematographer: Erich Kollmar
Editors: John Cassavetes, Maurice McEndree

WHY IS THIS FILM VISIONARY:
John Cassavetes was a force of nature. Like the members of the French New Wave, he too had seen the films of the Italian Neo-Realists and had understood that it was entirely possible to take unknown, inexperienced actors, natural locations, available or minimal light, and fashion these elements into a theatrical motion picture.

Mr. Cassavetes was first and foremost an up-and-coming actor who also taught a workshop for actors in New York, during the late 1950's. He must have, at some point, looked around at all of that raw talent and said to himself, "Why not make a film?" And that's exactly what he did.

Remember, this type of a production had never been attempted before in America and he had no one to reference as an example – no teacher, no mentor aside from the Neo-Realist Italian films that he had seen at various art houses in New York.

THE BASICS:
In 1957, Mr. Cassavetes used the improvisations from the actors in his workshop as the basis for his cast and the plot for his film. He pulled together a small group of inexperienced "volunteer" technicians and began to work on the film project that would eventually become *Shadows* – a film that was destined to become the foremost example of American Independent Filmmaking, garner tons of film festival acclaim for Mr. Cassavetes, and stand as a graphic example of how to make an independent film for many years to come.

Before most of the world even knew about the French New Wave, Mr. Cassavetes was already at work on his breakthrough film in the streets of New York. It's true that he shot the film twice – once in 1957 and again in 1959. After being displeased with the outcome of the first version, he re-shot and re-edited nearly half of the film, which eventually became the definitive version that everyone screens today.

The film's budget was claimed to be around $40,000, and a part of that budget was raised when Mr. Cassavetes went on the radio and asked for money. He appeared on the Jean Shepherd radio show and asked the listeners to send in a dollar or two to help with his production. He raised nearly a tenth of the budget from that program, and thankful for the help, he listed in the opening credits of the film, "Presented by Jean Shepherd's Night People." Basically he had pioneered "crowd-funding."

THE PRODUCTION:
Even though it was made in the 1950's during the uptight Eisenhower administration, it was a totally "outside of the box" production. Shot on 16mm in Black and White, it was a testament to the alienated "Beat Generation," of the 1950's that was questioning "the system," and all of its old-fashioned values.

In a time when films were dominated by white actors and nearly a decade before the Civil Rights movement, *Shadows* starred several African-

Americans. It also boldly attacked the taboo subject of an interracial love affair, boasted a largely improvised story, and a cutting edge Jazz Score by the saxophonist for the Charlie Mingus group, Shafi Hadi.

I worked with Seymour Cassell and he talked about volunteering to move equipment on the production and then spending months learning how to set up the lights, move the camera and load the film magazines. It was only years later that John finally considered using him as an actor in his highly acclaimed film, *Faces* for which Seymour received an Academy Award nomination.

THE CASSAVETES STYLE:
I met John on various occasion during the 60's, 70's, and 80's. First, when I was involved in the Cinematography and Editing of an unfinished and unreleased underground art film, *The Bach Train* in the late '60's, Mr. Cassavetes kindly let us use his editing room on the weekends to do some much needed re-cutting. Several of the crewmembers from that film went on to work on many of John's film and theatrical productions in the years to come.

I was personally disappointed not to have been able to DP one of his films, but John was primarily interested in using technicians who were inexperienced and who would work as "volunteers" for OJT (On the Job Training). I was, however, doing my best to be considered a "professional" Director of Photography and Editor, and being paid to do so in the mean streets of Hollywood.

THE AMERICAN INDEPENDENTS:
With *Shadows,* the doors had been opened, the way had been shown, and the template had been set for the emergence of the American Independent Film Movement. In a few years the names of Melvin Van Peeples, John Sayles, Spike Lee, Steven Soderberg, Robert Rodriguez, Kevin Smith, Neil La Bute, and others would come to the forefront as they carved out critical acclaim and careers for themselves by first making small 16mm films. Then, following the example set in the late 1950's by the maestro of American Independent Films John Cassavetes, they would go on to make bigger and better films.

THE AWARDS:
Shadows won the Critics Award at the prestigious Venice Film Festival and was nominated for three BAFTA Awards.

ONLINE RESOURCES:
Use Google Images & Google Video to find dozens of links...

Buy it on Amazon, Google Play, or iTunes.

Main Titles Video URL
http://www.imdb.com/video/screenplay/vi629604633/

THINKING OUTSIDE THE BOX:
Class Exercises:

1. After screening *Shadows*, each student should write an essay detailing what they liked and didn't like, their pros and cons.

2. John Cassavetes may have always considered himself to be an amateur filmmaker. Each student should research the definition and origins of the words "amateur," and "professional," and write an essay describing how those terms apply to the acting and directing careers of Mr. Cassavetes.

3. American Independent filmmakers like Melvin Van Peeples, John Sayles, Spike Lee, Steven Soderberg, Robert Rodriguez, Kevin Smith and Neil La Bute all made small 16mm first films. Each student should choose one of these filmmakers and write an essay naming and describing the film they made and the elements in it that can be linked back to *Shadows*.

4. The End Title card in *Shadows* reads: "The Film That You Have Just Seen, Was Entirely Improvised." Each student should write an essay describing the pros and cons about shooting a film under these conditions.

5. Each student should use the Internet to research Mr. Cassavetes directing career, find a film of his that they haven't seen and buy it, rent it or screen it online.

Chapter 11:

1960
BREATHLESS

Jean-Luc Godard
Breaking All The Rules

SPOILER ALERT!
Remember this film was made in 1960. The prevailing style of film production during that time was the big, wide-screen, perfectly lit, rock steady camera-on-a-dolly, star-driven, lavishly produced studio-film usually starring someone like Cary Grant, Rock Hudson, or Charlton Heston.

For a young upstart French film critic like Jean-Luc Godard, to take an American star, Jean Seberg, and put her into a film with a no-name cast, a production that didn't even have a script, that was shot without makeup, sound or even lights, was nothing short of totally revolutionary. To top it off, in place of a dolly, the director pushed his cinematographer around Paris in a wheel chair or in a canvas mail delivery cart!!!

That was not only unprecedented, it was absolutely unheard of, totally outside of the realm of sanity and as daring as someone today taking Ellen Page and starring her in a film made on a cell phone! Of course, in today's new paradigm climate that might not only be possible but acceptable. However, for Mr. Godard to do what he did in 1960 that was absolutely unheard of and unacceptable!

THE CREATIVE TEAM:
Writers: Jean-Luc Godard / François Truffaut
Director: Jean-Luc Godard
Cinematographer: Raoul Coutard
Editors: Cecile Decugis & Lila Herman

WHY IS THIS FILM VISIONARY:
Perhaps more that any other film in modern history, *Breathless* came smashing onto the art house screens in 1960 boldly stating that there was a New Wave that it was specifically French and that all of the old ways of doing things in the Cinema were now a thing of the past.

Jean-Luc Godard had taken the best elements from

the Italian Neo-Realists, his loathing of the old guard French studio films as well as his penchant for using improvisation, documentary-like locations, lighting and cinematography and woven of these disparate threads and entirely new cinematic tapestry. The old way of doing things had been suddenly and swiftly swept aside with the appearance of one small French film: *Breathless!*

THE BASICS:
There have been arguments as to whether or not Mr. Godard had a script, and he most certainly did not. Not by any classical definition of the term. What he had was a story by his colleague, Francois Truffaut and he had written several scenes, one of which may have read:

Ext. - Champs Elysees - Day
Jean Seberg sells the New York Times & meets Jean-Paul...

For everything else he only had notes, piles and piles of notes. Rather than wait for the inspiration to write a script, which seemed not to be happening, J-LG finally decided to go ahead and make the film without one. Instead of having a planned script, he would simply do his best to invent and improvise the film, writing scenes day by day as he went along. Also, to add to the spontaneity, Mr. Godard would often tell the actor's what lines he wanted them to say, <u>during the actual filming of the scenes</u>!

Breathless had a flagrant and total disregard for traditional filmmaking methods. In fact it seemed that Mr. Godard reveled in simply tossing all of those traditions out of the window. It's been said of his methods: "He drove a stolen truck over the rules of filmmaking, then backed up, and drove over them again."

THE PRODUCTION:
During an extended trip through Europe in the 1980's, I had the pleasure of meeting with the Cinematographer of *Breathless* and of many other great films of the French New Wave: Raoul Coutard. Our discussion lasted for several delightful hours and was punctuated by Raoul taking shots of whisky as we conversed through a translator. He graciously told me in answer to one of my many questions, exactly how Mr. Godard's version of the famous "Jump Cut" had come to pass...

It seems that Mr. Godard had told his Cinematographer that he wanted *Breathless* to look like reportage, like documentary news footage and that he did not want any of the usual movie lighting.

This forced Mr. Coutard to search for the fastest film stock that he could find, and he finally located an Illford stock that had been only used for still cameras. However, it only came in 50-meter lengths.

As a result, he had his assistants constantly following along behind him, loading magazines with these small rolls of 35mm film. Then whenever they would run out of film during a scene, Mr. Godard would simply say, "OK we have enough of that..." they would then move on to another sequence and hence the "Jump Cut."

Later, during the post-production Mr. Godard would simply cut large hunks out of various shots or scenes, whenever he felt that the material was too slow and in so doing, he enhanced the Jump Cut effect of the film even more. This is also one of the first films to ever shoot in the streets of Paris at Night using only Available Light and if you watch carefully during one of those night scenes, you can catch the first "High Five" ever to be captured on film.

THE AWARDS:
Breathless and Jean-Luc Godard won Best Director and Best Film honors at the Berlin International Film Festival, French Syndicate of Cinema Critics and the Prix Jean Vigo. Jean Seberg won a Best Foreign

Actress Award at the British version of the Academy Awards, the BAFTA.

ONLINE RESOURCES:
Use Google images & Google videos for dozens of links...

Buy it on Amazon, Google Play, or iTunes.

THINKING OUTSIDE THE BOX:
Class Exercises:

1. It's nearly impossible to judge the impact of this small French New Wave film today, over fifty years after it exploded onto the scene, but try. Each student should write an essay about all of the rule-breaking innovations that Jean-Luc Godard introduced in this groundbreaking film and how they are routinely accepted in mainstream films today.

2. Each student should write an essay comparing and contrasting The Bicycle Thief and Breathless. How are they similar, how are they different and which one has more impact today.

3. After the success of Breathless, Jean-Luc Godard became a media sensation, a film festival darling and a world-renown filmmaker. Each student should

write an essay describing what he meant when he said: "Film is the truth, 24 times a second."

4. Raoul Coutard was the outstanding Cinematographer behind many of Jean-Luc Godard's films as well as many other French New Wave classics like Jules & Jim. Each student should use the Internet to research Mr. Coutard's career and find a film of his that they can buy or rent on line and screen.

5. Ditto for J-LG. Each student should use the Internet to locate two more of Jean-Luc Godard's controversial films. Rent them or buy them on line and view them. Then write an essay about what you liked or disliked about his infamous, audience alienating style or lack thereof.

Chapter 12:

1960
PSYCHO

Alfred Hitchcock
An Ice Cold Shower

SPOILER ALERT!
This film is not for everyone. If you are squeamish about being hacked to death while taking a shower, or do not like to hear high pitched violins while blood is flowing down the drain, or would prefer not to be slashed and stabbed while exploring a sweet little old lady's ominous gothic home, then you may want to avert your eyes.

However, if you would like to watch the Maestro and Master Cinematic Artist, Alfred Hitchcock at work, as he literally gets his ticket buying, popcorn munching audience by their collective balls... Kindly, do not turn away.

By now nearly everyone on the planet has seen this film and its infamous shower scene. If you have not, under what rock have you been hiding for all of these years? And even if you have somehow missed this classic, we will attempt to reveal a few new wrinkles, none of them however are on the flawlessly voluptuous body of Janet Leigh!

THE CREATIVE TEAM:
Writers: Joseph Stefano / Robert Bloch
Director: Alfred Hitchcock
Cinematographer: John L. Russell
Editor: George Tomasini

WHY IS THIS FILM VISIONARY:
Psycho was not attempting to be "profound" or "important" or "new wave" or an "art film but it is still an outstanding and visionary film. Why? Because when this horror/thriller, dime-novel material, was in the hands of an absolute Cinematic Genius like Mr. Hitchcock, he was able to mold it into an audience-terrifying masterpiece, like no other before or since.

As we know, it has spawned many lesser attempts at its accomplishments since its release in 1960 and none of them have ever equaled it. I believe that the only films that have even come close are William Friedkin's *Exorcist* and Ridley Scott's original *Alien*. By the way, in 2001, those two huge multi-multi-million dollar productions, finished #3 and #6 behind *Psycho*, the little $800,000 masterpiece that finished #1 when the American Film Institute presented their 100 Years, 100 Thrills, Awards.

THE BASICS:
This film has sparked so much controversy so many books and articles have been written about it and its infamous "Shower Scene" that it certainly must have touched some sort of primal nerve, in both the critics and the audience's psyche. Quite an accomplishment for such a small, inauspicious production that had little more than an $800,000.00 budget (That was financed by Mr. Hitchcock himself!) was done on a spare 35 day schedule and utilized the crew from his TV Series, *Alfred Hitchcock Presents*.

THE PRODUCTION:
The production of *Psycho* took place at the Revue Studios, on the Universal Back Lot, from November 30th 1959 to February 1st 1960 with the shower scene being filmed from December 17th to the 23rd of 1959.

At Mr. Hitchcock's request, Saul Bass, who had designed the film's main titles also did the storyboards for the infamous shower scene, which were then carefully followed by Hitch and the entire crew. It's said that there are over 70 meticulous setups in this sequence, even though the actual murder takes only about 45 seconds of screen time.

It's also been reported that Janet Leigh had her private parts covered with moleskin and performed nearly all of the grueling filming of this horrific scene herself. Since Anthony Perkins was already in New York preparing a play, a body double in black makeup so that no features were distinguishable, was used for the knife wielding character of Norman's "mother."

Yes, a nude body double was used for Janet Leigh for several crucial beats during the bloody shower scene, including the hand reaching for the shower curtain. If your freeze that scene and turn down the contrast on your monitor you can clearly see that there are naked breasts out of focus in the background.

Bravo! Mr. Hitchcock for putting one over on the censors of that day. The blood effects that were utilized here and in nearly all black and white films during that time were done with chocolate syrup.

Janet Leigh more or less disputes that Mr. Hitchcock didn't discuss things with actors by stating that when he cast her he specifically told her: "I hired you because you are an actress! I will only direct you if A: You attempt to take more than your share of the pie. B: If you don't take enough. Or C: If you are having trouble motivating the necessary timed movement."

THE MUSIC:
Mr. Hitchcock and his writer Joseph Stefano originally thought that a Jazz score would be used for the film and at one point Mr. Hitchcock envisioned that the shower scene would actually play without music; composer Bernard Herman literally begged Mr. Hitchcock to let him do the shower scene. Then after seeing and hearing the results, Mr. Hitchcock doubled the composer's salary and later attributed over 30% of the films success and its effect on an audience to Mr. Herman's score which utilized only stringed instruments.

A SATURDAY MATINEE:
I was fortunate to see this film when it was first released at a normal Saturday afternoon matinee. The theater happened to be packed with 7 to 12 year old kids that had been dropped off by their parents, to go to the movies "on their own."

This was long before there was a ratings system and during that time, once a film was released, everybody from the cradle to the grave saw it. What I saw that afternoon left me speechless. I have never before or since witnessed such an audience reaction and I have also never seen a better example of the power of a film on the big screen, or of a Film Director, like Mr. Hitchcock, having his audience literally by the balls and totally under his control.

After the shower scene these kids were screaming, they were hiding their heads, they were literally crawling under their seats trying to get away from the horrors up there on the big screen: But nobody left the theater. Time and time again they were on their feet or standing on their seats screaming, "Don't go, don't go!!!" whenever anyone even thought of approaching the house or when near the end of the film, the character of Marion starts to go down the basement stairs...

That day, I ended up watching the audience nearly as much as I watched the movie and by the end, I finally understood exactly how powerful the movies were and how the masterful Film Director, Alfred Hitchcock, was able to totally manipulate and control his audiences.

Of course, no one took a shower for a very long time, some never again and when a father complained in a letter to Mr. Hitchcock, that his daughter would not take a bath after seeing the French film by Clouzot, Diabolique and now would not take a shower after seeing *Psycho*, Mr. Hitchcock replied with his customary humor, "Send her to the dry cleaners..."

THE AWARDS:
Psycho won the Golden Globe Award for Best Supporting Actress, it was nominated for the Directors Guild of America Award as well as four Academy Awards including Best Director, Best Cinematography and Best Supporting Actress.

ONLINE RESOURCES:
Use Google images & Google video for dozens of links...

Buy it on Amazon, Google Play, or iTunes.

Trailer / Video URL
http://www.imdb.com/video/screenplay/vi1492452121/

THINKING OUTSIDE THE BOX:
Class Exercises:

1. Mr. Hitchcock originally envisioned the shower scene to play silent. Play the scene that way then play

it again with the sound turned up. Now each student should write an essay about the roll that the music and sound design played in this scene and in an audience's experience of the film.

2. Clint Eastwood liked to use the phrase, "Don't overthink it... Just do it." With that in mind, each student should write an essay, comparing and contrasting: John Ford making *The Grapes of Wrath* and Alfred Hitchcock making *Psycho,* both for under 1 million dollars. Two Cinematic Artists, with very different taste, at the very top of their game.

3. As we stated, *Psycho* was made in 1960 for under one million dollars. Each student should write an essay giving their opinions why, despite spending many millions of dollars more, no one has been able make a better or a more frightening film.

4. Mr. Hitchcock has made several films in addition to *Psycho* that pushed sexual boundaries *Rope, Strangers On A Train* and *Vertigo*. Each student should choose one to research on the Internet, view it and write an essay on how it compares or contrasts with Psycho.

5. I've always thought that Mr. Hitchcock had quite a lot to say, or imply behind his technical facade of claiming to only do "Thrillers." That being the case,

each student should write an essay on what the philosophical implication are behind the Theme Music for his TV series, entitled: "Funeral March of a Marionette"?

V. The Confusion, The Bomb, & MTV

Chapter 13

1963
8½

Federico Fellini
A Director's Vision

SPOILER ALERT!
For some of you, this film may be difficult to appreciate. It is a film about filmmaking and about a filmmaker, a Director who has Director's block and who is not only in the midst of a production crisis, but also in the midst of a personal, spiritual, and emotional one. He is a liar, a cheater, a dreamer, and a visionary who is so obsessed by his personal

fantasies and memories that he uses them as material for his work. In short, he is an Artist who is suffering and striving and succeeding and failing right before our eyes.

8½ is at times a funny, fragmented, confused, private, personal, and universal work that, in the final analysis, is pulled off with the adept slight of hand of a master magician and the perfect balance of a dazzling high wire artist.

Like several of these top 50 films, this is probably not a film that you can comprehend with only one viewing. It has so much to offer on so many levels, that it is nearly overwhelming the first time through. But if you will allow yourself to be taken on a journey by a cinematic genius, to be led and informed and tricked and entertained my the maestro of maestros, then sit back and take in all the bravura and splendor of Federico Fellini's... *"Otto e mezzo"* or, *8½*.

THE CREATIVE TEAM:
Writer: Federico Fellini, Ennio Flaiano, Tulio Pinilli, Brunello Rondi
Director: Federico Fellini
Cinematographer: Gianni Di Venanzo
Editor: Leo Cattozzo

WHY IS THIS FILM VISIONARY:

If you look up the definition of a "visionary" you will find: "...A visionary person: inspired, imaginative, creative, inventive, ingenious, enterprising, innovative; insightful, perceptive, intuitive, prescient, discerning, shrewd, wise, clever, resourceful, idealistic, romantic, quixotic, dreamy..." That seems not only to be the definition of the many facets of the film, *8½* but also that of its flamboyant, "Fellini-esque" Director, himself.

If you are young or if this is your first viewing, *8½* may seem like a collection of nonsensical, meaningless, random scenes that are in no coherent order and that don't add up to a real story. If you are a filmmaker or part of the filmmaking process, the older you become and the more times you allow yourself the experience of *Otto e mezzo* the more profound, sincere, heartbreaking and universal it becomes. It is actually a Filmmakers Film.

THE BASICS:

On the first day of production, Maestro Fellini took a small piece of tape and placed it on the camera near the viewfinder, on it he had written: "Remember this is a comedy."

Nearly two decades before making *8½* Mr. Fellini had

been influenced by the Italian Neo-Realists and it showed in much of his early work especially the sparse and stark, "road picture" *La Strada*. Now however, after the astronomical success of *La Dolce Vita* had catapulted him into the stratosphere of a celebrity and the rarified position of being an "important director" it seemed that he might have run out of gas. He was bereft of a central idea, of a cohesive story and basically as Guido, the stand-in director for Fellini, in *8½* states to the paparazzi who pester him near the conclusion of the film: "I have nothing to say."

THE PRODUCTION:
But after all, he was the maestro Federico Fellini, and he had to perform, he had to make a statement, to make an important film, he had to say something. So out of his uncertainty, out of his *la bella confusione*, "The Beautiful Confusion," which happened to be the working title for *8½*, he began to create. Yes, it seems like Maestro Fellini even found beauty in his confusion.

He created a film about a Film Director, beset with doubts about the subject of the film that he was already making, that he was already in the middle of preparing. A Director surrounded by a cast and crew and having to make decisions regarding, actors screen tests, locations, wardrobe, script changes and bit parts, as well as fast talking his Producer who simply needed for the film to start production.

At the same time, he was in the midst of a mid-life spiritual crisis, being unfaithful to his wife, trying to hide his mistress, fantasizing either about his childhood memories, or his many and frequent affairs and ultimately longing for "The Ideal Woman" who could help him to escape, start over, and live a much simpler life.

Try to submit that as a treatment or story outline and see how fast the door would be hitting your backside. But this was Federico Fellini, and he either knew or imagined that he knew that he could pull it off. Production wise, this was an extremely difficult film to "board" or to plan and schedule, in order to film all of the various layers of fantasy, reality, movie making, dreams, childhood memories etc. First, each one needed planning well in advance: cast, crewed, clothed, made up, lit, rehearsed and finally filmed.

Also, Fellini being Fellini and thriving on spontaneity, he did not write much of the dialogue until during post-production; there was no final script, so he often had the actors moving around the various locations and sets, counting to themselves or mouthing meaningless phrases that he would then find the right words for later... Like they always warn you by saying: "Please... Do Not Try This At Home!"

THE AWARDS:
Ta Da! He did it! He pulled it off! *8½* garnered critical acclaim wherever it played. In 1963 it won Best Foreign Language Film from the National Board of Review and the New York Film Critics Circle Awards. In 1964 it won two Academy Awards for Best Foreign Film and Best Costume Design. In 1987 *Otto e mezzo* was voted The Most Important European Film Ever Made. In 2002 it ranked number three in the prestigious Sight & Sound Magazine's poll of the Top Ten Best Films Ever Made.

ONLINE RESOURCES:
Use Google Images & Google Videos for dozens of links...

Purchase the DVD at
www.criterion.com/films/150-812

Watch scenes or the Trailer at
Otto e mezzo
www.youtube.com

THINKING OUTSIDE THE BOX:

Class Exercises:

1. Each student should write an essay describing what they liked best about the film and what they liked least and why.

2. Each student should write an essay describing their favorite and least favorite scenes or sequences and why.

3. Each student should go online and find another of Mr. Fellini's films that they haven't seen and rent or buy it on line and view it.

4. After you have screened another of the maestros films, describe: What film you saw, what your reaction was to it and why.

5. Each student should write an essay, treatment or do a short film in the style of *8½* using autobiographical elements from their lives.

Chapter 14:

1964
DR. STRANGELOVE
Or: How I Learned To Stop Worrying And Love The Bomb

Stanley Kubrick
The Unimaginable As Satire

SPOILER ALERT!
Now we are in Stanley Kubrick territory. Or, as he was regarded by many of his contemporaries, the genius of all things cinematic or: Stan "The Man" Kubrick. We begin with *Dr. Strangelove*... a very black comedy about nuclear war. That right, it's a comedy! Could there be any subject more difficult to make funny than nuclear war? Alright... The Holocaust.

The comic dynamo, Peter Sellers, was originally going to play four roles in the film, but circumstances led to his only playing three. Each one, however, turned out to be a showstopper that caused audiences all over the world to fall out of their seats, convulsing with laughter.

It's been said that Mr. Sellers had so many improvisational flights of fantasy that ended up in the finished film, that both Mr. Kubrick and his co-writer Terry Southern, credit him with writing over 30% of the finished production.

THE CREATIVE TEAM:
Writers: Peter George / Stanley Kubrick / Terry Southern
Director: Stanley Kubrick
Cinematographer: Gilbert Taylor
Editor: Anthony Harvey

WHY IS THIS FILM VISIONARY:
Dr. Strangelove... began as a serious film, by a serious filmmaker, from a serious novel, "Red Alert" by Peter George. It was going to be a thriller based on the possibility of a nuclear war, but Mr. Kubrick, who had also read over fifty volumes of dense technical material in preparing for the film, soon discovered that the data and language being used bordered on the comic and the absurd.

Since Peter Sellers had given him a copy of Terry Southern's book *The Magic Christian*, which he had enjoyed, Mr. Kubrick brought in Mr. Southern to work on the final polish of what he had already written as a satirical comedy. To have the capacity and genius to poke fun at the horrendous subject of nuclear war and those who would wield its unimaginable power is what makes *Dr. Strangelove...* an extraordinary film masterpiece.

THE BASICS:
Based on the success of *Lolita*, Colombia Studios agreed to finance *Dr. Strangelove or: How I Learned To Stop Worrying And Love The Bomb*, only if Peter Sellers would play at least four (4) parts in the film. Mr. Kubrick agreed to their demand and as well as playing the British Officer Lionel Mandrake, the President of the United States Merkin Muffley and the titular character and ex-Nazi scientist Dr. Strangelove, Mr. Sellers also reluctantly prepared to play the role of Major (King) Kong, the B-52 Pilot.

Reluctantly, because he was afraid that he could not master the Texas accent. However, Terry Southern, who happened to be a Texan, recorded all of the character's dialogue onto a tape, which Mr. Sellers listened to repeatedly, night and day until he eventually did feel that he had the accent down cold.

THE PRODUCTION:

Mr. Sellers had actually done several successful days of shooting as Major Kong, when a leg injury prevented him from being able navigate the inside the B-52 set and Mr. Kubrick was forced to re-cast the role. All of Mr. Sellers scenes as Major Kong were eventually re-shot with the authentic western character actor Slim Pickins, playing the part to perfection.

More re-shooting also occurred on the War Room set concerning Mr. Sellers' role as the President, Merkin Muffley. Originally he was playing the part as being both effeminate and having a bad cold. However, these two affectations, when performed by Mr. Sellers amazing flights of improvisational fantasy, caused such episodes of unrestrained laughter from both the cast and the crew, that Mr. Kubrick finally had to tone down the performance.

He eventually re-shot the part of the President portraying him as being the only voice of reason among a room full of utter madmen. Mr. Sellers, was paid $1,000,000.00 for his three roles in Dr. Strangelove... which prompted Mr. Kubrick to quip, "I got three for the price of six."

THE WAR ROOM:

Mr. Kubrick had requested that the production designer Ken Adam, build a ceiling on the War Room set, not only for the sake of authenticity but also to force the Director of Photography, Gilbert Taylor to use the lighting that Mr. Kubrick had already designed, tested, and placed over the actors at the circular War Room table.

Even thought the film was photographed in black and white, Mr. Kubrick also had that same round War Room table covered with green felt, like a poker table, so that all the performers would understand that their characters were literally "Playing poker with the fate of humanity."

Dr. Strangelove... was the first example of Mr. Kubrick developing his style of building the lighting into his sets or locations, and he specifically told the DP Gil Taylor that he did not want to add any additional lights. This is a brilliant technique, which is also a very actor friendly and production friendly way of working.

I imagine that Mr. Kubrick arrived at this conclusion by starting out as a still photographer in New York and doing a lot of shooting on the streets, in the Jazz Clubs or on the Subway utilizing natural locations and available or practical light. Also having already worked with Peter Sellers, whose improvisations were considered to be the most valuable part of the production, building the lighting into the sets ensured that Mr. Sellers would not have to be stopped mid-improvisation in order for a technician to adjust the lighting. With this technique along with multiple cameras, Mr. Kubrick was able to shoot in any direction at any time and keep the actors, especially Mr. Sellers "in the moment."

DOCUMENTARY STYLE FILMING:
This was also one of the first times that I can recall seeing realistic simulated documentary war footage being used in a major studio film. The scenes where the Army is attempting to re-capture Burpelson Air Force Base were shot with telephoto lenses and with hand held cameras, peering through foliage or lying on the ground behind the defending troops, on an actual location and in available daylight. These techniques gave the scenes the exact look of authentic war footage that had been photographed by newsreel cameramen, during a military engagement.

A RISKY PRODUCTION:
This was a very ambitious, risky, and dangerous film to do at the time. It was scheduled to have its first preview screening on November 22$_{nd}$ 1963 – the infamous day of President Kennedy's assassination.

Due to the events in Dallas, the release of the film was delayed until 1964 – and a line from Major Kong was dubbed from "Dallas" to "Vegas." Look what had happened to the sitting President of the United States, after he had attempted to halt the U.S. Government and the Military Industrial Complex's plans for an ongoing war in Vietnam. That fact alone, is why this was a risky and dangerous film to attempt, but Mr. Kubrick soldiered on.

This film not only poked fun at the military but it also made those men, who were actually considering nuclear war as a logical choice in a future conflict, look like nothing short of madmen gambling with the ultimate fate of humanity. As a result, the Pentagon refused to have anything to do with the film and eventually even the studio, Columbia Pictures, backed away from it as best they could.

Once again, Fate or Destiny stepped in and *Dr. Strangelove...* became a huge international success both with the critics and more importantly with the public at large. I can recall seeing this film when it first came out and literally falling out of my seat in the balcony of the Pix Theater on Hollywood Boulevard, screaming with laughter at Peter Sellers as he stood up shouting, "Mien Fuhrer I can walk!" Mr. Kubrick and his film had succeeded mightily, in overcoming nearly insurmountable odds. As the actor Edmund Gwenn is reported to have said on his deathbed, "Dying is easy my dear, Comedy is difficult!"

THE AWARDS:
The film was nominated for four Academy Awards including Best Director and Mr. Kubrick won the New York Critics Circle Award as Best Director.

A PHILOSOPHICAL POST SCRIPT:
Stanley Kubrick, who already had major artistic notches in his belt *for Paths of Glory* and *Lolita*, had made another thought provoking movie for the ages, and by the way it would not be his last... Mr. Kubrick not only had a worldview, he also had a cosmic and universal one. As he had stated in his comments about nuclear war and humanity's bleak existence: "The destruction of this planet would have no significance on a cosmic scale. Our extinction would be little more than a match flaring for a second in the heavens. And if that match does blaze in the darkness, there will be none to mourn a race that used a power that could have lit a beacon in the stars to light its funeral pyre."

Dr. Strangelove or: How I Learned to Stop Worrying and Love the Bomb, a very funny film... from a deadly serious filmmaker.

ONLINE RESOURCES:

Use Google Images & Google Videos for dozens of links...

Buy it on Amazon, Google Play, or iTunes.

Trailer Video URL
http://www.imdb.com/video/screenplay/vi3114467609/

THINKING OUTSIDE THE BOX:
Class Exercises:

1. *Dr. Strangelove...* began as a serious project on a serious subject, but Mr. Kubrick discovered during his research, that the language and terms being used bordered on the absurd... Each student should write an essay or treatment about other contemporary problems that might benefit from laughter instead of a more serious tone.

2. I literally fell out of my seat, laughing at Peter Sellers last line in the film, "Mien Fuhrer, I can walk!" Each student should research Mr. Sellers on the Internet and write an essay about his comedic contribution to this and other of his many films.

3. Mr. Kubrick is famous for his many stylistic and technical accomplishments. Each student should write an essay describing exactly how he created the simulated documentary war footage for this film.

4. The circular table in the War Room is an example of Mr. Kubrick actually building much of the lighting for a scene into the set. Each student should write an essay giving their opinions on the pros and cons of this type of a lighting set up.

5. Mr. Kubrick was an extremely serious Artist and Filmmaker. Each student should write an essay regarding Kubrick's statement: "The destruction of this planet would have no significance on a cosmic scale..."

Chapter 15

1964
A HARD DAYS NIGHT

Richard Lester
The Fab Four

SPOILER ALERT!
Do not watch this film if you are not prepared to be mesmerized, dazzled and overwhelmed all over again by the Fab Four: The Beatles, the musical group that changed everyone and everything on the planet during the 1960's and 70's. You cannot possibly imagine the mind-blowing ecstasy and bouncing-off-the-wall euphoria that we all experienced back in the day, when viewing this freewheeling, black and white, day-in-the-life production, on the big screen. John, Paul, George and Ringo: the music, the fans, the excitement and right before our very eyes, the world's first Music Videos that would eventually evolve into MTV!

THE CREATIVE TEAM:
Writer: Alun Owen
Director: Richard Lester
Cinematographer: Gilbert Taylor
Editor: John Jympson

WHY IS THIS FILM VISIONARY:
Simply because this film was the first to take pop-music out of the jukebox, put it up on the big screen, and fuse it forever to the Art Of The Century: Filmmaking. Using black and white film, hand held cameras, and a documentary style to present the hottest young musical group on the planet to the movie-going public, took an extraordinary mastery of the filmmaking art and a cool and calculating vision: Mr. Lester had both. Whether by chance or design, *A Hard Day's Night* began the process; the beat of the music, the personalities of the Fab Four, and the power of the cinematic presentation all merged into an entirely new art form. An art form that started the snowball rolling downhill that soon became an avalanche, and lead directly to the concept of music videos and eventually, "I want my MTV!"

THE BASICS:
Richard Lester was an American child prodigy who was studying at the University of Pennsylvania by age

of 15. He began working in American television then moved to England, where Peter Sellers noticed him. Wanting to become a visionary filmmaker, he made an experimental short with Mr. Sellers called: *The Running, Jumping & Standing Still Film.* Which became a favorite of The Beatles. And as Fate would have it, he was later chosen by them to direct *A Hard Day's Night.*

This brilliant piece of pop-art filmmaking was presented more or less as a day-in-the-life of the Beatles; had it not been for this zany group's four distinct personalities constantly goofing, mugging, underplaying one-liners, and not ever taking themselves seriously, the film might have turned out to be a cautionary tale about four talented young musicians who had become prisoners of their own fame, living their celebrity lives on a treadmill that consisted of "...a train and a room, and a car and a room and a room and a room..."

Happily there was also the soundtrack, the songs, the music and the lyrics all sung by the lads that had the audiences of the 1960's tapping their feet, clapping their hands, and more or less forgetting for a while at least, the murder of President Kennedy, the growing war in Vietnam, student protests, civil unrest and the host of other troubles that awaited them outside the air conditioned confines of the theater.

THE PRODUCTION:
Filming began on March 2, 1964, and unlike nearly all of the feature films made before it, it was shot mostly in sequence. No doubt the director Richard Lester wanted to maintain as much of the semi-documentary, hand held style as possible so as not to stretch his new-to-acting cast too far and by not asking them to work out of sequence, certainly must have helped.

Today it's not uncommon for musical groups to spend countless hundreds of thousands, even millions of dollars on only one of their music videos. Back in the day, Mr. Lester made an entire film, that included over ten songs each with a different music video attached and the entire production cost only $500,000.00 and was completed during a six week shooting schedule.

The constant references to Paul's grandfather as being a "clean" old man, were because the actor playing the part, Wilfred Brambell, has starred in the 1960's English TV series, *Steptoe and Son*, where he was constantly referred to a "dirty" old man. In yet another example of our seeming lack of originality, *Steptoe and Son* was remade in the US in the 1970's as the hit TV Series, *Sanford and Son*.

The fans chasing the lads in the opening scenes at the train station are actual fans and, in keeping with the semi-documentary style, when George unexpectedly falls down while being chased, the faux pas was kept in the finished film. George also met his future wife, Patricia Boyd, during the filming since she was playing one of the schoolgirls on the train.

The title of the film came flowing out of Ringo's mouth as a one of his many malapropisms dubbed by his mates as "Ringo-isms," and struck everyone as exactly right for the title of the film: *A Hard Day's Night.* This witty and inventive production not only led directly to many other British thrillers and comedies, it also spawned the US TV series *The Monkeys*, and as Roger Ebert has stated: "Today when we watch TV and see quick cutting, hand-held cameras, interviews conducted on the run with moving targets, quickly intercut snatches of dialogue, music under documentary action and all the other trademarks of the modern style, we are looking at the children of *A Hard Days' Night.*"

THE AWARDS:
A Hard Day's Night was nominated for two Academy Awards, Best Screenplay: Alun Owen and Best Score

Adaptation: George Martin. In 2004 Total Film magazine chose it as the 42nd greatest British film of all time and it ranks number one on Rotten Tomatoes lists of Top Ten Certified Fresh Musicals.

ONLINE RESOURCES:
Use Google Videos & Google Images for dozens of Links...

Buy it on Amazon, Google Play, or iTunes.

THINKING OUTSIDE THE BOX:
Class Exercises:

1. While the film is still fresh in you mind, each student should write and essay about their likes, dislikes and what worked and didn't work for them.

2. This film contained the first Music Videos of popular songs, which led directly to MTV. Each student should write an essay about what other influences this film had on popular culture and entertainment.

3. The Cinematographer, Gil Taylor also shot Dr. Strangelove... Each student should compare and contrast his black and white work in both films. What makes the cinematography in each film different and

how is it similar?

4. Each student should write an essay about what song and music video is their favorite and why.

5. Each student should check out the Director Richard Lester on IMDb, select one of his other films, watch it and write an essay about how and why his style and vision changed.

VI. Global & Personal Conflicts

Chapter 16:

1965
THE WAR GAME

Peter Watkins
The Unimaginable As Documentary

SPOILER ALERT!

Like Hiroshima Mon Amour before it, The War Game is a devastating, semi-documentary film on the horrendous effects of nuclear war. It was made in England by Peter Watkins for BBC television and was supposed to be seen by the British public on August 6, 1965, the twentieth anniversary of the nuclear attack on Hiroshima. However, because the film was in direct opposition to the Official British Government policy that a nuclear war was survivable, it's broadcast was delayed indefinitely and it was not shown on the BBC until 1885.

This film is not for the timid or the squeamish, since it's presented like news footage, or a documentary of an actual nuclear attack on England. As one viewer stated after a screening in Toronto: "...I recall people coming from the small theater with shocked looks on their faces, one couple I recall the man was being sick at the curb, others seemed to have just blank stares on their faces."

THE CREATIVE TEAM:
Writer: Peter Watkins
Director: Peter Watkins
Cinematographer: Peter Bartlett, Peter Suschitsky
Editor: Michael Bradsell

WHY IS THIS FILM VISIONARY:
Because it boldly told the world that nuclear war, was an horrific, unimaginable option of modern warfare, that is was not survivable, that those in charge of the government had been and were continuing to lie to the public about it and that the human cost would be unfathomable. Using the style of a matter-of-fact, made for television news magazine it presented its anti-nuclear point of view in graphic and nearly

unwatchable detail. It was a stunning and startling account of what might actually happen in a nuclear attack that was so chillingly presented that the running time of under fifty minutes wasn't a problem, since the experience of watching it, actually felt as if you had just seen a two hour feature film.

THE BASICS:
Peter Watkins was an outspoken and unique film artist who style is both entertaining and in your face since he likes to mix dramatic and documentary content together. By 1963 his work had been noticed by the head of the documentary department at the BBC. When he was offered his choice of assignments, he requested to do a film about the affects of nuclear war. His request was turned down. However, after the success of his BBC project *Culloden*, he was allowed to proceed with his nuclear war production, which became *The War Game*.

The finished 48 minute film caused so much controversy within the BBC that it's broadcast was delayed in order for it to be shown to representatives of the British Cabinet. Subsequently, Mr. Watkins resigned from the BBC and their official statement regarding their not showing the film was: "The effect of the film has been judged by the BBC to be too horrifying for the medium of broadcasting."

Let's reiterate: the British Government's position on the matter was, that the effects of a nuclear war were survivable; however seeing a film about it, was simply too horrifying for them to broadcast!

THE PRODUCTION:
Mr. Watkins brilliantly directed the film in what has become known today as the "News Magazine" style, which consists of incorporating the elements of documentary footage, man-in-the-street interviews, commentary by public figures and a voice-over narration. In the case of *The War Game* the documentary footage consisted of recreations by Mr. Watkins, his documentary crew and his non-actor cast, of what might have actually occurred during and after a nuclear attack on Great Britain.

Shot on 16mm black and white film, the production used many of the key elements of documentary and independent filmmaking: natural locations, available or practical light, non-actors and an episodic, organic story. The film presents in horrific and graphic detail what could happen to ordinary citizens and the infrastructure of society in the case of a nuclear attack even showing the shooting of civilians by the police to either control rioting or to dispose of untreatable victims who had been burned beyond help or recognition.

After the cancellation of the public broadcast by the BBC, the controversy over the production was so intense that several screenings were arranged for politicians and the press. It was here that Fate and Destiny once again played a part in making sure that this extraordinary film reached the public. The notable film critic Kenneth Tynan called the film, "...the most important film ever made."

From there the film's celebrity was carried on by the Campaign for Nuclear Disarmament and it was widely shown not only in England but also represented Great Britain at the 1966 Venice Film Festival.

THE AWARDS:
The War Game and Peter Watkins received a "Special Prize" at the 1967 Venice Film Festival. The film also won the BAFTA Film Award and UN Award and was awarded the 1967 Academy Award for Best Documentary Feature.

ONLINE RESOURCES:
Use Google Videos & Google Images for dozens of Links...

Buy it on Amazon, Google Play, or iTunes.

THINKING OUTSIDE THE BOX:
Class Exercises:

1. After screening the film, each student should write an essay about what they liked best or didn't like about the film and what worked or what didn't work for them and why.

2. Each student should write an essay comparing and contrasting the films: *Hiroshima Mon Amour* and *The War Game*.

3. Out of the three films that we have studied concerning nuclear war: *Hiroshima Mon Amour, Dr. Strangelove* and *The War Game*, each student should write an essay about which film they felt was most effective and why.

4. Each student should go online and locate Peter Watkins film, The Battle of Culloden which uses the same style on a war taking place in the 1700's. After screening it they should write an essay comparing and contrasting it with *The War Game*.

5. The students should team up and make a short digital or HD film using the "News Magazine" style about a topic that they think should be addressed.

Chapter 17:

1966
PERSONA

Ingmar Bergman
Cinematic De-con-struc-tion

SPOILER ALERT!
This is another very serious film from a very serious filmmaker. It is a film about the positive and the negative, the light and the darkness, the verbal and the silent, the real and the imagined. A film about being and nothingness, about the illusion of cinema... Simply, it is a film by Ingmar Bergman.

Persona is not easily explained or analyzed, although many have tried and much has been written and theorized about this enigmatic production. Viewing it is, however, an enriching experience that somehow speaks directly to your soul and your subconscious in the same manner as great piece of music.

If you have never seen this film, you have inadvertently overlooked one of the true milestones in Cinematic Art from the last century, and I hope that as of now you will begin to appreciate its many profound achievements.

THE CREATIVE TEAM:
Writer: Ingmar Bergman
Director: Ingmar Bergman
Cinematographer: Sven Nykvist
Editor: Ulla Ryghe

WHY IS THIS FILM VISIONARY:
Persona has been described by film critics as a masterpiece and as one of the century's great works of art. In 1972, the prestigious film magazine, *Sight and Sound*'s poll of the Ten Greatest Films of all time, ranked Ingmar Bergman's Persona at number five. Bergman himself has stated that "… in Persona… I had gone as far as I could go… working in total freedom, I touched wordless secrets that only the cinema can discover…"

"Deconstruction" is the major word to keep in mind when approaching this film. It is a personal, difficult, violent, sensual film by a major film artist at the very peak of his powers and cannot possibly be understood, comprehended, or appreciated in one viewing. Personally, I have been watching this film ever since it was first released in 1966, and for me, it just seems to gets better, richer, and more meaningful with each passing year.

THE BASICS:
Can you even begin to imagine the cinematic bravado and balls that it took to write and direct a feature film about two women alone in a deserted beach house and one of them doesn't speak? Do they represent the "body" and the "soul" of the same woman? After all, one of the characters is named "Alma" the Spanish word for "soul." Or, are they two separate characters, the Nurse "Alma" who is looking after the Patient "Elisabet," an actress who has ceased to "perform" to "act" or even to speak?

Right. This is cinematic work of "Art" with a Capital "A," and as such it is open to any and all interpretations. It is like attempting to answer the question, "Exactly why, and exactly at what, is the Mona Lisa smiling?"

However, from the very first frame to the very last it is also a film about the process and the medium of film and filmmaking. The opening shot is the fading in from black, heating up and coming together of the "positive and negative" parts of the Carbon Arcs that were used to supply the light for film projectors, way back in the day.

The closing shot is the "positive and negative" parts of the Carbon Arcs separating, cooling down and fading once again to black... In between these polar opposites of heat and cold, of light and darkness, we are constantly being startled out of our cinematic reverie by Mr. Bergman and reminded of the fact that all of this "...sound and fury signifying nothing..." that what we are watching is merely an illusion in a darkened theater up on a silver screen. In fact, the only word that the silent Elisabet speaks near the end of the film is, "...nothing."

THE PRODUCTION:
The film opens with the heating up of the carbon arcs of the film projector, then we see the film unspooling from the reel, the "Start" mark and the seconds counting down 9... 8... 7 at the "2 pop sound" there are 4 frames of an erect penis, then the film begins with an upside down cartoon of a woman washing her breasts, that scene gets stuck in the projector and then continues, a bit from a silent film of a man being scared by someone in a skeleton outfit, a shot of a spider, a sheep is bled to death and disemboweled, a

nail is driven through a man's hand, then the hand relaxes. Still Photographs of a snow-covered landscape, an old man, an old woman and a young boy covered with sheets, are they corpses or are they sleeping. A phone rings and the old ladies eyes pop open: In A Jump Cut! The young boy wakes up and begins to read a book, then looks up and reaches toward a movie screen showing the out of focus images of the two actresses from the film we are about to see. Finally the Main Titles appear and are intercut with flash cuts of what we have just seen as well as the boy, Liv Ullman and Bibi Anderson the two actresses about to appear in the film. *Persona* has just been introduced by a tone poem that celebrates the endless possibilities of the cinema.

Time and time again, Mr. Bergman reminds us that we are only viewing an illusion, a projection on a screen. At a crucial dramatic moment, the film itself suddenly stops in the projector, tears and burns. It's only a cinematic special effect, but since this was always a possibility with the old-style film projectors, while I was watching the film for the first time, during the 1960's, I actually thought that this was happening during the screening!

Later, close ups of the faces of the two female stars are merged with another cinematic special effect, into one misshapen face, after we are literally forced to sit through "the dailies" of a scene.

The same scene was shot twice in order to do the "coverage" on both of the actresses. That extraordinary scene is played in its entirety first as a medium shot and several close ups of the patient Elisabet listening to the dialogue. Then the very same scene is played again <u>in its entirety</u> this time showing the same coverage on the nurse Alma speaking the dialogue.

When I realized that this was happening during my first viewing of the film, it nearly sent me running out the theater in total frustration. Mr. Bergman later stated, that he could not choose between the two takes of which parts to use, so he simply used them both.

Persona, also contains one of the most erotic scenes ever filmed and all it consists of is the character of Alma curled up in a chair, telling the character of Elisabet a sensual story about how she and another girl, one summer day, had casual sex on a beach with two random teenage boys. This is another tribute to Mr. Bergman and his total mastery over his actors' performances as well as over all of the ineffable elements of filmmaking.

FIN:
Near the end of the film we see a film crew on a crane filming the character of Elisabet... Is this a flashback to the actress at work, or a flash-forward? Has she finally decided to "act" to "perform her part" in the world again?

Then the character of Alma folds up the bedding, puts away the lounge chairs and leaves on a bus... The carbon arcs separate, the white-hot light fades to black and the movie, *Persona* is over.

This uncompromising and unique cinematic experience is an enigmatic, stunning, stark, troubling, sensual, and ultimately profound film about the illusions of filmmaking, the illusions of the real and the imagined, as well as the human condition of being and nothingness...

A Film By: Ingmar Bergman.

AWARDS:
Persona won the 1967 National Society of Film Critics Awards for: Best Film, Best Director and Best Actress, Bibi Anderson. Also, during the making of the film, the director Ingmar Bergman fell in love and began a long affair with the other star of the film, Liv Ullmann.

ONLINE RESOURCES:
Use Google Images & Google Videos for dozens on links...

Buy it on Amazon, Google Play, or iTunes.

THINKING OUTSIDE THE BOX:
Class Exercises:

1. *Persona*, is a masterpiece, a work of Cinematic Art, but what did you think of it? Each student should write an essay about their thoughts, feelings, likes, dislikes, pros, cons.

2. This is a film that, for the most part, takes place at a secluded beach house, stars two women, and one of them doesn't speak. Each student should write an essay about the inherent difficulties of writing such a script and then of making such a film.

3. Each student should use the Internet, to find and watch the opening of the movie through the main titles... Then write an essay about what you thought this abstract, enigmatic sequence meant in relation to the entire film.

4. During his life, Ingmar Bergman was considered to

be a very serious filmmaker who dealt with the un-commercial and philosophical topics of: human isolation, the silence of god toward human suffering and the inevitability of death. Each student should write an essay listing any contemporary directors that have taken Mr. Bergman's place and if there are none, why not? Then list any "un-commercial and philosophical" topics that you would like to see made into a film.

5. Each student should use the Internet to research Ingmar Bergman and select one of his films that they haven't seen and buy it, rent it on line and view it.

Chapter 18:

1966
THE BATTLE OF ALGIERS

Gillo Pontecorvo
Occupation & Insurrection

SPOILER ALERT!
This film is a docudrama about the battle fought by the Algerians for their independence from French Colonial rule during the years 1954 to 1960. It was so accurately directed and photographed as a "reproduction" of actual events, a disclaimer had to be placed on all of the American prints stating "not one foot" of actual newsreel or documentary footage was used in the production.

Mr. Pontecorvo and his Cinematographer Marchello Catti used many techniques established by the Italian

Neo Realists and the French New Wave to give the film a realistic look: black and white film, natural locations, available or practical light, non-actors, and an organic, episodic story structure. The film contains literally thousands of Algerian extras and, due to the director casting mostly non-actors for their look, many of their lines had to be re-recorded by actors in post-production; but their visual, visceral and emotional effect in the film was perfect.

THE CREATIVE TEAM:
Writer: Gillo Pontecorvo, Franco Solinas
Director: Gillo Pontecorvo
Cinematographer: Marcello Gatti
Editor: Mario Morra, Mario Serandrei

WHY IS THIS FILM VISIONARY:
Because it was presented with such extraordinary cinematic skill and in such a perfect semi-documentary style, it felt like the audience was actually peering over the shoulders of the combatants on both sides of this highly charged, graphic, slice-of-life account of modern urban guerrilla warfare.

Even though it was made in 1966 it nearly has the feel of a reality television show like *Cops* and at the time, it was very graphic in it's portrayal of acts of torture and the random killing of innocent civilians, which has unfortunately become the trademark of today's terrorist and anti-terrorist activities.

THE BASICS:
The script was based on a book written by one of the producers and stars, (who is actually playing himself in the film, Saadi Yacef) during the time that he was imprisoned by the French for being a FLN commander. (*Front de Libération Nationale,* or National Liberation Front) The script went through several drafts mainly because the financial backers of the production did not want the film to be overly biased either toward the French or the Algerian point of view. As a result, the script ended up presenting, fairly and graphically, the cruelty, suffering, and atrocities perpetrated by both sides that occurred in that tragic urban conflict.

THE PRODUCTION:
Mr. Pontecorvo accurately portrays the ruthless and violent acts of terror by the FLN guerrillas and by the French anti-terrorist paratroopers who often tortured, beat, and murdered their victims in an attempt to put down the growing popularity of the FLN. The atrocities committed by both sides were presented and the films fair portrayal of these events has been lauded as one of its most outstanding features.

Although the film was originally banned in France for several years and all of the scenes depicting torture by the French were cut from its original release, over the years the film's popularity seems to have grown. The film is said to have been used as something like a training film by the Black Panthers, the Irish Republican Army and others, and as such it has inadvertently contributed to the urban guerrilla war tactics that these factions have often employed.

However, when I recently viewed this production having the 20/20 hindsight of both a post-Vietnam, post-Iraq war perspective, it seemed to me more like a cautionary tale about why our own country or any country should not be getting involved in urban warfare, as well as not taking part in imperialist, regime change or nation building activities anywhere on the planet.

THE AWARDS:
The Battle of Algiers has won worldwide acclaim, and was even screened at the Pentagon in 2003 as an illustration of the problems we were going to face in our occupation of Iraq. The film won the Venice Film Festival Grand Prize, The International Critics Award, The United Churches of America Prize and is the only film in history to be nominated for an Academy

Award in two separate non-consecutive years: it was nominated for the Best Foreign Film in 1966 and for Best Screenplay and Best Direction in 1968.

ONLINE RESOURCES:
Use Google Videos & Google Images for dozens of links...

Buy it on Amazon, Google Play, or iTunes.

THINKING OUTSIDE THE BOX:
Class Exercises:

1. While the film is still fresh in your mind, each student should write an essay about what they liked or didn't like about the film, what worked best or least for them and why.

2. This film shows some very graphic scenes of torture and some of these same techniques were used by the Argentine Military during the "Dirty War by the US in Abu Ghraib Prison and even by Jack Bauer on "24": Each student should write an essay about their pro or con opinions about this seemingly acceptable military practice.

3. This film also raises some very important questions about "occupation and insurrection." This is an age

old conflict going back to the Roman Empire, The British Empire, Spain, France, Israel and more recently America's interest in Central America, Asia and the Middle East: Each student should write an essay about their beliefs about when, where, and for what reason one country should occupy another.

4. This film is renowned for utilizing some very serious semi-documentary techniques. Each student should write an essay describing what the filmmakers did and how they achieved the look of the film.

5. The students should work together and create a short "semi-documentary" digital film production.

VII. In A Class By Itself

Chapter 19:

1969
2001, A Space Odyssey

Stanley Kubrick
Beyond The Infinite

SPOILER ALERT!
This is the one. The "greatest of the great," that you've heard so much about for so long and that you still find too tedious and boring to sit through! You're right. Yes, this film is too long and in places too slow. Yes, this _is_ your grandfather's space movie! However, without *2001...* there would never have been *Star Wars*, or *Close Encounters Of The Third Kind*, or *ET*, or *Aliens...* This is the film that set the standard for all of the rest: Do I have your attention now?

2001... was the forerunner, the avant-garde. This was the visionary film that showed the world what outer space looked like and did so without the assistance of CGI effects. More importantly, this is probably the most significant, most far reaching, and most philosophical piece of cinema ever put up there on the big 70mm Cinerama Screen!

In a way, it's not really fair. Having to see this film after *Star Wars* and all of the other action-packed space films that it influenced does make it seem much too slow. When I saw it, when we all saw it, back in the day, it was the hippest and most outlandish item on the planet. It was "The Ultimate Trip!" We sat in the front row, we grooved, we dug it, we got it, and we loved it. Now, it's your turn.

THE CREATIVE TEAM:
Writers: Stanley Kubrick, Arthur C. Clarke
Director: Stanley Kubrick
Cinematographer: Geoffrey Unsworth
Editor: Ray Lovejoy

WHY IS THIS FILM VISIONARY:
2001, A Space Odyssey showed the audiences of 1969 the past and future of the human species in the overall scheme of Time and Space and pondered the

unimaginable possibilities that might await a conscious human entity in an unknown and unknowable universe.

At the core of this film is Mr. Kubrick's belief that, "Most astronomers and other scientists interested in the whole question are strongly convinced that the universe is crawling with life; much of it, since the numbers are so staggering, (is) equal to us in intelligence, or superior, simply because human intelligence has existed for so relatively short a period."

THE BASICS:
Personally, I believe that there are only three films that stand head and shoulders above the all the rest of the films for the past 100 years. We have already discussed the first two, *Intolerance* and *Citizen Kane* and now we come the third, *2001, A Space Odyssey*. It could be argued, that *2001...* is the greatest of them all simply because it succeeded in covering so much totally uncharted territory.

The film is broken into three sections:
Part I: <u>The Dawn of Man</u>: Here primitive man, first meets the presence of The Monolith, which leads directly to the discovery of tools and weapons. Cut to: Millions of years later and the discovery, by a more

modern primitive man, of The Monolith buried on the moon, which sends its piercing signal towards Jupiter and brings us to…

Part II: <u>18 Months Later:</u> Where we follow a space crew on their Jupiter Mission led by the all-too-human, neurotic, and murderous HAL 9000 computer. After a physical and mental battle with HAL over the territory of the spaceship leads to one of the astronauts lobotomizing it, we reach the finale.

Part III: <u>Jupiter and Beyond The Infinite:</u> Where once again The Monolith leads mankind through an Inner and Outer Space trip and into the unimaginable resolution of his journey where he is ultimately reborn as the Star Child of Time & Space, now viewing the earth from a galactic point of view…

PHILOSOPHICAL BLOCKBUSTER:
This unprecedented film nearly defies any form of rational description since it is, on the one hand, a Big Road Show 70mm Blockbuster Movie and on the other, a visual tone poem about the existence of mankind in the universe from his first primitive ape-like origins to his galactic rebirth. We must simply pause and ask ourselves; "How the F#@! did this film ever get made?"

This astounding production contains concepts and theories that can give rise to whole philosophies. To my knowledge, none of this territory had ever been covered before, nor has it been since, in either a Hollywood or an Independent or even an Experimental Film. As Mr. Kubrick has stated, "The feel of the experience is the important thing, not the ability to verbalize it. I tried to create a visual experience which directly penetrates the subconscious content of the material." And I might add that made the experience of this film much like listening to a great piece of music mainly because it was scored with great pieces of music.

IN THE BEGINNING:
How exactly did Mr. Kubrick accomplish this extraordinary production? Basically, he willed this film into existence by first engaging the highly recognized science fiction author, Arthur C. Clark, to do a novel that would become the script for his next film.

They worked on the story though most of 1964, and by Christmas of that year the novel was more or less complete. As Mr. Clark has stated, "...the existing manuscript, together with his own salesmanship, allowed Stanley to set up the deal with MGM and Cinerama, and *Journey Beyond The Stars* (the original title) was announced with a flourish of trumpets." By April of the next year 1965, Mr. Kubrick had changed the title to: *2001: A Space Odyssey* and as Mr. Clark has also stated, "As far as I can recall, it was entirely his idea."

THE PRODUCTION:
On December 29, 1965 the production began shooting at Shepperton Studios in England utilizing 70mm film and Panavision 65 Cameras. This studio housed the 60 feet wide, by 120 feet long, by 60 feet deep pit for the Tycho excavation on the moon. Mr. Kubrick was already "behind schedule" because that set had to be torn down by the first week of January 1966 to make way for another expensive production and he had only a few days to shoot this crucial scene.

After it was completed, the production moved to MGM-British Studios in Borehamwood, England for the remainder of the filming, which was described by Herb Lightman in his American Cinematographer article as being a "...huge throbbing nerve center... with much the same frenetic atmosphere as a Cape Kennedy blockhouse during the final stages of countdown."

METICULOUS PLANNING:
Mr. Kubrick used a tedious and fragile "retro-

reflective" front projection system to shoot the Dawn of Man sequence with the ape-men, because that was the best that was available at that time. Today of course, blue screens, green screens, and Computer Generated Images or CGI effects have replaced rear and front projection systems.

Amazingly, Mr. Kubrick actually did all of his special effects photography on the original camera negatives fearing that using dupes would not look good on the huge Cinerama screen. This involved the most painstaking, meticulous care and planning because often one effect, A Planet, would be shot using only a part of the negative, the film would then be rewound to a First Frame Mark, and then weeks or even months would pass before the next effect, A Space Vehicle Passing By, was scheduled to be shot using another part of that same piece of original negative... Talk about having to be absolutely accurate and perfectly precise.

IN CAMERA C.G.I. EFFECTS:
The other remarkable production achievements included the creation of a rotating space ship interior where the astronauts could experience normal gravity. Here, Mr. Kubrick created all of his weightless effects (that would be done today by CGI technology) totally on the set in real time and on the film inside

the Panavision 65 Cameras. Once again you will notice, like with *Dr. Strangelove...*, that all of the lighting was built into the sets – especially on the rotating interior.

If you look very carefully you can see that many of the weightless effects were done by simply locking the camera to the entire set and then rotating both the set and the camera while the actor stayed in one place held by gravity... absolutely brilliant!

This cinematic technique for creating a "weightless" effect was based on what the Director Stanley Donen did in the MGM Classic Film, *Royal Wedding*, where Fred Astaire dances up one wall and across the ceiling and back down another wall.

THE BEST CUT IN FILM HISTORY:
And what I believe is also The Best and Most Meaningful Cut In Film History, occurs in *2001...* when the Dawn Of Man sequence transitions into space. Kindly Note: this cut does not transition the film from Part I into Part II, it is a continuation of Part One: The Dawn Of Man, and it only serves as a transition to a more modern primitive man. I also believe that this cut is the most important and philosophical cut in the history of filmmaking simply because of what it implies.

EXT – Earth / Dawn Of Man - DAY

The ape-man throws his bone/weapon into the air and we...

CUT TO:

EXT – Outer Space / 3 Million Years Later – DAY

As a space satellite/weapon replaces the bone/weapon in the frame....

That flash forward of three million years, implies that the primitive human intelligence and motivation, that caused the bone/weapon to be launched, also caused the space satellite/weapon to be launched and that modern man still has the same instincts as his primitive forefathers. He has progressed technologically but not spiritually or emotionally, and he is still battling others of his own species over territory.

For Mr. Kubrick, all of uncivilized and civilized human history from barbarians to space travelers, is rendered simply as a: Cut To: From The Dawn of (Primitive) Ape-Man to The Future of (Primitive) Modern-Man... Everything in between is simply a rehashing of the same old story. Mankind fighting himself over territory, race, religion, language, possessions, trade routes, human slavery, gold, silver, silk, opium, and oil...

Whether it's the ape/men fighting over the territory of the water hole, or the modern/men arguing with the Russians over territory on the moon, Man is still the same animal only the tools and technology have changed: the bone/weapon has now become a space/weapon! Those are some of the implications of that CUT TO: Welcome to Mr. Kubrick's rather bleak view of humanity, and by the way, it's going to get bleaker.

THE MUSIC:
You cannot possibly imagine the effect of seeing the opening of 2001, A Space Odyssey for the first time. Watching in 70mm the sunrise over earth from our POV behind the moon, with Richard Strauss's glorious "Thus Spoke Zarathustra" blasting on the sound track. As it finished, I turned to a friend and said, "Let's leave now, it can't possibly get better than that..." but of course I was wrong, I was very, very wrong.

It got much better, and richer, and more meaningful, always accompanied by the most amazingly appropriate music. The discovery of the weapon, the flash forward to 2001, the docking at the space station, the battle with HAL, on and on through the light trip and the star child... So much of this film is simply, Music and Visuals... or as it was billed, during 1960 and '70: "The Ultimate Trip!"

ARTHUR C. CLARK:
For some final thoughts on *2001, A Space Odyssey*, I would like to use a long quote from an article by Arthur C. Clark, which I found on the website: http://www.visual-memory.co.uk/amk/ which is called: The Kubrick Site. This is about how the famous Most Meaningful Cut In Film History came into being:

"The skull-smashing sequence was the only scene not filmed in the studio; it was shot in a field a couple of hundred yards away, the only time Stanley went on location. A small platform had been set up, and Moonwatcher (Dan Richter) was sitting in this, surrounded by bones. Cars and busses were going by at the end of the field, but as this was a low-angle shot against the sky, they didn't get in the way, though Stanley did have to pause for an occasional airplane."

"The shot was repeated so many times, and Dan smashed so many bones, that I was afraid we were going to run out of warthog (or tapir) skulls. But eventually Stanley was satisfied, and as we walked back to the studio he began to throw bones up into the air. At first I thought this was sheer *joi de vivre*, but then he started to film them with a hand held camera, no easy task. Once or twice, one of the large, swiftly descending bones nearly landed on Stanley as he peered through the viewfinder; if luck had been against us the whole project might have ended then. To misquote Ardrey, "That intelligence would have perished on some forgotten Elstree field..."

"When he had finished filming the bones whirling against the sky, Stanley resumed the walk back to the studio; but now he had got hold of a broom, and started tossing that up into the air. Once again, I assumed this exercise was pure fun; and perhaps it was. But that was the genesis of the longest flash forward in the history of movies: three million years, from the bone to the artificial satellite, in a twenty-fourth of a second."

THE AWARDS:
2001 A Space Odyssey was nominated for the Director's Guild of America Award, won three BAFTA Awards and was nominated for four Academy Awards, Mr. Kubrick won for Best Special Effects.

ONLINE RESOURCES:
Use Google Images & Google Videos for dozens of links...

Buy it on Amazon, Google Play, or iTunes.

Trailer Video URL
http://www.imdb.com/video/screenplay/vi2230453017/

THINKING OUTSIDE THE BOX:
Class Exercises:

1. You did it! You finally sat through this amazing cinematic experience for the first time, or maybe for the tenth time... Each student should write an essay about his or her impressions of the film. Did you like it or not, does it still work or not. What did you like the best, the least... Your analysis, thoughts, emotions, and feelings.

2. Each student should write an essay and draw sketches to explain how Mr. Kubrick accomplished all of his "weightless effects" in the camera. How does the stewardess appear to walk up the side of the space shuttle? How do the astronauts appear to jog around the circular ceiling of their space ship?

3. Some may say that this is sacrilegious, but If you were able to "re-cut" this film today... Each student should write an essay describing what you would do. Be specific on exactly what and where you think that 2001 might be improved simply by doing a little

"tightening up."

4. What effect did the music have on you? Each student should write an essay about the choice of music, where it was used and how it affected your overall experience of the film.

5. Mr. Kubrick has stated: "Most astronomers and other scientists interested in the whole question are strongly convinced that the universe is crawling with life..." Each student should write an essay about what they think this quote means and if it is true, what implication would that have on all of our belief systems.

VIII. The Year Of Dubious Bad Taste

Chapter 20:

1971
Sweet Sweetback's Baadasss Song

Melvin Van Peebles In Your Face

SPOILER ALERT!
If you are easily offended, or if crude, blatant sexuality, violence, ghetto slang, disrespect for authority and semiprofessional filmmaking aren't what you like to see up on the big screen, then this film may not be to your liking. Personally, I'm a big fan.

Like, the John Cassavetes film *Shadows, Sweet*

Sweetback's... may not be one of the best films ever made, but it is an important film, simply because of the changes that were brought about by its groundbreaking production. After it was released, it showed filmmakers and film distributors alike that there was indeed a black audience who would support black films by black filmmakers.

What this guerrilla production lacks in a cohesive narrative or even its semiprofessional filmmaking style, it more than makes up for in sheer audacity, raw nerve and in-your-face anti-establishment rhetoric. "He (The Man) bled your sister, He bled your brother... But he won't bleed me!"

THE CREATIVE TEAM:
Writer: Melvin Van Peebles
Director: Melvin Van Peebles
Cinematographer: Bob Maxwell
Editor: Melvin Van Peebles

WHY IS THIS FILM VISIONARY:
Melvin Van Peebles is a visionary as well as an Artist and an unstoppable creative force. Before he became the Producer, Writer, Director, Star, Editor and Composer of *Sweet Sweetback's...* Mr. Van Peebles was a college graduate with a degree in English, an author, playwright, actor, musician, singer, and

novice filmmaker who also spoke French. He had already lived in France, and had published books and starred in films while staying there.

In the 1970's, after starring in *Watermelon Man*, Columbia Pictures offered him a three-picture deal. Instead of signing and settling into the comforts of a Hollywood contract, Mr. Van Peebles took $70,000 from whatever remained of the money he had made at the studio and began shooting his own hybrid 16mm version of a Neo-Realist, New Wave, Independent, Underground, Sexploitation Film.

He chose to get into the streets with a non-union, half third world crew, make a film that starred "The Black Community "Brer Soul," and was "...about a brother getting the Man's foot out of his ass." Or as the dedication at the beginning of the film reads: "This film is dedicated to all the Brothers and Sisters who had enough of the Man."

What follows is an in your face, surreal, psychedelic, anti-establishment rant that was so blatant in its language, sex and violence that it was finally, "Rated X By An All White Jury" before it achieved its limited release.

THE BASICS:

This truly was a guerrilla film. It was shot in 19 days using natural locations, a lot of available light or garishly lit interiors, and a mostly untrained and inexperienced cast and crew. They used inexpensive equipment while telling an episodic story that was right off the streets of South Central LA.

In order to keep the unions away, Mr. Van Peebles told them that he was making a pornographic film, and by the way, he nearly succeeded in doing so. He used his own thirteen-year-old son, Mario, in a simulated sex scene, where the young Sweetback looses his virginity to a prostitute. He also shot a lot of un-simulated sex scenes with himself and an array of women, so many in fact that he contracted gonorrhea. Then had the audacity to apply to the Director's Guild for Workman's Compensation, claiming that he had been "injured on the job." He won the claim and used the money to buy more film stock! This dude was the original guerrilla filmmaker!

Melvin Van Peebles persevered "by any means necessary" to make the film and the statement that he wanted to make.

THE PRODUCTION:
Since he was using non-actors and an inexperienced crew Mr. Van Peebles decided to shoot his scenes in

"globs" that is, in their entirety in a single day. This would avoid the novice cast from showing up the next day wearing the wrong wardrobe or having gotten an unwanted tattoo or haircut.

He did whatever he had to do to get the job done. He starred, produced, wrote, directed and did his own stunts. There's an apocryphal story about shooting with several bikers, who wanted to leave before the scene was over and one of them was so dumb as to pull a knife. Mr. Van Peebles was reported to have snapped his fingers and several of his crewmembers immediately appeared, armed with rifles. Obviously, the bikers stayed and Mr. Van Peebles completed the scene.

POST PRODUCTION:
This is where the film that the audience ended up seeing was truly finished and with a $50,000 loan from Bill Cosby, Van Peebles was able to finish his film his way. Usually a guerrilla film does not have the luxury of doing re-shoots, pick-up shots, or inserts, so Van Peebles used this to his advantage and presented his various scenes in a jump cut, superimposed, and kaleidoscopic style that struck a sympathetic note with his young, hip, sometimes high, and disenfranchised audience.

When it came to composing the music, once more Van Peebles persevered. Since he could not read music, he numbered all of the keys on his piano so that he could remember and write down the numbers that he used to create each melody! Through friends he was introduced to the as-of-yet-undiscovered group, Earth, Wind & Fire. After they had made their musical contribution Van Peebles played their music, which was now the soundtrack from *Sweet Sweetback's Baadasss Song*, on urban radio stations to help to promote his soon to be released film.

He even sacrificed the vision in one of his eyes by looking too closely at the aperture of the bright Moviola light when checking how a superimposition would look when he placed two separate pieces of film together. Yes, Melvin Van Peebles persevered "by any means necessary" to make the film and the statement that he wanted to make.

THE RESULT:
No distributor in America wanted to touch this poorly made, blatantly sexual, anti-establishment, and controversial film. However, the persistent Melvin Van Peebles was able to find two theaters that were willing to play it, one in Detroit and one in Atlanta. From day one, it was slow going, but once the word got out, the film broke house records every night that

it played even though it had received an "X Rating" (By An All White Jury) and went on to gross over $4,000,000 dollars domestically and nearly $10,000,000 worldwide.

Melvin Van Peebles had, simply by the strength of his persistence, kicked open the door and paved the way, for the era of "Blacksploitation Films" that followed and eventually led to a vast array of African American films and filmmakers. By simply "doing his own thing" Melvin Van Peebles had not only run interference he had carried the ball into the end-zone, making it a whole new ballgame for the likes of Spike Lee, Fred Williamson, John Singleton, Richard Pryor, Carl Franklin, Robert Townsend, the Wyans brothers, the Hughes brothers, Tyler Perry, F. Gary Gray and a host of others.

THE AWARDS:
The only well deserved Award that this film ever received along with the adulation of "The Black Community" was the undying gratitude of all of the subsequent African American Film Artists that have followed in its very bold footsteps.

ONLINE RESOURCES:
Use Google Images & Google Videos for dozens of links...

Watch Free On Line:
www.movieandtvonline.com/.../sweet%20sweetback%20badass%20song

View Trailer or Scenes:
www.youtube.com

Buy it on Amazon, Google Play, or iTunes.

THINKING OUTSIDE THE BOX:
Class Exercises:

1. Each student should write an essay about their reaction after seeing this film for he first time and what were their pros and cons.

2. Each student should write an essay about what they think worked best in the film, what they think did not work and why.

3. Since they are both flawed but groundbreaking films, each student should write an essay comparing and contrasting *Sweet Sweetback's...* with John Cassavetes film, *Shadows*.

4. Each student should go online and research all of Melvin Van Peebles other work, then locate some of

it, check it out and write an essay about whatever they liked best.

5. Each student should view Mario Van Peebles film *Baadasss,* in which he stars as his father in a film about the making *Sweet Sweetback's...* Then write an essay comparing and contrasting Melvin's film and Mario's film.

Chapter 21:

1971
The Devils

Ken Russell
The Politics Of Religion

SPOILER ALERT!
This is a very serious work of Art, by a very serious Film Artist, Ken Russell, that happens to deal with some of the worst, most perverse and profane twisting of human instincts and institutions imaginable. It deals with the corruption and perversion of organized Religion into an orgy of envy and torture, the debasement of Government and Politics into a means of greed and power, and the psychological perverting of Human Sexuality into repressed mania, jealousy and revenge.

Beware & Be Warned! This film is not for the faint of heart. It is an extravagant and over-the-top Art Film that is being wielded by its Director as a weapon of enlightenment, to inform, incite and inflame your senses, and may ultimately cause you to squirm in your seat with revulsion at its brazen, bold and uninhibited revelations.

THE CREATIVE TEAM:
Writer: Ken Russell. Aldous Huxley, John Whiting
Director: Ken Russell
Cinematographer: David Watkin
Editor: Michael Bradsell

WHY IS THIS FILM VISIONARY:
To be politically correct, you should never get into a brawl over Politics or Religion, and if you happen to add the sensational element of Perverted Sex to the mix, then you have created many of today's headlines. However in 1971 society was a bit more constrained and Ken Russell's film, *The Devils*, provoked so much indignant rage from the Catholic Church that it was banned in Italy and it was decreed that its stars, Vanessa Redgrave and Oliver Reed were to be thrown into jail if they ever set foot in that country.

Even though this was during the "Tricky Dick" Nixon administration prior to Watergate, Ken Russell ventured daringly into these taboo subjects basing his script on the characters, records, and historical facts that occurred during the "possessions of Loudun" in France in the early 1600's.

Viewed in the light of today's Breaking News, Ken Russell's film The Devils, although gut wrenching and disturbing, mostly got it right. Our headlines scream about the world-wide abuse of children by the Catholic Church, as well as sex trafficking, prostitution, sweetheart deals, insider trading, no-bid contracts, and payoffs by Wall Street and in Washington by Lobbyists for Major Corporations.

Most of these above institutions have proven themselves to be pillars of corruption, dealing in bribes, bailouts, war profiteering, lies, cover ups obscene bonuses in the office, and obscene conduct in the bedroom. So much for Mr. Russell being over the top!

THE BASICS:
The film boasts the acting talents of Oliver Reed, Vanessa Redgrave, and a host of wonderful character actors all of whom are giving some of the most flamboyant performances of their artistic lives. The Production Design by Derek Jarman echoed Fritz Lang's Metropolis instead of the realities of the 1600's. The Cinematography by David Watkin was as stunning and startling as the modern atonal and

unsettling musical score by Peter Maxwell Davies.

The entire production was infused with major artists on every level of production, doing their very best work. Yes, *The Devils* is excessive, brazen, revolting, over the top, and jaw dropping, but that is all the more reason that it should be shown and appreciated instead of being censored. But censored it was, chopped, cut, re-edited, reviled, and it's still going on, even to this very day.

THE PRODUCTION:
Ken Russell has said that this was his only political film, and that every extravagant frame of it was <u>based on the facts of the original historical events.</u> Those events caused such a sensation at the time, that tourists came all the way from Paris to witness the public exorcisms... <u>That's right - The Catholic Church had, "public exorcisms."</u> And some accuse Mr. Russell of being excessive!

At it core, *The Devils* is about a man going against the will of the State. That man is a Priest named Grandier whose womanizing and influence in the city of Loudun went against the will of both Cardinal Richelieu and Louis XIII, who wanted to destroy the fortifications of the city to prevent the Protestants from an uprising and to better prevent its citizens from being "self governing."

The Church and The State both conspired along with the sexually repressed head of the local convent Sister Jeanne, to bring up this handsome, charismatic, womanizing, and outspoken Priest on charges of witchcraft. What followed were episodes of torture and orgiastic nuns running amuck, until those in power had achieved the ends, and the results they wanted.

More or less like our recent leaders torturing twisting the truth so that the American public would believe in the existence of WMD's, Weapons Of Mass Destruction, in order that our Government could invade Iraq and have the result that Wall Street, Halliburton, and The Military Industrial Complex all wanted. However, by 2015 nearly everyone agrees that this destabilization of the Middle East has caused much more international carnage by the emergence of the radical ISIS than was ever expected.

FINALLY:
Even today the censorship of this film continues, for fear of offending the contingent of far right wing, Christian Fundamentalists. In a time when people are being beheaded on the Internet, Warner Home Video still refuses to release the DVD of a movie from 1971,

The Devils. If you think that policy by Warner Home Video is a steaming pile of BS, why don't you simply call or email them about it!

Warner Home Video
Email address: whv@b3custserv.com.

Phone Number: (800) 364-6928

Regular Mail: Warner Home Video P.O. Box 30620Tampa, FL 33630-0620

THE AWARDS:
Ken Russell won The Best Director Award from The Italian Syndicate of Film Journalists and The National Board of Review, USA.

ONLINE RESOURCES:
Use Google Images & Google Videos for dozens of links...

View the Trailer or Scenes from *The Devils*:
www.youtube.com

Search out the Documentary about the censoring of The Devils: Hell On Earth – The Desecration and Resurrection of Ken Russell's *The Devils.*
www.youtube.com

THINKING OUTSIDE THE BOX:
Class Exercises:

1. After screening the film each student should write an essay about their personal reaction and feelings as well as their pros and cons about the production.

2. Each student should write an essay about the scenes that shocked them the most, what scenes were the most effective, what were the most disturbing, and why.

3. Each student should write an essay about what the meaning of the film is from the Director's perspective as well as what the film means to them personally.

4. Each student should research "The Possessions at Loudun on the Internet and write an essay detailing if in fact, all of the events depicted in the film are based on historical facts.

5. This was an extraordinary film that caused a storm of controversy. Each student should write an essay or treatment describing a controversial subject that they would like to explore or have explored in a film.

Chapter 22:

1971
A CLOCKWORK ORANGE

Stanley Kubrick
Ultra Violence

SPOILER ALERT!
I already warned you that Mr. Kubrick's view of mankind was bleak, well now it is about to become pitch black. In his previous film *2001, A Space Odyssey* he viewed humanity as a modern ape/man, technically proficient, yet still emotionally primitive.

A Clockwork Orange's original tag line on the one sheet movie poster read: *"Being the adventures of a young man whose principal interests are rape, ultra-violence and Beethoven."* Is it possible to have a more un-politically correct, cynical, and desolate view of humanity than that?

So hold on tight: this is going to be another controversial and mind-blowing ride. Once again it will be music, the lovely Ludwig Van, who will accompany and underscore all of the wanton sex, violence, and the sapping of our hero's free will: "Viddy well, little brothers, viddy well!"

THE CREATIVE TEAM:
Writers: Stanley Kubrick / Anthony Burgess
Director: Stanley Kubrick
Cinematographer: John Alcott
Editor: Bill Butler

WHY IS THIS FILM VISIONARY:
This is another Stanley Kubrick film that tackles another "big premise" - that of Man's Free Will. Whether a man should be able to Choose to do good, or if he should be Conditioned to do good, by the state in order to make him a more productive member of society, which in turn, would turn him into, *A Clockwork Orange*.

This is a difficult premise that Mr. Kubrick handled deftly with his extraordinary wit, style, cynicism and bravura filmmaking. The film was an instant critical success, however, there were several incidents of rape and murder committed by punks in England, who cited *A Clockwork Orange* as "influencing" them.

Most of these moronic felons no doubt had the same lager sodden IQ as the out-of-control soccer thugs in that country who repeatedly cause death and destruction in the name of "football" wherever they go. But Mr. Kubrick and his groundbreaking film were given all of the blame and after he and his family had received several death threats, Mr. Kubrick pulled the film from circulation in England and forbade it from being shown there until after his death.

THE BASICS:
When Mr. Kubrick's extraordinary "X-Rated" film had its US premier at the Pacific Theater on Hollywood Boulevard in 1971, I was actually the first person in line. So I bought two tickets and I still have the unused ticket #0001 filed away as a piece of priceless memorabilia while I used ticket #0002 to go inside and view this startling and extraordinary production.

Having already seen Mr. Kubrick's rather jaundiced take on humanity in his productions of: *Paths of Glory, Lolita, Dr. Strangelove* and *2001...* I thought that this would most certainly be another satirical black comedy on the human condition and of course, I wasn't disappointed.

I was however, amazed and stunned when all of the

articles accusing Mr. Kubrick of "too much sex and violence" began to appear. Didn't they get the part about the film being satirical? To me, everything about *A Clockwork Orange*, was so stylized, that accusing it of having too much sex and violence, was like saying that there's too much sex in the Greek Tragedies or too much violence in the Roadrunner Cartoons!

Certainly, Little Alex performing *"Singing in the Rain"* as part of the attack on the writer and the rape his wife, or the erotic scene with the two teenage girls from the music shop being shot at 6 frames per second and scored with *"The William Tell Overture"* (Which everyone recognized as The Theme from The Lone Ranger, "Hi Ho Silver...") blaring on he soundtrack, let the viewers know that this was a stylized satire! Mr. Kubrick was overdramatizing these violent and erotic elements for both a comic and cathartic effect and not so that the audiences would be titillated by them.

NAPOLEON'S WATERLOO:
A Clockwork Orange did however, have a much more pleasant beginning. In the same way that Peter Sellers had given Mr. Kubrick Terry Southern's book *The Magic Christian*, which had led to their collaboration on *Dr. Strangelove*... Mr. Southern had given him a

copy of Anthony Burgess's novel, *A Clockwork Orange.*

After doing the tedious, grueling and meticulously complex production of *2001, A Space Odyssey* and after his long researched production of *Napoleon* was cancelled, due to the bad box office performance of a similar production, *Waterloo*, Mr. Kubrick began in earnest on *A Clockwork Orange.*

THE PRODUCTION:
Filming began during September of 1970 and wrapped on April 20, 1971, the film was released later that fall, which made it the fastest Kubrick film ever to be shot, edited and released.

Mostly as a reaction to having to deal with the painstakingly precise production of *2001...* this film was, designed to be shot simply on natural locations and with a small crew. As opposed to the over $10,000,000.00 budget on 2001... *A Clockwork Orange* is estimated to have cost around $2,200,000.00. This figure gives you a clue as to how small his core team actually was, since that small budget still allowed Mr. Kubrick to have nearly an eight-month shooting schedule.

The small budget, along with several other factors, like using natural locations, a wheelchair for several of the dolly shots and often a hand held camera and mostly practical lights, has caused me to refer to this production as "Almost a Guerilla Film." I say "Almost" because Mr. Kubrick still had a very long shooting schedule and often did fifty takes per set up as was his accustomed style.

Still, only four sets were build, two in a rented factory and two in a large tent behind the location for the writer's home: 1. The Room where Alex is Checked Into The Prison and 2. The Korova Milk Bar, were built in the factory. 3. The Mirrored Hallway entrance to the writer's home and 4. The Bath Room in the writer's home, where Alex sings *"Singing In The Rain"* in the bathtub, were built in the tent behind that location. Nothing, not one frame of film, was shot in the studio.

MENTORED BY THE MASTER:
It was only by sheer luck (or was it Fate and Destiny?) that I was able to study this film in detail and, indirectly, be mentored by Mr. Kubrick and his Cinematographer, John Alcott. It happened while I was still a fledgling filmmaker during the 1970's and it led to an epiphany that completely changed my approach to Lighting and Cinematography.

In the mid 1970's I was editing a very small feature

that I had also photographed and our lab was the MGM labs in Culver City, California. Back in the day, you needed "fill leader" whenever you were building your sound tracks, which usually consisted of unused and discarded 35mm film prints. When I ordered my next box of fill leader from the MGM lab, the gods of production smiled and the lab by sheer chance, sent me nearly an entire 35mm print of *A Clockwork Orange,* with French Subtitles.

Remember, this was back in the 1970's when there were no VHS tapes, no DVD's and the only way to study one of your favorite films or filmmakers, was to go to a screening in a theater. Needless to say, after the screening, the projectionist could not and would not go back and replay your favorite scenes for you to study and analyze.

I was ecstatic at receiving Mr. Kubrick's extraordinary film and I immediately took all of my work off of the old upright Moviola and re-placed it with Mr. Kubrick's masterpiece. Then I spent the next several hours running my favorite scenes forward and back, forward and back, forward and back... A happy, eager, enthralled student, being able to study the maestro, up close and personal...

WAIT A MINUTE!!! I quickly hit the break on the

Moviola! I was running the scene where "Little Alex" kills the "Cat Lady" with the large sculptured phallus, and I saw that Mr. Kubrick was chasing them around the room, with a 18mm lens on his hand held Arriflex 2C camera. I could clearly see on the Moviola screen, all four walls, the floor and the ceiling of the practical location and to my astonishment there were absolutely NO MOVIE LIGHTS!

This discovery was not only astounding it was revolutionary, remarkable, and totally outside of the box! This was no student film or a Roger Corman production; this was a big, Warner Brothers, Stanley Kubrick Production that had been nominated for four (4) Academy Awards. I immediately isolated the frames where I could see the practical lights and studied them on the Moviola... Mr. Kubrick had simply designed several small lighting sculptures that contained what appeared to be a series of 100 or 150-watt bulbs. He then had placed them around the room, plugged them into to wall sockets and Ta Da! The set was lit! Lights... Camera... Action!

ZAP!!! The maestro's brilliant work had caused my fledgling filmmakers consciousness to have an epiphany! I immediately studied the rest of the film, and realized that this groundbreaking technique was being used in nearly every scene. Then I adapted this style, as the most practical, actor friendly and production friendly method of lighting and shooting: Anytime, Anyplace, Anywhere.

When I took the time to study the rest of Mr. Kubrick's films both before and after *A Clockwork Orange* and discovered that he had not only pioneered, but had also implemented this technique over and over again.

IF IT'S GOOD ENOUGH FOR MR. KUBRICK:
I put the lessons learned from the maestros Kubrick and Alcott to good use in both my first Big Budget, Big Star, Studio Film, *Bronco Billy,* and in the small Independent film, *Bloodsport*, and I might add, that it led to my having some of the most extraordinarily productive shooting days imaginable.

On the Warner Brothers feature, *Bronco Billy* I was able to accomplish between 45 to 55 set-ups per day on a Big Studio, Big Star feature. While on the independent film, *Bloodsport* I was able to average 70 set ups during a week of shooting Martial Arts scenes, along with a record high of 93 set ups, that stood for many years.

I even wrote an article during the 1990's for The American Cinematographer Magazine's "Let There Be

Light" series, entitled: "If It's Good Enough For Mr. Kubrick..." wondering why this actor friendly and production friendly technique wasn't being used more often in Hollywood? Trust me, the answer to that question could be the subject of another book.

However, by the new millennium the Director and Cinematographer team of Alfonso Cuaron and Emmanual Lubezki began using this style of lighting in both their small independent Mexican road movie *E Tu MaMa Tambien* and their big studio, bit budget, big star Sci Fi feature *Children of Men*. It was also utilized by the Director and Cinematographer team, of Jean-Marc Vallee and Yves Belanger on both of their Academy Award productions *Dallas Buyers Club* and *Wild*.

Talk about Mr. Kubrick being ahead of his time, read this quote from Michael Ciment's book "Kubrick" published in 1982, the quote was from a previous interview with Mr. Kubrick regarding the 1971 release of *A Clockwork Orange:* "The State sees the specter looming ahead of terrorism and anarchy, and this increases the risk of its over-reaction and a reduction in our freedom..."

How prescient was Mr. Kubrick? Since we can now thank the Bush/Cheney administration for taking his predictions and turning them into our country's "Patriot Act." Which led to the NSA and later to Edward Snowden's revelations about how evasive and ubiquitous their spying had become on the emails and phone records of the American Public!

THE AWARDS:
The film won the New York Film Critics Circle Award for Best Film and Best Director it was nominated for the Director's Guild of America Award, three Golden Globe Awards, seven BAFTA Awards and four Academy Awards.

ONLINE RESOURCES:
Use Google Images & Google Videos for dozens of links...

Buy it on Amazon, Google Play, or iTunes.

Trailer Video URL
http://www.imdb.com/video/screenplay/vi3502113049/

THINKING OUTSIDE THE BOX:
Class Exercises:

1. Even for Stanley Kubrick fans, this is a bizarre, brutal, erotic, violent and thought provoking film.

Each student should write an essay about their analysis, thoughts, feeling, pros and cons, likes and dislikes of this production.

2. *2001, A Space Odyssey* was a painfully precise special effects studio film, *A Clockwork Orange* was an on location gun and go film that doesn't even have a single dissolve in it. Each student should write an essay comparing and contrasting the advantages and disadvantages of both of these types of productions.

3. "The Lovely Ludwig Van..." Each student should write an essay describing the effect that the music in this film has on the protagonist, "Little Alex" as well as the overall effect it has on the audience and you, personally.

4. Even though Alex gets his human nature back, I'm not sure that's a definitive answer to the question of man's "choice." Each student should write an essay about whether it's better to be a despicable human being who has the ability to choose or someone who has been conditioned by the state to be a productive member of society.

5. Mr. Kubrick received a lot of bad press and harassment about having too much sex and violence in *A Clockwork Orange.* In light of what you can find

and view on the Internet today, each student should write an essay about what they think "too much sex and too much violence" is and when and where and for whom, is it appropriate.

IX. Four International Visions

Chapter 23

1974
THE CONVERSATION

Francis Ford Coppola
A Matter Of Privacy

SPOILER ALERT!

At the time of its release, *The Conversation* was thought to be an indictment of the Nixon Administration's bugging of the Democratic Headquarters at Watergate, but Mr. Coppola has stated that he wrote the script nearly a decade before that political debacle, after seeing the Michelangelo Antonioni film, *Blow Up*. That film had featured a dramatic revelation being discovered by blowing up a still photograph larger and larger, while in *The*

Conversation, Mr. Coppola used basically the same technique only this time making a recorded conversation clearer and clearer thus eventually giving the words a much different and more sinister meaning.

This is a very troubling film, in that it deals with the technology of the 1970's being able to listen in on nearly anyone's private conversations anywhere and at anytime. If you couple the technical facts of this film with Tony Scott's 1998 film *Enemy Of The State*, in which Gene Hackman was basically playing a similar character 25 years later, you have today a world wide web of global positioning devices, cell phones, wiretapping, social media, online services and satellite surveillance that enables the conversations, family histories, financial and medical records of any citizen to be instantly scrutinized by any number of government agencies most notably the NSA who does so ubiquitously, simply by waving the red flag of "national security."

THE CREATIVE TEAM:
Writer: Francis Ford Coppola
Director: Francis Ford Coppola
Cinematographer: Bill Butler
Editor: Richard Chew

WHY IS THIS FILM VISIONARY:
This is the production that brought the reality of the Nixon Administration's surveillance activities out of the closet and rubbed them into the faces of the American public. Although that was not the director's intent, *The Conversation* was serendipitously the right film at the right place at the right time and its effect was overwhelming. The Rights of privacy, intimate conversations, the sanctity of the home, freedom of speech, behind closed doors had all been swiftly swept aside by the aggressive governmental use of clandestine surveillance. Naturally the American public was upset!

THE BASICS:
What appears to be a casual conversation between a man and a woman walking through the park during their lunch hour is being filmed and simultaneously recorded by multiple cameras, microphones and tape recorders. Over the course of the film the man hired to make this recording, (Harry Caul / Gene Hackman) uses the latest technology to make what they are saying become clearer and clearer. Finally he comes to conclusion that their innocent conversation is instead a murder plot.

Indeed there is an assassination, one that he is unable and unequipped to stop, but the most sinister and troubling scene in the film is the last one, where he is attempting to find the surveillance device that has now been placed in his apartment. The character of Harry Caul had been established as being someone who was absolutely the top man in his field and one who had dedicated himself to his work even to the detriment of his own personal and social life. For this surveillance expert <u>not</u> to be able to find the bug in his own home, made the ominous threat of "big brother is watching" a very real concern in the 1970's.

Today it's 1000 times worse and most recently, the leaks of "classified" information by Edward Snowden regarding the NSA have caused voices to be raised in protest. However, it seems that as long as the American Consumer can have the latest version of their iPhone, an endless supply video games, downloadable apps and cable TV they seem content to let the eavesdropping by the US Government continue, and to surrender their right to privacy for the convenience of having a GPS device that can direct them to the nearest Costco.

THE PRODUCTION:
Even though the script was written in the 1960's Mr. Coppola was not able to get the film financed and into production until 1973, after the overwhelming

success of *The Godfather*. The film boasts an amazing cast of then not so established character actors including John Cazale, Fredric Forrest and Teri Garr. Harrison Ford has a pre-Indiana Jones, small pivotal role in the film and the later acclaimed Academy Award winning actor, Robert Duvall plays an uncredited part of the corporate director who hires Gene Hackman.

Pardon my candor, but what was troubling the much-acclaimed Academy Award winning Director of Photography Haskell Wexler? I revere him as an extraordinarily talented Cinematographer with a list of films that seems to go on forever. However, it appears that he may have had at times, very strong and inflexible opinions about certain elements of various productions.

Early in his career in 1963, he worked with the legendary Director Eli Kazan on his semi-biographical film, *America, America*. Even though Mr. Wexler was much lauded for his Cinematography, Mr. Kazan has stated publicly that he did not care to ever work with him again. After several days of shooting on *The Conversation*, Mr. Coppola found it necessary to fire Mr. Wexler over creative differences. Again in 1975 he was fired from, *One Flew Over The Cuckoo's Nest* by Milos Forman. On both occasions he was replaced by the talented and versatile DP Bill Butler who would go on to film Spielberg's blockbuster *Jaws*.

The Editor and Sound Designer on the production was Walter Murch. His work was stunning and exceptional and of course he would go on to do outstanding work on the films, *The Godfather II, Apocalypse Now, The English Patient, The Talented Mr. Ripley* and many more.

THE AWARDS:
In 1974 The Film won the Palm d'Or at the Cannes Film Festival and was nominated for three Academy Awards: Best Picture, Best Sound and Best Original Screenplay. In 1995 the Library of Congress for being "culturally, historically and aesthetically significant" selected *The Conversation* for preservation.

ONLINE RESOURCES:
Use Google Images & Google Videos for dozens of links…

Buy it on Amazon, Google Play, or iTunes.

THINKING OUTSIDE THE BOX:
Class Exercises:

1. After watching the film, each student should write

an essay about what worked for them and what did not work as well as what they liked best and liked least and why.

2. Knowing the technological advances in surveillance that have occurred between 1974 and today, each student should write an essay about the average American's assumption of privacy and what they are supposed to be able to do "behind closed doors."

3. Mr. Coppola made *The Conversation* after being inspired by viewing Michelangelo Antonioni's film *Blow Up*. Each student should write an essay about how they might have been inspired by a film they've seen, to create something similar but entirely different.

4. Since Gene Hackman plays a similar character, in both films, each student should screen *The Conversation* and *Enemy Of The State*, then write an essay comparing and contrasting the two films.

5. The students should team up and make a short film, using some of today's small "hidden cameras"

Chapter 24:

1974
SWEPT AWAY,
By An Unusual Destiny In The Blue Sea Of August

Lina Wertmuller
The Bare Essentials

SPOILER ALEERT!
Those politically correct critics who have characterized this film as, "...the most outrageously misogynist film ever made..." have simply missed the point altogether or are too obtuse to "get" this film's brilliant female writer/director, or the meaning of her outstanding film.

Yes, there is violence against a woman. Yes, there is almost a rape. Yes, there is the subjection of a woman to a man's will... But all of this must be viewed within the entire context of what the extraordinary Female

Writer / Director, Ms. Wertmuller was saying in her brilliant film.

When you look at this exceptional film, do so realizing that this is not a man's perspective that is being presented, this is the vision of a woman who is telling us of her observations, her point of view of our rather frail and tentative relationships as men and women, within the context of the much larger socio-political landscape.

THE CREATIVE TEAM:
Writer: Lina Wertmuller
Director: Lina Wertmuller
Cinematographer: Giulio Battiferri, Giuseppe Fornari, Ennio Guarnieri, Stefano Ricciotti
Editor: Franco Fraticilli

WHY IS THIS FILM VISIONARY:
Swept Away... is a remarkably brilliant production, made by an accomplished female Director who was also an Assistant to the Maestro of Maestros, Federico Fellini. This film says nearly everything that there is to say about the human condition when it comes to: survival, politics, race, class, economics and especially the man/woman relationship.

Amazingly, all of that is presented to us as expertly

packaged as a travel brochure, with nearly 75% of the film following the plight of a beautiful Italian couple, from totally different backgrounds, lost at sea in a small skiff and then cast away on a deserted Mediterranean island.

With *Swept Away...* Lina Wertmuller, managed to strip away all of the trappings of society and civilization leaving our two heroes, Raffaella and Gennarino with only the Bare Essentials. By skillfully doing so, she was able to reveal to us her illuminated vision of exactly what's going on with the human condition.

THE BASICS:
Raffaella is blonde from the north of Italy, Gennarino is dark, from the south. She is a rich, educated, cultured, Capitalist-Fascist. He is a poor, street-smart, coarse, Socialist-Communist. She rules the world on her yacht, bosses him around, ridicules him and she and her girlfriends coldly sunbath topless in front of him. He must serve her every whim as her lowly deck hand, suffer her ridicule and control his hot blood at the sight of her naked breasts. She is a loud, opinionated white bitch while he is her silent, subservient dark slave.

Clearly this is a film has been carefully structured to

show the audience the struggle between regions, classes, education, culture, economics, politics and gender. By the way, Act I of this milestone and masterpiece, is one of the very best "set ups" ever written for all of the "what goes around comes around" cosmic-joke action and punch lines that follow in Acts II and III.

Naturally, these two polar opposites are *Swept Away by an Unusual Destiny in the Blue Sea of August...* Lost in a skiff and then cast away on a deserted Mediterranean Island where the poor dark southern communist servant is now in charge of their survival and he makes the rich blonde northern capitalist bitch pay for all of her injustices in spades.

He knocks her around, and with each slap, blames her ruling class for a different social ill, for the inflation, for not being able to use hospitals, for the price of oil and gasoline. He nearly rapes her but holds back, saying that she must "fall in love" with him first, that he wants from her "passion or nothing!"

Does she actually fall in love with him? Or, does he fall in love with her? Or, do they both fall in love... Do they swear never to go back, to the social-economic-political-regional-gender traps of their society? But then finally he forces them to go back to prove that their love can stand the test and by so doing he gets the full and final brunt of this topsy-turvy, class-struggle, economic-struggle gender-struggle... cosmic joke.

THE PRODUCTION:
This is one film that looks like it was a joy to make, shooting mostly on a yacht and what doubled for a deserted island somewhere off the coast of Italy. It appears not to have been done with a large crew, but instead with a team of very efficient professionals.

As was the Italian custom the entire film was dubbed, that is, all of the dialogue spoken by the cast was recorded in post-production. This makes shooting much more efficient, because you never have to wait to shoot until it's "OK for sound." Instead you just get what is called a "guide track" that you can use to dub the dialogue to later.

In the case of the two leading actors, Giancarlo Giannini and Mariangela Melato, they both do an extraordinary job of post syncing their dialogue, since they both were given a torrent of insults to spew at each other, which they usually did in both a fury of emotion and at break neck speed. And then they were able to rerecorded it all again in Post Production to perfection! Outstanding work!

I'm not sure why there are four different Cinematographers listed on Swept Away... but they all did an amazing job of making each sequence in the film look stunningly beautiful and totally believable. Perhaps one was only shooting on the yacht and another was only shooting the various establishing shots, sunrises and sunsets on the island. There is really no way to tell.

However, in researching each Cinematographer on the Internet, it appears as if Mr. Battiferri and Mr. Fornari were both primarily camera operators who worked as Cinematographers on Swept Away... and that Mr. Riccioto was mostly a Cinematographer for television. However, the gentleman with all the film credits, including The Garden of the Finzi-Continis for Mr. De Sica and Ginger and Fred for Mr. Fellini, was Mr. Guarnieri and I can only conjecture that he was the main Cinematographer for all of the dramatic scenes on the production.

FINALLY:
This is a film that is like a fine Italian wine that simply grows richer and deeper with age. I have watched this film many times since it was first released in 1974 and I just watched it again today online doing research for this chapter. And I watched the entire

film in Italian, even though I do not speak the language. That's how compelling and visually exciting this extraordinary film actually is.

ONLINE RESOURCES:
Use Google Images & Google Videos for dozens of links...

Buy it on Amazon, Google Play, or iTunes.

Or view the entire film or scenes at:
www.youtube.com

THINKING OUTSIDE THE BOX:
Class Exercises:

1. Each student should write an essay about their reaction to seeing the film, how did they feel about it and what were their pros and cons.

2. Each student should write an essay about all of the various big ideas that are portrayed in the film: class, education, economics, region, politics, gender etc.

3. Each student should go online and find some other Lina Wertmuller films to rent or buy and screen including: *The Seduction of Mi Mi* and most especially: *Seven Beauties*.

4. Each student should do research and write an essay about how many successful female film directors there have been and do they think that Kathryn Bigelow owes a tip of her director's hat to Ms. Wertmuller.

5. *Swept Away...* Used two people on a deserted island to discuss a lot of important ideas and each student should write an essay or treatment using this a similar template, to discuss several big ideas that they would like to make a film about.

Chapter 25:

1974
AND NOW MY LOVE

Claude Lelouch
Amazingly Hand Held

SPOILER ALERT!
In America, this is a fairly obscure French film. It is in black and white and color, it has subtitles and it is partially a period piece that starts out at the beginning of the 20th century with a man cranking an early version of a motion picture camera. Yes, the film is partly about the Director's love of filmmaking.

It is also a film about love that traces the history of the two lovers, who will only meet in the last scene of the film. It begins with the girl's grandparents during World War I and then to her parents who were Jewish refugees after World War II. The young man is an orphan of the streets, a delinquent and petty thief who educates himself while in jail and eventually becomes a filmmaker. We are moving between these two lives and along the way the film is also detailing the major events of the decades that span the timeframe of the film as well as the coming of age of motion pictures.

A very ambitious production to say the least, and one that boasts some of the finest hand held camerawork in film history. That is what we are celebrating: Mr. Lelouch and his amazing moving camera that at times actually becomes another character in the film.

THE CREATIVE TEAM:
Writers: Claude Lelouch / Pierre Uytterhoeven
Director: Claude Lelouch
Cinematographer: Jean Collumb
Editor: George Klotz

WHY IS THIS FILM VISIONARY:
In its scope, invention, imagination and realization it is truly a remarkable film. Claude Lelouch is a French cinematic artist and filmmaker who has written and directed over forty feature films. He burst onto the film scene in 1966 with a small feature called *A Man and A Woman* and over the decades since he has demonstrated an unrivaled cinematic bravura.

He shot *A Man and A Woman* on 35mm film in 15 days for around $80,000. The actors did their own make up and wardrobe and improvised the dialogue, since there was no formal script. The film was shot in black and white and color, which caused a sensation at the time. When asked why he had used both black and white and color film, Mr. Lelouch simply replied, "...because we ran out of color." By the way, this small independent production went on to win the Academy Award in 1966 for the Best Foreign Language Film.

Almost eight years later in 1974 *And Now My Love*, was released in France and one year later it was released in the US. As we have pointed out it was an audacious production, but the most audacious part of it was the way that it was shot. Several years before the Steadicam was introduced, Mr. Lelouch was using long hand held takes in which the camera became a choreographed participant in the action. His extraordinary use of the hand held camera sets him apart from nearly every other Director and Filmmaker in Cinematic history.

THE BASICS:
In order to do these kinds of long, moving, hand held shots, you need you use available light or have the lighting built into the sets or locations like Mr.

Kubrick likes to do. However the most astounding aspects of many of Mr. Lelouch's "one shot takes" was that they also contained hundreds of extras all dressed in full period costumes!

Even with all of those logistics, the scenes were only shot with one camera that covered all of the action in a single take. From purely a production standpoint alone, this takes a very huge amount of cinematic bravado and a very large set of cinematic balls: Mr. Lelouch seems to have both.

There are many outstanding, long hand held one shot takes in this film, but one of my favorites takes place early in the film in the trenches of World War I. A woman has just given birth to a son and then we Cut To: The trenches where a messenger is looking for the father to give him the news. The hand held camera follows as the messenger weaves his way through the narrow, grimy trenches, lined with dozens of battle weary soldiers, some wounded, some dead, some ready to fight. On and on, the messenger treks looking for the father as explosions are going off. Finally the camera moves left as dozens of men suddenly charge out of the trenches and into battle. Weapons fire, more explosions, men dying on and on the camera follows the charge, finally coming to rest on the father, working at documenting the battle with his hand cranked movie camera. The messenger runs up and gives him the news and as he shouts "It's a boy!" Suddenly a shell hits and an explosion blows the father away while the camera is left burning on its tripod. But the shot is still not over. Now waves of men attack running through the smoke and past the burning camera to carry on the battle. After they pass, then the shot ends.

Can you imagine the logistics of doing this kind of a battle scene with hundreds of extras in period costume, firing weapons, smoke, explosions, the camera covering seemingly hundreds of yards of terrain... ALL IN A SINGLE HAND HELD ONE SHOT TAKE! Believe me there are many more shots as astounding as this one, in this incredible film.

THE DISASTROUS FUTURE:
In some versions of this outstanding film there is a disastrous final reel, after the lovers meet, on the airplane, where Mr. Lelouch fantasizes about their uncertain life together in a sterile future society.

If this scene happens to come up when you are viewing the film, Skip Over It Immediately!!! And get back to the final exchange between the two lovers, on the airplane, this was how the film was originally released in the US... and how this wonderful love story should and must end.

FINALLY:
While doing research on the Internet I discovered a small 9 minute film that Mr. Lelouch recently made called Rendezvous, where he seems to drive at top speed through the pre-dawn streets of Paris... It is another one-shot take! Check it out below and be astounded once again...

ONLINE RESOURCES:
Use Google Images & Google Videos for dozens of links...

Buy it on Amazon, Google Play, or iTunes.

Also Watch: Rendezvous
http://www.youtube.com/watch?v=wij_-YuHcdg&feature=player_embedded

THINKING OUTSIDE THE BOX:
Class Exercises:

1. This is a very complex story and set of characters, with the leading actors playing all of their relatives. While it's still fresh in your mind... Each student should write an essay tracing the character of the girl from her grandparents and the boy from his life of

petty crime, until the two lovers meet.

2. There are more than a few astounding hand held one-shot takes in this film. Each student should choose their favorite, then watch it several times and write an essay about what they think was involved in the production being able to accomplish the shot.

3. The director Alfonso Cuaron and his cinematographer Emmanuel Lubezki who did *Y Tu Mama Tambien* and *Children of Men* owe a lot to the work of Claude Lelouch. Each student should view these films again and write an essay comparing and contrasting *And Now My Love* with the work of Alfonso Cuaron.

4. There may not be another love story that has attempted to cover as much chronological territory and is as uniquely constructed as *And Now My Love*. Each student should write an essay about their feelings, thoughts and what were the pros and cons and what worked and did not work and why.

5. Each students should make a small HD film using the same style and unique hand held camerawork used by Mr. Lelouch in *And Now My Love*.

Chapter 26:

1975
BARRY LYNDON

Stanley Kubrick
Candlelight By NASA

SPOILER ALERT!
Barry Lyndon is not my favorite Kubrick film. It is a long, difficult, ponderous film to watch, and much of it is set at a tedious pace. This is largely due to Mr. Kubrick's insistence on beginning many scenes with a very long 500mm to 50mm Zoom Back, that seems to go on and on forever. Even though it's sacrilegious to say, I've told myself that I could easily trim an hour out of this film and never touch an important scene or line of dialog, simply by addressing the pacing and dissolving through many of these repetitive zooms.

That being said, I must admit that this is a ravishingly gorgeous film to look at and while it did not do well at the US box office, it was a huge hit in Europe and even played at one theater in Paris for over a year.

THE CREATIVE TEAM:
Writers: Stanley Kubrick, William Makepeace Thackeray
Director: Stanley Kubrick
Cinematographer: John Alcott
Editor: Tony Lawson

WHY IS THIS FILM VISIONARY:
It is simply one of the most stunning visual masterpieces ever photographed and one that faithfully recreates the period that it is dealing with down to the last button and thread of a detail. When it came to the look of the film and the lighting of the interior scenes, Mr. Kubrick and his Director of Photography, the great John Alcott, wanted to remain true to the period and shoot mainly by candlelight.

As part of his ongoing research into every and all things of interest, Mr. Kubrick had discovered several lenses developed by Zeiss for NASA that had an unbelievable aperture of f .7; the normal lenses at the time had an aperture of f 2.8 or f 2.2 and the Super Speed Lenses, which were not available until the late 1970's would eventually give filmmakers an aperture from f 1.0 or f 1.4. Finding a lens that opened up several stops wider than what was then available, "100% more exposure…" as Mr. Kubrick has stated, is what made their shooting by candlelight even remotely possible.

THE BASICS:
I believe that *Barry Lyndon* was undertaken to utilize some of the many years of research that Mr. Kubrick had done on his never to be realized production of *Napoleon.* The studio, Warner Brothers, as Columbia had done in demanding four roles from Peter Sellers before financing *Dr. Strangelove…* told Mr. Kubrick that they would finance this film, only if he managed to get a Top 10 Box Office Name in the staring role as *Barry Lyndon.*

At the time in 1974, there were only two actors in The Top 10 that could play the part. After, it had been turned down by Robert Redford it was taken up by Ryan O'Neal who did the very best work of his career in this role. As fate would have it, this was the one and only time that Mr. O'Neal was ever in the Top Ten and it was as a direct result of previously starring in the film, *Love Story* with Ali MacGraw.

THE PRODUCTION:
Began in May of 1973 and shot for a total of 300 days over the next two years. The film was finally finished

and released in December of 1975. Ever the perfectionist, Mr. Kubrick was reported to have, on more than one occasion: first, shot a sequence, edited it, screened it and then finally decided to shoot it again. He also made sure that every article of clothing every prop and every vehicle used in the film were authentic down to the very last detail.

NASA LENSES:
After Mr. Kubrick managed to acquire the NASA lens, a lot of work still needed to be done. First carefully adapting his Mitchell BNC camera to take the newly acquired Zeiss lens and then once that had been accomplished, in working out the focus.

This was a major hurdle, since the wider the aperture of the lens, the less depth of field, or area that is in critical focus in front of the lens. A host of tests were done and the camera assistant eventually needed an elaborate video monitor system, with the actors carefully placed at critically measured distances to make it all come together, but obviously it did.

AVAILABLE LIGHT:
The other photographic choice was to use natural exterior daylight when shooting outside; and for the masterful long shots and establishing shots presented throughout the film it worked beautifully. Where it

did not work as well, was in the bare knuckles fight scene between Barry and another soldier.

Knowing Mr. Kubrick's style, I'm sure that this scene was shot over the course of several days, if not weeks, and even a person as exacting as Mr. Kubrick was not able to control the ever-changing daylight provided by, "The Big Gaffer In The Sky." By watching carefully you can plainly see several continuity jumps in the lighting, since during the course of the shooting, the sky went from magic hour, to overcast, to clear and from hard light to soft light and back again, on many occasions.

Often for their interiors, since they were shooting in what was considered a museum and they could not bring in any lighting equipment, Mr. Kubrick and Mr. Alcott would use mini-brutes shining through tracing paper to create the feeling of natural light. Most of the time it worked perfectly, however, in one scene, the duel between Barry and Lord Bullington, late in the film, you can spot a slight faux pas, that was undoubtedly an "artistic choice."

The scene was shot using Tungsten balanced film instead of Daylight balanced film and since they used a warmer (tungsten) light to augment the natural (blue) daylight, you can spot the flaw by looking at several small windows in the background that show the natural (blue) daylight shining through, while the actors are illuminated by a warmer tungsten glow.

THE AWARDS:
Once again, Mr. Kubrick's amazing vision had triumphed and Barry Lyndon, while not successful with the American audience, was highly regarded by its peers and went on to win four Academy Awards: Cinematography, Music, Costumes, and Art Direction. It was also nominated for Best Adapted Screenplay, Best Director and Best Picture and went on to achieve major international acclaim.

ONLINE RESOURCES:
Use Google Images & Google Videos for dozens of links...

Buy it on Amazon, Google Play, or iTunes.

Trailer Video URL:
http://www.imdb.com/video/screenplay/vi247005465/

THINKING OUTSIDE THE BOX:
Class Exercises:

1. With this film still fresh in mind, each student

should write an essay about their thoughts and feelings, their pros and cons.

2. This film is a ravishingly beautiful film to watch and contains some outstanding, award winning cinematography. Each student should write an essay describing in detail the process that Mr. Kubrick and Mr. Alcott had to go through to achieve their outstanding work.

3. If you see a Trailer for this film, you marvel at all of the breathtaking scenes. However, I believe that the pace of the film is far too tedious and hurts the overall effect. Each student should write an essay describing in detail, how they could improve the pace of the film and tighten it up, without touching any major scenes or important dialogue.

4. Mr. Kubrick and Mr. Alcott had to go through an exhaustive process in order to shoot by candle light, today it's routinely done by my students utilizing the latest HD or DSLR technology. Each student should write an essay describing the difference between filmmaking back in the day and with today's more technically advanced and democratized process.

5. We have studied four of Mr. Kubrick's films, *Dr. Strangelove, 2001... A Clockwork Orange* and *Barry*

Lyndon. Each student should write an essay discussing their thoughts and feelings about which film is their favorite and why.

X. Words & Music

Chapter 27

1976
NETWORK

Sidney Lumet
The Boob Tube

SPOILER ALERT!
Even though my background is in the production side of filmmaking, directing, cinematography and editing, I have always told everyone, that I consider the hardest job in show business, sitting in front of the blank page or computer screen and typing the words: "Fade In."

What Comes Next? That is why it's the hardest job. That's the hard part, coming up with 90 or 100 or 120 pages of polished Drama, Comedy or Action that contains all of the characters and dialogue, that will become either the outline that will evolve or the bible that will be reverently followed.

Network is being celebrated primarily for the written word, for its outstanding Screenplay by Paddy Chayefsky, which I believe was not only extraordinary but also visionary, very far ahead of its time and very far "outside of the box."

THE CREATIVE TEAM:
Writer: Paddy Chayefsky
Director: Sidney Lumet
Cinematographer: Owen Roizman
Editor: Alan Heim

WHY IS THIS FILM VISIONARY:
The venerated Director, the late Sidney Lumet was a supremely subtle stylist and absolutely one of the best Directors of actors on the planet. In my humble opinion, during the 1970's he should have won the Academy Award for Best Director at least five times. Namely for his outstanding work on the films: *Serpico, Murder On The Orient Express, Dog Day Afternoon, Network* and *Equus*. I can still recall physically throwing something at the television set when the Academy Award for Best Actor went to Richard Dreyfuss for Neil Simon's sappy *The Goodbye Girl* instead of going to Richard Burton for the best

performance of his career in Peter Schaffer's and Mr. Lumet's psychological drama, *Equus.*

However, *Network* is not a being discussed here because of its Acting, Directing, Cinematography or Editing, even thought Mr. Lumet's masterful work, along with each of those other Arts and Crafts, was brilliantly and flawlessly executed to award winning perfection. Instead we are addressing the Script: The extraordinary words put onto the page after "Fade In" by the unparalleled Screenplay Writer, Paddy Chayefsky.

THE BASICS:
While this film is widely acknowledged to be a "Satire on the Television Industry" both the Director Sidney Lumet and the Writer Paddy Chayefsky have stated for the record, that it was specifically a reflection of what was happening or that would be happening, in the medium of television, based entirely on their real life observations and experiences. Mr. Lumet has actually compared the film to reportage.

As we know much of what *Network* prophesied in the 1970's has come true many times over on today's 24-hour 500-channel, yet still mostly mindless, boob tube. News programming, which began with the high standards of reporting the facts and of journalistic truth, has become, as predicted, nearly pure entertainment. If you happen to watch the half-truths, biased blathering and outright lies that pass for "fair an balanced news" on Fox Television you are used to hearing editorial opinions that contain bigoted, right wing, scare tactics that are outright lies and border on racist, fascist hate mongering. Of course, that's not only my opinion, I can recall my news source for may years Jon Stewart's *The Daily Show* which was all over Fox News for its lying underhanded conduct.

THE POWER OF THE WORDS:
Contrary to what some laymen may believe, the actors do not make up the dialogue in a film as they go along. Unless the director has specifically asked them to "improvise" they are performing the words that have been carefully and patiently set down by the Writer. In the case of *Network*, these words were astoundingly powerful and to demonstrate exactly how powerful they were: Beatrice Straight who won the Academy Award for Best Supporting Actress for this film, was on screen for only a total of 5 minutes and forty seconds!

This still stands as the record for the briefest performance ever to win an Academy Award. Ned Beatty worked on the production for one day and received an Academy Award Nomination and Peter

Finch, who died before the Academy Awards took place, became the first actor to ever win the Best Actor Award posthumously until Heath Ledger won in 2008. Of course all of the performances were outstanding. However, these examples are a testament to Mr. Chayersky's Extraordinarily Powerful Writing!

THE MONOLOGUES:
Watch the entire film but pay special attention to two examples of some of the best written monologues in cinema history: Peter Finch's "I'm as mad as hell..." scene and what I consider to be the very best monologue ever recorded on film, Ned Beatty's "You have sinned against the primal forces of nature..." scene.

Network directed by Sidney Lumet requires repeated viewings. The words written by Mr. Chayefsky for Ned Beatty's character Arthur Jensen should be read and memorized. Both the film and the words should be passed on from generation to generation, because they predicted with crystal clarity, how much the ominous worlds of Corporate Greed, Political Power, and Big Business were, and now are dictating exactly how the Economy of our planet, our nations and our lives are being run... TODAY!

Read the words here and then pass them on:

Arthur Jensen

"You have meddled with the primal forces of nature, Mr. Beale, and I won't have it, is that clear?! You think you have merely stopped a business deal—that is not the case!

The Arabs have taken billions of dollars out of this country, and now they must put it back. It is ebb and flow, tidal gravity, it is ecological balance!

You are an old man who thinks in terms of nations and peoples. There are no nations! There are no peoples! There are no Russians. There are no Arabs! There are no third worlds!

There is no West! There is only one holistic system of systems, one vast and immane, interwoven, interacting, multivariate, multi-national dominion of dollars! Petro-dollars, electro-dollars, multi-dollars!, reichmarks, rubles, rin, pounds and shekels!

It is the international system of currency that determines the totality of life on this planet! That is the natural order of things today!

That is the atomic, subatomic and galactic structure of things today! You get up on your little twenty-one inch screen, and howl about America and democracy. There is no America. There is no democracy. There is only IBM and ITT and AT&T and Dupont, Dow, Union Carbide and Exxon. Those are the nations of the world today...

We no longer live in a world of nations and ideologies, Mr. Beale. The world is a college of corporations, inexorably determined by the immutable by-laws of business.

The world is a business, Mr. Beale! It has been since man crawled out of the slime, and our children, Mr.Beale, will live to see that perfect world in which there is no war and famine, oppression and brutality --one vast and ecumenical holding company, for whom all men will work to serve a common profit, in which all men will hold a share of stock, all necessities provided, all anxieties tranquilized, all boredom amused..."

<u>That is the power of a writer who is telling it exactly like it was and still is today!</u>

THE AWARDS:
Network won three of the four Academy Awards for Acting, which tied the record with the Elia Kazan film, *A Streetcar Named Desire.* It also became the last film to receive four Academy Award Acting nominations, which tied it with the films: *Who's Afraid of Virginia Woolf, Reds,* and *Coming Home.*

Network won a total of four Academy Awards: Best Actor in a Leading Role - Peter Finch. Best Actress in a Leading Role - Faye Dunaway. Best Actress in a Supporting Role - Beatrice Straight and Best Original Screenplay Paddy Chayefsky. *Network* also won the Golden Glove Awards for: Best Motion Picture Actor-Drama: Peter Finch. Best Motion Picture Actress-Drama: Faye Dunaway. Best Director: Sidney Lumet and Best Screenplay: Paddy Chayefsky.

ONLINE RESOURCES:
Use Google Images & Google Video for dozens of links...

Buy it on Amazon, Google Play, or iTunes.

THINKING OUTSIDE THE BOX:
Class Exercises:

1. *Network* was a powerful script that became a

powerful film. Each student should write an essay about their thoughts, feelings, pros, cons, likes and dislikes of the film. Does it still hold up after all these years?

2. Is Writing the hardest job in show business? With all of the information available, scripts on line, endless "how to" books and courses on screenwriting, why are there still so few good scripts? Each student should write an essay giving their answers to these two questions.

3. Sidney Lumet has directed literally dozens of great films and great performances. Each student should check out his resume on the Internet, select one they haven't seen, view it and write an essay about it and what it means to you.

4. What surprises me about *Network*, is that is remains current and insightful. Each student should write an essay concerning why and also what there is about this film that keeps it so seemingly up to date?

5. In the theater they say, "If it's not on the page, it's not on the stage." Each student should write an essay discussing how this phrase relates to the resume of Sidney Lumet.

Chapter 28:

1980
Stardust Memories

Woody Allen
The Loyal Opposition

SPOILER ALERT!
Even though Woody Allen is a comedian he is also a brilliant and serious writer and filmmaker. *Stardust Memories,* which has been called a homage to Fellini's *8 1/2* could also be seen as a homage to his favorite director, Ingmar Bergman, because there are scenes in this film that are simply that outstanding, chilling and meaningful.

Comedies and comedians rarely get the nod when it comes to handing out awards, so it's easy to overlook Mr. Allen's seriousness in the wake of all of his slapstick antics, zingers and one-liners. But if you look carefully at even one of his early funny films like

Every Thing That You Always Wanted To Know About Sex, But Were Afraid To Ask, you can see that Mr. Allen is stylistically using each sequence in the film as an excuse for doing a spoof on a different genre of filmmaking: The Monster Film, The Sci-Fi Film, The Romantic Comedy, The Urban Drama, The European Art Film, etc. etc. This takes a lot of filmmaking insight and mastery to pull off this technique as seamlessly as it was done.

THE CREATIVE TEAM:
Writer: Woody Allen
Director: Woody Allen
Cinematographer: Gordon Willis
Editor: Susan E. Morse

WHY IS THIS FILM VISIONARY:
Stardust Memories is an outstanding cinematic achievement that; while paying homage to both Ingmar Bergman and Federico Fellini, also turns its unflinching Black and White cinematic gaze on a film director's midlife crisis. We follow him through a weekend retrospective of his "early funny" films, as he parries a cacophony of questions and demands thrust upon him from friends, fans, critics, wannabe's and hangers on.

At the same time the director is searching for

meaning to his existence, the proper ending for his latest film, the right woman to share his life with and the will and inspiration to continue to fill that large empty screen with more sound and fury... that may only signify, Nothing. During this bizarre journey, we are also given a peek behind the scenes, into many of the traps and trappings of a celebrity's lifestyle. So much so, that by the final frame we may not even want to wish that circumstance on our worst enemy.

THE BASICS:
Woody Allen is the most prolific filmmaker of our time and in this computer age he still writes all of his scripts on his trusty, old portable typewriter. Over the past forty years, he has averaged a film a year, writing, directing and starring in over 40 motion pictures and as of 2010 and on into 2011, 12, 13 & 14, 15, 16 there's no sign that he's about to slow down.

In the early 1970's after establishing himself as a comedic talent, he soon began to use his film work to ask hard and important questions about the existence of God, and a world where, day after day, terrible crimes not only go unpunished, but the perpetrators seem to thrive as in his film, *Crimes & Misdemeanors.*

I've always thought that an insightful way of studying Mr. Allen would be to screen a double bill featuring,

Stardust Memories and *Deconstructing Harry*: The first being the creative life of the Director, the second being the creative life of the Writer. To paraphrase the maestro himself, "...two subjects on which Mr. Allen is an absolute expert."

Mr. Allen believes that his films should speak for themselves. In other words for the DVD release of each film there are no interviews, no commentaries, no behind the scenes, no "the making of" documentaries. If you want insight into his films, look at his films. That's right, we are totally on our own.

THE PRODUCTION:
There are three outstanding scenes that seem to set the tone and subtext for this unique and important film that on the surface appears to be a "comedy." First: The opening scene in Stardust Memories is a showstopper, because it is Fellini by way of Bergman. Like 8 1/2 it starts in what we suppose is a dream, but then like many of Bergman's films we discover that it is about a bleak and hopeless existence... A man (Woody Allen) sits alone on a train. The coach is full of crying, morose, misshapen and bereft people. He looks out the window and sees another train containing a good-looking, happy, affluent, partying crowd. A beautiful woman (Sharon Stone) blows him a kiss, he wants to change his ticket, there's been

some mistake, right? Shouldn't he be on the other train?

Suddenly both trains lurch and start up, then when he tries to leave his coach the door will not open, the emergency cord comes off in his hand, sand is running out of a random piece of luggage and as he bangs on one of the window to get out... The entire scene, Fades to White.

Now we see a seemingly endless trash dump and slowly all of the misshapen passengers from the man's coach arrive walking in from the left side of the frame. Then as the man follows and steps into a huge close up he sees: All of the good-looking passengers from the other train walking in from the right side of the frame... Now he realizes that no matter what train you're on in life, everyone is going to end up at the same pile of trash, the same garbage dump of... Death! Then we see... Film Leader!

It was only a movie, a screening of our heroes' latest movie and now his producers and the studio execs bellow about how much they dislike it, how they will take it back, re-shoot it, re-cut it... They hate it! And that's just for openers.

Second: Early on we are introduced to an important

ex-girlfriend, Dorrie (Charlotte Rampling) and realize that our hero seems to be drawn to troubled, neurotic bordering on psychotic woman who bring a lot of baggage along with them. Nearly three quarters of the way through the film we see a searing portrait of Dorrie, presumable as our hero visits her in a mental institution. The entire scene plays in only a Close Up of Dorrie and it repeatedly Jump Cuts her from emotion to emotion as she continually asks, "Are you seeing anyone..." over and over again, along with other disjointed remarks. It is a scene that might well have been done by the maestro Ingmar Bergman himself. It is a dispassionate, passionate portrait of someone on the emotional razors edge of reason. Each time I see it this scene seems to be so raw and unsettling that it is like viewing outtakes from the Bergman classic, *Persona*.

Third: The final scene of the film. As the crowd, consisting of all of the actors in the film file out of the theater, an elderly Jewish couple shuffle by and the man says; "From this he makes a living? I enjoy a nice melodrama..." So the audience will have a nice smile to exit on, right?

Absolutely not, the film is not over. For several beats the theater is entirely empty as we stare from the back row, at the blank movie screen... Is That All?

No... Not quite...

Now, the character of the director (Woody Allen) comes back down the center isle to look for and find his dark glasses that he's left behind. He puts them on and starts to exit then, almost as an afterthought he glances back then turns to face the large empty silver screen...

He looks at it motionless, for nearly 15 seconds... An eternity of screen time, before finally, slowly turning away and seemingly with the weight of the world on his shoulders, trudges back out into his life to make his next film.

That scene never ceases to deeply move and astound me, that look at the empty screen is one of the most profound and emotional pieces of filmmaking that I have ever seen. Is he thinking: What have I done? Or, What should I have done? Or, What will I do? Or, Is this even worth doing at all? Whatever those thoughts are, this is a one-of-a-kind cinematic moment and one, I venture to say, that even the maestros Bergman and Fellini would not have even dared to attempt!

THE AWARDS:
Stardust Memories was nominated for a Writers Guild

Award but did not win. However, even though Mr. Allen has no interest in awards of any kind especially the Academy Awards, he holds the record for the most nominations for Writing and Directing with 21 and for nominations for Best Original Screenplay at 14. He has also directed 15 different actors to Academy Award nominated performances.

ONLINE RESOURCES:
Use Google Images & Google Videos for dozens of links...

Buy it on Amazon, Google Play, or iTunes.

View the Trailer and various scenes on:
www.youtube.com

THINKING OUTSIDE THE BOX:

1. Each student should write an essay about how they feel about this film. Whether it's your first time or tenth time seeing it, how did it affect you and what are your likes and dislikes, your pros and cons.

2. Each student should write an essay theorizing about why Mr. Allen still writes all of his scripts on an old portable typewriter.

3. Each student should write an essay comparing and contrasting *Stardust Memories* with *8 1/2*.

4. Each student should also view *Deconstructing Harry* then write an essay comparing and contrasting that film with *Stardust Memories*.

5. Each student should go online and research Woody Allen's immense body of work then choose a film that they haven't seen and rent or buy it on line and view it.

Chapter 29:

1980
Raging Bull

Martin Scorsese
Cinematic Redemption

SPOILER ALERT!
In *Raging Bull*, only about 10 minutes of the film's 129 minutes takes place inside the boxing ring, but when you are there it is an exceptional experience and one that you will definitely not forget. I can still recall seeing the film when it first came out and for the first time in my life, actually feeling the force of the punches hitting me in the chest during the screening. Later I discovered that all of the punches were original sounds created by smashing tomatoes and melons. After they were used, the tapes of those sound effects were destroyed so that they could not be used by anyone ever again.

Aside from the extraordinary technical achievements, this is a film about redemption by a director who was actually living it and experiencing it during the time that he was making the film. In 1978, Martin Scorsese had a substance abuse issue and that substance cocaine had nearly caused his death from an overdose. While recovering in the hospital, his long time friend Robert De Niro visited him and told him that he had to clean up his act and to start by Directing *Raging Bull*.

Mr. Scorsese refused not understanding the complexities of the film and basically, not wanting to do a "sports movie." However, finally, due to Mr. De Niro's tenacity, he agreed and later claimed that doing this film is what turned his life and his career around.

THE CREATIVE TEAM:
Writer: Paul Schrader, Mardik Martin
Director: Martin Scorsese
Cinematographer: Michael Chapman
Editor: Thelma Schoonmaker

WHY IS THIS FILM VISIONARY:
No film before or since has ever depicted what occurs inside the boxing ring with such power, violence, blood-spurting reality, surrealism and poetry. Shot

almost entirely from the Point Of View of being inside the ring with the fighters, the spectacle was also at times literally a blood bath for the ringside co-stars and extras viewing the brutal onslaught.

For the final LaMotta vs. Robinson fight, it's reported that Mr. Scorsese was having trouble visualizing how the scene should be shot and edited and consulted the famous shower scene in *Psycho* as a guide. This can clearly be seen in the shot of Robinson raising his punishing right glove in nearly the same size frame and angle as the infamous silhouetted knife attack. Talk about that often used phrase "He murdered 'em" when one fighter dominates another, being right on the money.

This is a brutal story about a brutal man, Jake LaMotta, in a brutal game, 1950's prize fighting that was notoriously dominated by the mob. A bloody, vicious, violent, profane script, character and film but according to Mr. Scorsese's Catholic upbringing, not without the possibility of redemption. As the opening dedication in the film reads, "...once I was blind, but now I can see..."

THE BASICS:
This film is a tribute to Robert De Niro's insight and tenacity. He is the one who first read the

autobiography of Jake LaMotta, wanted to play the part and took it to his pal Martin Scorsese. After he initially turned it down, Mr. De Niro interested the producer Irwin Winkler who said that he would sign on only if Mr. Scorsese would sign on. Recovering from his near fatal drug overdose and with Mr. De Niro's persistence, finally Mr. Scorsese came on board.

Later when the script needed some last minute surgery, Mr. De Niro and Mr. Scorsese went into seclusion in the Caribbean for two weeks and emerged with the final draft for which they both still remain, un-credited. During pre-production it was Mr. De Niro who found Joe Pesci and who suggested shooting the early LaMotta years first, then shutting down so that he could put on sixty pounds for the end of the film. He also went though grueling and intense physical training to become a prizefighter and even entered three authentic boxing matches, winning two of them.

Has an actor, any actor, ever done more in the pursuit of a part or in the pursuit of the team to realize the production in which he wanted to play that part? Star, collaborator and un-credited co-writer and co-producer: Talk about an actor who was never waiting in his trailer!

THE PRODUCTION:

Raging Bull began shooting in Los Angeles in April 1979, capturing most of the scenes for the LaMotta early years and all of the fights, before shutting down for several months so that Mr. De Niro could tour Northern Italy and put on the extra pounds necessary for the LaMotta later years.

Shooting a fighter's POV inside the ring had certainly been done before, but Mr. Scorsese wanted to use this technique nearly exclusively in covering all of the fight scenes in Raging Bull. That was not the only unique item that he pulled out of his bag of cinematic tricks. At various times he used dance choreography, different size boxing rings, hand held cameras, slow motion, Dutch angles and facial prosthetics that sprayed blood several feet into the air.

Basically, Mr. Scorsese got right down to the real "nitty gritty" of what a fighter, felt, sensed, saw and experienced during a match by taking total creative and dramatic license with the material; it was truly a revelation. If you look at the film of the actual LaMotta vs. Robinson fight, yes it's a great fight but it's just another prizefight. However, this same material in the hands of Mr. Scorsese becomes something other. Something, not only dramatic, but heroic, frightening, horrific and epic. In the words of Mr. Hitchcock, it becomes: "Pure Cinema."

By the last reel, the vile, profane, blood-soaked, vulgar, violent life of Jake LaMotta, had been converted into something mythic, poetic, emotional and eternal by the masterful filmmaking of Martin Scorsese and by the final fade out, that harsh, brutal reality had been transformed by the maestro into cinematic redemption.

THE AWARDS:
Although it opened to mixed reviews and did not do well at the box office, it eventually was nominated for many awards including eight Academy Awards, wining two for Best Actor and Best Film Editing. It was nominated for seven Golden Globe Awards winning for Best Actor and for three National Society of Film Critics Awards, winning for Best Director, Best Cinematography and Best Supporting Actor.

ONLINE RESOURCES:
Use Google Images & Google Videos for dozens of links...

Buy it on Amazon, Google Play, or iTunes.

View the Trailer, scenes or the entire film online at:

www.youtube.com

THINKING OUTSIDE THE BOX:

1. This Film has been called violent and profane. Each student should write an essay discussing their reaction to the film, their pros, cons and feelings after viewing it.

2. Robert De Niro basically willed this film into existence. Each student should write an essay about the importance of having strong, determined collaborators on any film production.

3. Each student should write an essay comparing and contrasting the infamous shower scene from *Psycho* and the final attack on LaMotta by Robinsion in *Raging Bull*.

4. Each student should write an essay about "cinematic redemption." Does the vary act of transforming and abstracting any "reality" into a "film" somehow change the original material into something epic, mythic, poetic, even heroic and spiritual.

5. Each student should go online and view the final LaMotta vs Robinson fight, then view the scenes

recreating it in Raging Bull. Finally, write an essay about Martin Scorsese's use of artistic and dramatic license in interpreting and transforming "reality" into "Pure Cinema."

Chapter 30:

1981
CHARIOTS OF FIRE

Hugh Hudson
A Triumphant Score

SPOILER ALERT!
Many of our Milestones in Cinema... selections are films that primarily celebrate the work of the Director, with some consideration given to the Cinematographer, Editor and Writer, since these are the arts, crafts and disciplines that clearly shape "The Look" of what we end up seeing larger than life up on the silver screen.

There have been times, like with *Network,* when we concentrated on the words of the Writer over these other elements and there are also many historical examples where an important musical score has elevated a small film to a triumphant success. *Chariots Of Fire* is one of those films.

Do not misunderstand. This particular film is flawlessly Produced, Written, Directed, Photographed and Edited, but if you were to remove the music you would simply lose the film entirely. Its soul, its richness and emotion would literally evaporate into the ether. Without the musical score by Vangelis to underscore these other important contributions and bind them together, the film would simply lose much of its emotional power.

THE CREATIVE TEAM:
Writer: Colin Welland
Director: Hugh Hudson
Cinematographer: David Watkin
Editor: Terry Rawlings
Composer: Vangelis

WHY IS THIS FILM VISIONARY:
The musical score for *Chariots of Fire* has been called, "One of the most memorable soundtracks of all time..." and "a landmark" by award winning writer and radio producer, John Diliberto who goes on to state, "... just go back to this 1981 film to relive a perfect marriage of image and music. Vangelis captures the heroism, grandeur, and pain of this

racing drama, from the opulent main "Titles" theme with its echoing snare drum and piano cadences to the electronically abstract setting of Sir Charles H.H. Parry's choral work, "Jerusalem." Vangelis's score hangs suspended between orchestral lushness and electronic mood, sweetness tempered by the underlying psychological themes of the film..."

THE BASICS:
This is a wonderful and wonderfully made film about champion athletes who push themselves to extraordinary limits to achieve both physical and spiritual greatness. Many of the races were covered in Slow Motion, which emphasized the physical, heroic and spiritual commitment of the runners. That, along with the stunning electronic score by Vangelis, gave this period piece a very modern and special energy.

THE PRODUCTION:
For some reason, the brilliant work of the Director Hugh Hudson has often been overlooked in this film. Possibly it is due to all of the deserving praise given to the Art Direction, Wardrobe, Cinematography and especially the Music by Vangelis. However, if you want to witness the enormous contribution of Mr. Hudson, look no farther than the race in which Mr. Abrams wins the famous 100-meters at the 1924 Olympics. The entire race is presented in two shots. A

normal-speed take of nearly the entire race seen in a very long shot and then a closer medium shot in slow motion of Mr. Abrams breaking the string at the finish line and winning! But then Mr. Hudson presents us with the race again, this time is Slow Motion and with Close Ups of the other runners all exerting a super human effort in order to win and finishing with a Close Up of Mr. Abrams winning again and blurring out of focus and into history...

The Directorial Choices of camera placement, lens size, camera speed and finally in the Editing, by using the coverage to play the race again, non-linearly and in Slow Motion, were all in themselves stunning Directorial achievements. It still puzzles me to this day, how *Chariots of Fire* could win the Academy Award for Best Picture and not win for Best Director? Who exactly made the Directorial Choices that enabled the film to become Best Picture?

Colin Welland the Writer attributes 40% of the films success to the score by Vangelis. The Director, Hugh Hudson, calls his music the "most important element" that not only blends perfectly with the film, but which ushered in a new "electronic" trend in film scoring. Prior to this production, many larger film productions had a 100-piece orchestra playing their various themes. Here you simply had one man, Vangelis and his electronic synthesizer.

The Producer David Puttnam, who was originally a "socialist" but who is now however, referred to as, "Lord" Puttnam has stated that the contrast between Vangelis's electronic score and the Gilbert and Sullivan songs within the film, helped contribute to its success.

Vangelis himself has reminded us that "music is the language of the soul," and if you speak to the audience's soul, you will be understood. To put it simply, that is exactly what Vangelis did with this profound and eloquent electronic score he spoke directly to our souls.

AWARDS:
This small film with the big score, and by big I mean emotionally big not number of instruments in the orchestra big, achieved astounding international acclaim and success. The Director, Hugh Hudson, was nominated for the Palme d'Or at the 1981 Cannes Film Festival and for an Academy Award for Best Director. *Chariots Of Fire* was nominated for six Academy Awards and won four, Best Picture, David Putnam Producer. Best Music Score, Vangelis. Best Original Screenplay, Colin Welland and Best Costume Design, Milina Canonero.

ONLINE RESOURCES:
Use Google Images & Google Videos for dozens of links...

Buy it on Amazon, Google Play, or iTunes.

Trailer Video URL:
http://www.imdb.com/video/screenplay/vi3434938649/

THINKING OUTSIDE THE BOX:
Class Exercises:

1. After screening the film each student should write an essay about how the film affected them their thoughts, feelings, pros, cons, likes and dislikes.

2. We've already discussed that by turning off the sound, you can really analyze a film and begin to understand how much the sound and especially the music contributes. Each student should view several of the important scenes with music, starting with the main titles and then play them again, without the music. Finally write an essay about exactly how much you think that the music contributed to this film.

3. There have been three films so far, where we have

drawn attention to the use of music. *Psycho, 2001, A Space Odyssey* and *Chariots of Fire.* Each student should write an essay comparing and contrasting how the music was used to enhance each one.

4. The electronic music by Vangelis and the use of Slow Motion and non-linear editing in the races by Terry Rawlings, were two modern elements in an otherwise period film. Each student should write an essay describing their thoughts and feelings about this and whether or not they felt that it worked.

5. Chariots of Fire won four of the six Academy Awards that it was nominated for: Best Picture, Best Screenplay, Best Music, Best Costumes, But not Best Director... Each student should write an essay about why they think that "The Academy..." does not seem to believe that having the Best Picture is a direct result of having the Best Director.

XI. Film Of The Century

Chapter 31:

1991
JFK

Oliver Stone
The Assassination Of Democracy

SPOILER ALERT!
This brings us to perhaps the most controversial and most important film of the 20th Century. A film that in 1991 forced us to once again look back and remember the blatant murder and political assassination of President John F. Kennedy that took place in Dallas, Texas on November 22, 1963.

JFK finally, graphically showed what many of us had

already suspected for many years; that the single most forward thinking President in our history and one who at the time, was already planning to disband the CIA, curtail the Military Industrial Complex and get us out of Vietnam, one who was spreading good will among the peoples of the world, was brutally murdered, gunned down and assassinated in the streets of Dallas, Texas. More importantly, this atrocious crime was a political coup could not have taken place, without the sanction and assistance of the US Government, most notably within the Military the Secret Service and the CIA.

If you doubt the involvement of the Secret Service in this tragedy, simply Google: "JFK Assassination Secret Service Stand Down, November 22, 1963," and watch the video showing the two agents who were supposed to be riding on a specially built platform at the rear of JFK's limo, being urged to "stand down" by one of their own men in charge of the President's protection that fateful day. Had those two agents been standing on the rear platform behind JFK. The minute a shot was heard they would have thrown themselves over the President. Thus preventing the murder as well as the political coup. Kindly remember that these government agencies are the very same people who have been lying to you about this event for decades.

THE CREATIVE TEAM:
Writers: Oliver Stone / Zachary Sklar / Jim Garrison / Jim Mars
Driector: Oliver Stone
Cinematographer: Robert Richardson
Editor: Joe Hutshing & Pietro Scalia

WHY IS THIS FILM VISIONARY:
JFK is an elaborate and extraordinary film and as Mr. Stone has stated: "...I see the models as Z and Rashomon, I see the events in Dealey Plaza taking place in the first reel, and again in the eighth reel, and again later, and each time we're going to see it differently and with more illumination..."

To assist him in this immense undertaking, he enlisted the great Director of Photography, Robert Richardson who, in some cases utilized as many as seven cameras, five 16mm and two 35mm, and up to 14 different film stocks to achieve the kaleidoscope of emotions, events and recreated footage needed for the production.

Mr. Richardson has stated that, "...Oliver disdains convention, he tries to force you into things that are not classic. There's a constant need to stretch... For some shots, you could have multiple crews shooting at once, five cameras at the same time in different formats..."

THE BASICS:
We have already perceived several times, how Fate and Destiny can often play a role in a films success. In this instance, while Oliver Stone was attending a Latin American Film Festival in Havana Cuba, he was given a copy of Jim Garrison's book, *"On The Trail Of The Assassins"* by it's publisher, Ellen Ray. After reading it, he bought the film rights and coupled this book with Jim Mars' *"Crossfire: The Plot That Killed Kennedy"* as well as many other volumes of research, to write the script for *JFK.* Mr. Stone felt that he needed and wanted to make a film that was counter to The Warren Report, since he felt like many Americans, that it was simply a whitewash, a bed of lies and "...a great myth..." *JFK* was his correction of that myth.

MTV had already been around for ten years and many of its music video techniques had made their way into TV commercials, but this was one of the first times that the mixing of 8mm, 16mm, 35mm color and black and white film, and video, was being used in a big studio, big star, big budget wide screen Hollywood movie.

THE THEATRICAL IMAGE:
Back in the day the old classic Hollywood Directors of Photography loved to discuss the merits of, "The Theatrical Image" which was usually a 35mm, rock solidly mounted, perfectly composed, lavishly lit, sumptuously produced wide screen film. Mr. Stone's film, JFK, effectively did away with that concept by bringing the new and more radical cinematic language of music videos and commercials to the big screen to tell the multifaceted story of the political assassination portrayed in *JFK*.

THE PRODUCTION:
The "establishment" really wanted this production to fail and actually launched a battery of attacks on Mr. Stone and the film: <u>While it was still in production!</u> Many leading newspaper like The Washington Post, The New York Times, The Miami Herald and the Chicago Sun-Times attacked either Mr. Stone personally or the validity of the production, one even going so far as to call foe Film Studio (Warner Brothers) censorship in order to "...blunt the highly charged message of a filmmaker like Oliver Stone..." Apparently these so called "journalists" approved of freedom of the press, but not freedom of the filmmaker!

To answer his critics, Mr. Stone eventually released a

593 page book entitled, *"JFK - The Book Of The Film"* documenting nearly every page of the script and all of the exhaustive research which basically justified nearly every claim that he had made in this groundbreaking production. He also, particularly in his commentary on the Directors' Cut DVD, points many of the places were he was using conjecture, supposition or dramatic license to make his point and acknowledges that there are several items in the film where he can be proven wrong... But then he pointedly asks, what about the other hundred or more allegations that no one has been able to disprove?

I believe that the most important amateur 8mm film ever shot and possibly the most important filmed document of the last century is the Abraham Zapruder film of President Kennedy's assassination. This one piece of 8mm film, which is less than a minute long, completely refutes the erroneous "single assassin" theory contained in the thousands of pages and multiple volumes of the Warren Report. It also disproves the "magic bullet theory" by showing that the first shot to hit President Kennedy was the shot in the throat that came from the front. Simply run the film frame by frame and count the shots...

BANG! BANG! BANG! BANG! BANG! BANG!

1.The first shot from the Book Depository, as has been proven, hit a streetlight pole beneath the window, and missed the car completely. 2. The second shot came from The Front, The Grassy Knoll and hit the President in the throat since he can clearly be seen as the limo emerges from behind the road sign, sitting upright and grasping at his throat. The shock of this shot likely rendered him unconscious as, 3. The third shot from the Book Depository hit the President near the base of his neck in his back and in a downward trajectory. 4. The forth shot also from the Book Depository missed the car and ricocheted, causing a fragment of cement to hit a bystander near the underpass. 5. The fifth shot which was the Kill Shot, came from The Front, The Grassy Knoll and hit JFK in the right temple blowing his blood and brains BACK AND TO THE LEFT and onto the vehicles trunk. 6. Moments later the sixth shot, came from the Book Depository and struck Governor Connolly you can clearly see him react suddenly, after the fatal head shot from The Grassy Knoll.

There was no "Magic Bullet" there was no bullet that entered the THE PRESIDENT'S BACK in a downward trajectory then turned upward and exited his throat!!! The throat shot was from the front and was the first shot to hit him! **Watch The Film!** Yes someone was firing from the Book Depository. Was it Lee Harvey

Oswald, probably not! Wasn't he the same stooge who couldn't hit a right wing general sitting immobile in his dining room several months earlier? It makes no difference. There were at least TWO (2) shooters, front and back. Thus there was, by definition, a conspiracy and one at the highest levels of the US Government to eliminate the sitting President of the United States: John Fitzgerald Kennedy.

PERSONALLY:
I remember this time very vividly and November 22, 1963 had a huge impact on my life, in fact it still does. In my opinion the evidence points to the fact that radical elements in the American Government, the Military, the Secret Service and the CIA, not only allowed it to occur, but sanctioned it, enabled it, then covered it up and have never, allowed the American public to determine the truth about this appalling Political Coup! And isn't this the same CIA, who in 2014, was under investigation for destroying the taped records of them torturing prisoners!!!

To check out the CIA's involvement in this type of treachery just Google their various collaborations in "Regime Changes" all over the globe: View for yourself, the many political coups, assassinations, torture and death squads that they were behind and that resulted in the overthrowing of popular governments in Iran, Central America, South America, Vietnam and South East Asia usually in cooperation with the Mafia! In relation to the CIA's involvement in the Kennedy Assassination, as the brilliant journalist Bill Moyers has stated: "When anything goes... in dealing with foreign heads of state... that way of thinking can come home to roost."

Yes, the US Government claimed "...the presidents brain has disappeared..." then attempted to whitewash this abomination with the fraudulent and contrived, Warren Report. The very same US Government that has continued to lie to the American people about this assassination for decades, in fact, they are still lying about it today only now they're attempting to do so with computers, re-creations and with the establishment's new "single assassin" hawkers: Vincent Bugliosi, Gerald Posner and the curator of The Sixth Floor Museum at Dealey Plaza, Gary Mack. All of whom want you NOT to believe your eyes when you see the throat shot and the kill shot ALL coming from The Grassy Knoll and instead believe that there was only one (1) shooter as well as a "magic bullet." They are all establishment shills and beneath contempt!

Finally, in the late 1960's the New Orleans prosecutor Jim Garrison led the way to uncovering this web of deceit, by introducing the Zapruder Film into evidence in his New Orleans trial of Clay Shaw. Soon others like the (Pre Fox News) TV Journalist, Geraldo Rivera and the brilliant satirist Mort Saul, began to show the unsuspecting American public this astounding piece of film.

Of course, the US government had already locked this vital piece of evidence away, deep in a vault, in the Time/Life Building in New York City. Insuring that the American people could and would not see for themselves, the bullet from The Grassy Knoll blow the President's brains onto Elm Street as his head was snapped, "Back and to the left! Back and to the left! Back and to the left!"

REAPING THE WHIRLWIND:
After that fateful day, November 22, 1963 America's Innocence was officially over, shattered and blown away, as was our faith in an honest and benevolent government. America had sown the wind and now she would now reap the whirlwind as the apocalypse of the 1960's descend across our shattered nation.

* Now would come all of the unrest and descent and protests with our cities on fire: **"Burn Baby Burn!"**

* Now would come the Free Speech Movement and

the Kent State murder of students by the National Guard: **"Make Love, Not War!"**

* Now would come the riots and the blood on the hands of Mayor Daley's Police Force at the Democratic National Convention in Chicago: **"The Whole World Is Watching!"**

* Now would come the Hippies and the Summer of Love and the drug culture: **"Turn On, Tune In, Drop Out!"**

* Now would come the ant-war, anti-Vietnam protests that divided our entire nation: **"One, Two, Three, Four, We Don't Want Your Fucking War!"**

* The message was loud and clear and Lyndon Johnson would not seek another term as President. Perhaps he was tired of hearing the chant: **"LBJ, LBJ, How Many Kids Did You Kill Today?"**

I hope that those of you, who were not even born when this American tragedy occurred, are finally beginning to comprehend the kind of devastation that this murderous and treasonous political coup had and continues to have on our nation!

Kindly remember, to carefully read the scroll at the

end of the film *JFK*, which reads in part: *"In 1979 Richard Helms, director of covert operations in 1963, admitted under oath that Clay Shaw had worked for the CIA."*

Bingo! That was the whole point of Garrison's trial! Clay Shaw was AKA Clay Bertrand! Clay Bertrand was Clay Shaw, Shaw/Bertrand knew Oswald, Shaw was CIA... Oswald Was A Patsy! The Prosecution Rests!

The scroll at the end of the film continues: *"A Congressional investigation from 1976 to 1979 found a "probable conspiracy" in the assignation of John F. Kennedy and recommended that the Justice Department investigate further."*

As of 1991 when the movie *JFK* was released, the Justice Department had done nothing. As of this writing, well over fifty years after the assassination, the files of the House Select Committee on Assassinations are still locked away until the year 2029.

Always remember the words of Kevin Costner's character, Jim Garrison in his final courtroom summation as his gaze finally came to rest looking directly into the camera, looking at the audience, looking at you and me and the generations to come...

"Do not forget your dying king... Nothing as long as you live will be more important...
It's up to you!"

THE AWARDS:
The initial release began slowly, but the $40,000,000 feature found its audience finally grossing over $200,000,000.00 domestically. It also directly led to the signing of the *JFK* Act. It won the American Cinema Editors Award, was nominated for the DGA Award and won the Golden Globe Award for Best Director, it was nominated for eight Academy Awards, including Best Picture, Best Director and won for Best Cinematography and Best Editing.

ONLINE RESOURCES:
Use Google Images & Google Videos for dozens of links...

Buy it on Amazon, Google Play, or iTunes.

Trailer Video URL:
http://www.imdb.com/video/screenplay/vi937361689/
THINKING OUTSIDE THE BOX:
Class Exercises:

1. We may never know what actually happened. However, each student should write an essay about their thoughts and feelings about the film *JFK,* what worked and what didn't, the pros and cons.

2. The Zapruder Film is an important historical record. Each student should go online and view the original "shaky" Zapruder Film and also watch the digital "steady" version, then write an essay answering for themselves; where and when the President was hit and where the fatal head shot came from.

3. If as nearly everyone believes, there were at least two shooters. Each student should write an essay about why the US government spent so much time and money and now "computer analysis" to attempt to prove the, "lone assassin" single shooter and "magic bullet" theories?

4. Google the "Dallas, Parkland Hospital Doctors," and listen while they discuss the President's head wound caused by a bullet coming from the front, and blowing away the back of his head.. Both the Warren Commission and the 1970's Conspiracy Committee skipped over this evidence and never even listened to the original doctors. Each student should write an essay about why they think that this testimony was

never taken and what conclusions can be drawn from that fact.

5. Today, with Terrorism, Ethnic Cleansing, Beheading on the Internet, world wide devastation as well as the elimination of the Middle Class, the ongoing greed of Wall Street, the millions of dollars being spent by Corporations Lobbying to buy US Senators and Congressmen, so that Big Oil, Big Pharmaceuticals and Big Arms Corporations can all making billions of dollars of profit each quarter, while taking advantage of tax loopholes and not even putting a portion of 1% back into the countries infrastructure or education: Each student should write an essay that answers the question: With this amount of blatant political Crime and Corruption facing us each day. Does anyone still have the time to care about the assassination or President John Fitzgerald Kennedy?

XII. New Guerrilla Filmmakers

Chapter 32:

1992
El Mariachi

Robert Rodriguez
Brilliant Simplicity

SPOILER ALERT!
By now everyone knows the urban legends surrounding the groundbreaking film, *El Mariachi*, its infamous director, Robert Rodriguez and the self-proclaimed, *"Rebel Without A Crew"* book that detailed its production.

However much hype it generated, its importance cannot be underestimated since many of its revolutionary guerrilla filmmaking techniques have become modern day production shortcuts that bear repeated examination and implementation by the young independent guerrilla filmmakers of today.

This smallest of small films began as a throw away production, that Mr. Rodriguez basically did "for practice." It was turned down by the very local Mexican TV stations that he hoped would show it, but eventually his persistence and perseverance paid off and it became the pot of gold at the end of the rainbow for this brilliant, self taught, guerrilla filmmaker.

If you think that you want to become a filmmaker but you haven't done it as yet… If this story doesn't inspire you to gather all of your resources and do it immediately, then perhaps you should just resign yourself to living in your parent's basement, indefinitely!

THE CREATIVE TEAM:
Writer: Robert Rodriguez
Director: Robert Rodriguez
Cinematographer: Robert Rodriguez
Editor: Robert Rodriguez

WHY IS THIS FILM VISIONARY:
Reread the above "The Creative Team" information

again! RR became an entrepreneurial filmmaker before the term had even been invented! From the standpoint of successful guerrilla filmmaking, of making a very small film that would give the filmmaker a very big professional payoff and career, there are very few films that can compare with *El Mariachi*. This film accomplished exactly what a guerrilla film should accomplish and at the time, Mr. Rodriguez did it the old fashion way: On his own and using 16mm film.

During the 30 days that he spent making $100 a day, volunteering for a medical experiment, he wrote the script, by devising "The Rodriguez List," and met another volunteer who would play the villain in the piece, Peter Marquardt.

He ended up doing every single job on the production himself, except acting; he did the writing, the directing, the cinematography, the special effects, the editing and the post-production. He even undercut his original budget of $9000 by not wasting film and only doing one take per set up, thus coming in under schedule and under budget at about $7,200!

He had previously decided not to shoot sync sound because the time that it would take to roll the sound, roll the camera and slate them both would take up too much film! This was the kind of pre-production planning and penny pinching precision that bordered on genius when it came to making a guerrilla film, way back in the last century.

THE BASICS:
Using what has come to be known as "The Rodriguez List" he wrote his script around a list of items that he knew that he could use, borrow or find access to For FREE! A bar, a jail, a hotel, a bus etc... Many of his weapons were toy guns, others were borrowed from the local police and his squibs were condoms filled with fake blood and backed by a weight lifting belt so that the small explosive charges used for the effect, would not hurt the non actors that he used in front of the camera.

Mr. Rodriguez estimates that most of his budget went to film stock, processing and tele-cine costs and that all that he actually spent, if you take away the film costs, for his less than three-week production, was around $600. That's an interesting sum, because that's the same amount that was reportedly spent on doing the "pilot" for *It's Always Sunny In Philadelphia.* That's what those amazingly crazy actors involved in that production spent on their antics that were shot on home video over a weekend... I guess that Mr. Rodriguez was running a much tighter ship, in order to make his $600 stretch to under three weeks.

THE PRODUCTION:
Many of his cast, were simply passers by who were grabbed off the street, his dolly was a broken down wheelchair and his camera car was a pickup truck. The actor's dialogue was done by first shooting a take on film, then immediately afterwards doing a take only for sound using a small hand held-tape recorder. Later all of these "wild lines" were edited into the actor's mouths during post-production. His lighting equipment consisted of either available light or two 200-watt clip lights. You simply cannot get much more bare bones or hardcore guerrilla than that!

FINALLY:
Once again the gods of production smiled... After editing tape to tape, hand syncing all the dialogue, finishing the film and having it rejected by the local Mexican TV stations in Texas, somehow, the Trailer made its way to someone's desk in Hollywood. It became a "talked about" item around town and finally Columbia Pictures stepped in and bought it. They invested over $1,000,000 to cover doing a more professional post-production sound track, a 35mm blow up and advertising.

The rest, as they say is history...

THE AWARDS:
El Mariachi won the Independent Spirit Award, The Sundance Film Festival and by that time, Mr. Rodriguez had a very firm grasp on the ladder that was leading straight to his success as a major independent filmmaker.

PS:
It's refreshing to report that Mr. Rodriguez did not "Go Hollywood" in fact when the DGA told him that he could not give a co-director credit to Frank Miller, who had worked along side him and whose original work had inspired *Sin City*, he told that Hollywood Guild exactly were they could go.

No he did not move to Beverly Hills, purchase a big house an expensive car or hang out at The Viper Room. Instead, he remained in Austin, Texas as an independent regional filmmaker. He converted his three-car garage into a post production center and expanded his "Troublemaker Studios" to a warehouse, where RR has successfully produced a host of R rated action and G rated kids films, all of them done in his inimitable style: "Cheep, Fast & In Total Control!"

If you want to become a guerrilla filmmaker, you've

just read exactly how to DO IT!

ONLINE RESOURCES:
Use Google Images & Google Videos for dozens of links...

Buy it on Amazon, Google Play, or iTunes.

Watch the Trailer or Scenes at:
www.youtube.com

THINKING OUTSIDE THE BOX:
Class Exercises:

1. Each student should write an essay about their feelings after seeing this film, their likes, dislikes, pros and cons.

2. Each student should write an essay about why they think that a film of this size, with this story and cast, and these meager production values, was able to become so successful.

3. Each student should write an essay comparing and contrasting *Sweet Sweetback's Baaadasss Song*, which cost $70,000.00 and *El Mariachi*, which cost $7,000.00.

4. Each student should make a "Rodriguez List that is, write an essay or develop a treatment utilizing what they have at their disposal, through friends or family for free, in order to make a film.

5. Each student should use their cell phone or home digital camera to make a small film that they can edit on their computer with iMovie and show to their friends or family or use to generate interest in doing a larger film...

Chapter 33:

1997
In The Company Of Men

Neil LaBute
Barbed Wit

SPOILER ALERT!
Neil LaBute is a writer's writer. He is unparalleled in his ability to write compelling characters who are totally human but who will none-the-less, totally creep you out. Mr. LaBute began his journey to filmmaking first as a playwright at Brigham Young University and later as a Drama Professor. After waiting over a year for someone who had taken a film option on one of his plays, he decided that he should try to mount a production himself.

He had heard the stories about young independent filmmakers using credit cards or raising $25,000 to make their first film through friends. When one of his friends happened to receive an insurance settlement, for $35,000, that inspired and enabled Mr. LaBute to do the same. His production was totally under the radar since he was teaching Drama and Film at Indiana University in Fort Wayne at the time.

Although he was a first time filmmaker, he still managed to adapt his play, raise the money, assemble the production team and put the film in the can, on only a two week shooting schedule. An amazing accomplishment for an inexperienced first time director!

The film's rough cut was submitted and accepted for the 1997 Sundance Film Festival; then he and his producers had to come up with another $100,000 to finish the post production sound and make a 35mm blow up in order to make the Festival's January deadline. Needless to say, they did it and the result caused an unstoppable word of mouth sensation.

THE CREATIVE TEAM:
 Writer: Neil Labute
Director: Neil LaBute
Cinematographer: Tony Hettinger
Editor: Joel Plotch

WHY IS THIS FILM VISIONARY:

Very few, if any, first films or first time directors have exploded onto the scene with so much sensation and controversy, especially by utilizing a very small guerrilla film made with a no-name cast and very little money. This is the production that made an instant star out of Aaron Eckhart and a writer-director phenomenon out of Neil LaBute.

The material contained in In *The Company Of Men* is so dark and troubling that it caused its director Mr. LaBute, to be immediately labeled a misanthrope and a misogynist and even had women telling its star, Mr, Eckhart, how much they hated him, personally! So much for the so-called fringe benefits and perks of celebrity.

The ultimate goal of any production is to be so compelling that your viewers are totally enthralled. Any material that can at the same time cause an avalanche of controversy and sensation is obviously doing something right.

THE BASICS:
Chad: What's the difference between a golf ball and a g-spot?
Howard: I don't know.
Chad: I'd spend twenty minutes looking for a golf ball!

Two frustrated macho corporate sleazebags fed up with women in general, decide to "...do something about it..." They pick a lonely, vulnerable, deaf secretary that they both start a relationship with in order to jerk her around emotionally... Why? Because they can! Twisted, yes. But also a scathing, compelling critique of the worst that human behavior has to offer. This film can be like watching a high-speed chase that you know will end badly but that you simply cannot turn away from no matter how hard you try.

Amazingly, a novice writer-director like Mr. LaBute was able to put up on the screen, material that had the passionate impact of works by directing giants like Elia Kazan or Ingmar Bergman. The result being that you end up feeling as though someone has just delivered an emotional fist to your guts. This is truly mature subject matter that may not be for everyone, but it marked the debut of a truly world-class Filmmaker.

THE PRODUCTION:
Mr. LaBute has stated that he began totally out of "ignorance." That may be true, but he quickly became a master of filmmaking during his very first production. Having a crew of less than twenty-five people, a regional cinematographer and a two-week

shooting schedule didn't dampen his enthusiasm. He rose to each and every challenge, as he rehearsed and coached his unknown cast to the performances of their young lives.

Once again we can see how the power of a screenplay and a writer's words can shape an actor's performance and provoke an audiences reaction to the material. A young filmmaker can have no greater ally, than having a unique, and controversial script to begin with.

AWARDS:
In The Company Of Men won the Filmmakers Trophy at The Sundance Film Festival, Best First Film from the New York Film Critics Circle Awards and the Independent Spirit Awards, Best Debut Performance and Best First Screenplay.

ONLINE RESOURCES:
Use Google Images & Google Videos for dozens of links...

Buy it on Amazon, Google Play, or iTunes.

View the Trailer, Scenes and Interviews at:
www.youtube.com

THINKING OUTSIDE THE BOX:
Class Exercises:

1. Each student should write an essay about their reaction to seeing this film for the first time, what were their feelings, their pros and cons.

2. Each student should write an essay about what worked best and what worked least for them in this film and why.

3. Each student should write an essay or an original treatment that describes a character or characters that are truly flawed yet compelling, controversial and watchable.

4. Each student should attempt to find, rent or buy the DVD of Neil LaBute's three one-act plays: Bash - Latter Day Plays and once again witness the power of a writers words to inspire the actors performances. (Produced by Showtime in 2002, they claim to have no DVD's of Mr. LaButes work for sale.)

5. Each student should write an essay about how important it is to have the best and most unique script possible when making a film and how does that compare with all of the other important elements.

Chapter 34:

1998
The Celebration

Thomas Vinterberg
Digital Dogma

SPOILER ALERT!
As some have recounted in March of 1995... Drunk, debunking and disavowing all of the decades of groundbreaking work done by the Italian Neo-Realists, the French New Wave, and the American Independents, the pretentious *enfant terrible* of Denmark cinema, Lars von Trier and his colleague Thomas Vinterberg spent all of 45 minutes coming up with their sparse, "Vow of Chastity." This "Vow" set down the precepts of their new, "new wave" DOGMA 95 and to this day you can literally count on one hand, the number of films that have actually followed the rules and utilized this so called, "vow."

Later in 1995, at the 100 Year Anniversary of Cinema celebrated in Europe, Mr. von Trier showered the delegates with pamphlets containing the Dogma 95 "ten commandments." They read as follows:

VOW OF CHASTITY
I swear to submit to the following set of rules drawn up and confirmed by DOGMA 95:

1. Shooting must be done on location. Props and sets must not be brought in (if a particular prop is necessary for the story, a location must be chosen where this prop is to be found).

2. The sound must never be produced apart from the images or vice versa. (Music must not be used unless it occurs where the scene is being shot.)

3. The camera must be hand-held. Any movement or immobility attainable in the hand is permitted. (The film must not take place where the camera is standing; shooting must take place where the film takes place.)

4. The film must be in color. Special lighting is not acceptable. (if there is too little light for exposure the scene must be cut or a single lamp be attached to the camera).

5. Optical work and filters are forbidden.

6. The film must not contain superficial action. (Murders, weapons, etc. must not occur.)

7. Temporal and geographical alienation are forbidden. (That is to say that the film takes place here and now.)

8. Genre movies are not acceptable.

9. The film format must be Academy 35 mm.

10. The director must not be credited.
Furthermore I swear as a director to refrain from personal taste! I am no longer an artist. I swear to refrain from creating a "work as I regard the instant as more important that the whole. My supreme goal is to force the truth out of my characters and settings. I swear to do so by all the means available and at the cost of any good taste and any aesthetic considerations.

Thus I make my VOW OF CHASTITY
Copenhagen, Monday 13 March 1995.
On behalf of DOGMA 95,
Lars von Trier, Tomas Vinterberg

***

It must also be noted that the very next year Mr. von Trier released Breaking The Waves, a film that broke nearly every commandment in his so-called "vow of chastity." In my opinion, the only film of any merit to come out of all of this grandstanding and self-promotion was Thomas Vinterberg's Dogma #1, *Festen*, or *The Celebration*.

THE CREATIVE TEAM:
Writer: Thomas Vinterberg, Mogens Rukov
Director: Thomas Vinterberg
Cinematographer: Anthony Dod Mantle
Editor: Valdis Oskarsdottir

WHY IS THIS FILM VISIONARY:
This production was far ahead of its time, since it was shot on tape with a Sony Hi-8 home video camera. It adhered to many of the Dogma 95 rules, including the use of a natural location that suited the story and available or practical lighting throughout as well as a mostly hand-held camera.

Tomas Vinterberg teamed up with a Director of Photography who dared to go into these uncharted waters on a feature film, the creative and courageous

Anthony Dod Mantle. You will be seeing his name several more times in our upcoming Milestones... since he has boldly aligned himself with filmmakers who are thinking far outside of the box and using new and cutting edge modes of capture and delivery to tell their stories.

This is the first professional feature film that I know of that was shot entirely on home video and still had wide success, film festival acclaim, and international distribution.

THE BASICS:
Back in the early 1980's, I had the pleasure of preparing a feature film in Stockholm, Sweden. It was my first trip to Europe, I took a lot of great photographs and discovered to my awe and amazement that in the downtown parks surrounded by high rise office buildings, women of all ages often sunbathed topless during their lunch breaks!

That was the good news! The bad news was that at the time, the home entertainment situation in that part of the world was very bleak. The highlight of an evening of television, if there happened to be anything scheduled at all, was usually a documentary about a Finnish Farmer.

Apparently by 1998 television was still bleak in Denmark, since Thomas Vinterberg found himself with some free time and ended up listening to the radio. As luck and timing would have it, he happened to hear a young man telling of a supposedly real incident that became the inspiration for his screenplay for Dogma #1 *Festen* or as we know it, *The Celebration*.

The story concerned a large family gathering for the sixtieth birthday of their father; then when one of the sons stood up to give a toast, he accused the man of sexually molesting both him and his sister, which had caused her to recently commit suicide.

Later, after the suicide note is read from the sister the son asks their father "Why? Why did you do it?" The patriarch callously replies, "That's all you were good for." So much for his ideas about nurturing!

THE PRODUCTION:
During the production, Thomas Vinterberg remained true to the Dogma 95 Vow of Chastity using only: a natural location that contained the necessary props, no artificial lighting, no weapons, no music, no post production sound or special effects, no superficial action, the film was in color, in the Academy Aperture and took place in the here and now. However, he later

"confessed" to erring when he covered a window for the shooting of one scene.

When you screen the DVD of this film, kindly watch the behind the scenes "making of" documentary. On it you will also catch Anthony Dod Mantle "cheating" as he captures part of one scene on a home made jib arm, that he created by taping the Hi-8 camera to a broom handle!

This subject of sexual abuse by a father or a father figure must be more common than anyone suspected and seems to have struck a sympathetic chord world wide, since the script of The Celebration has been adapted to the stage, translated and played successfully all over the world: In English, Dutch, Danish, German, Greek, Finnish, Italian, Spanish, Swedish, Polish, Hungarian, Estonian and Afrikaans.

THE AWARDS:
Among many awards, *The Celebration* won the Jury Prize at the Cannes Film Festival, The Discovery of The Year at The European Film Awards, The Independent Spirit Awards, The Best Foreign Film at The Los Angeles Film Critics Association Awards, the New York Film Critics Circle Award and the Audience Award at the Rotterdam International Film Festival.

ONLINE RESOURCES:
Use Google Images & Google Videos for dozens of links...

Buy it on Amazon, Google Play, or iTunes.

Check out the Trailer and various Scenes at:
www.youtube.com

THINKING OUTSIDE THE BOX:
Class Exercises:

1. Each student should write an essay about what their feelings were after seeing this film, what were their pros and cons.

2. Each student should write an essay about their reaction to the Dogma 95 rules and do they find the "Vow of Chastity" to be a positive or a negative concept for film production.

3. Each student should write an essay comparing and contrasting all three films discussed in this section: *El Mariachi, In The Company of Men* and *The Celebration.*

4. Each student should write an essay or a treatment concerning a "hard to look at" topic like sexual abuse, which they would like to educate the public about.

5. Each student should shoot a short HD or Digital Film using whatever equipment they have and abiding by all of the Dogma 95 rules.

XIII. World War II Revisited

Chapter 35:

1993
Schindler's List

Steven Spielberg
The Holocaust

SPOILER ALERT:
If you believe in Fate and Destiny, then this is the film that Steven Spielberg was born to make and the film that he desperately tried for nearly a decade not to make. Sid Sheinberg president of MCA had purchased the rights to the book *Schindler's Arc* in 1983 after Mr. Spielberg had shown interest in the project. Then over the years, Mr. Spielberg offered the film to a host of important directors in an attempt to avoid

directing it. The list included Martin Scorsese, Roman Polanski, Sidney Pollack and Billy Wilder.

Apparently, Mr. Spielberg was concerned about his own maturity in being able to take on a subject as formidable as the Holocaust, but finally by the early 1990's with a new wave of Holocaust deniers on the horizon and the Bosnian Genocide fresh in everyone's mind he decided that the time was right for him to proceed.

THE CREATIVE TEAM:
Writer: Thomas Keneally, Steven Zaillian
Director: Steven Spielberg
Cinematographer: Janusz Kaminski
Editor: Michael Kahn

WHY IS THIS FILM VISIONARY:
Because it caused the world to, once again, address the horrific facts of The Holocaust. To view with nearly documentary, black and white clarity both the absolute evil and the immense good that humanity can be capable of by fulfilling the premise of the film, which is based on a quote from the Talmud: "Whoever saves one life saves the world entire." If you happen to Google that phrase, the name Oskar Schindler will come up. We can only hope that, in focusing our attention on this one horrendous

episode in human history, Mr. Spielberg has saved the word entire... from ever repeating it again.

THE BASICS:
For over ten years, the script went through several incarnations the original draft was done by Thomas Keneally the author of the novel and was over 220 pages long. The writer of *Out of Africa* Kurt Luedtke, became involved for several years but eventually resigned and finally the draft done by Steven Zaillian, when Martin Scorsese was attached to direct the film, became the version that Mr. Spielberg used and expanded upon.

At long last the audiences of the world were going to see A Film By Steven Spielberg. A film that was not a blockbuster, a genre film, a benevolent space alien fantasy, an overblown comic book action adventure or a film that featured a faceless killer in a 18 wheeler, an unstoppable shark or rampaging dinosaurs. This was a film in the tradition of the best of European and American Cinema, a thought provoking, gravely serious emotionally rich and moving film. A film that for the first time, deserved to be called: A Film By Steven Spielberg.

THE PRODUCTION:

Shooting began in and around Cracow Poland in March of 1993 and the movie was shot on black and white film. This was done over the protests of Universal Studios chairman Tom Pollock who requested that Director Steven Spielberg and his Cinematographer Janusz Kaminski shoot on color negative and print in black and white, in order that later versions of the film might be released in color. However, Misters Spielberg and Kaminski held their ground and the film was made for the ages in all versions and in all media in black and white.

Mr. Spielberg did not expect this film to be successful and he did not care. For the first time he was working without all the trappings of a Hollywood production and making this film like an artist with a limited palette. No crane, no zoom lens no Steadicam and no storyboards. This was however, a horrendous production for him emotionally and he has thanked his wife and children on numerous occasions for saving his life every day during the production. "I was hit in the face with my personal life. My upbringing. My Jewishness. The stories my grandparents told me about the Shoah. And Jewish life came pouring back into my heart. I cried all the time."

To help him through this ordeal his friend Robin Williams would call every few weeks and attempt to make him laugh. This production however, was no laughing matter for Mr. Spielberg; in fact he had requested that screenwriter Steven Zaillian expand the liquidation sequences in the Jewish ghetto to the point that there were "almost unwatchable."

Then there was the little girl in red. The only speck of color in this somber black and white production: A symbol of life, of renewal, of hope, of a possible silver lining to the dark cloud of these unspeakable atrocities? No! Absolutely Not! As Mr. Spielberg has stated, "America and Russia and England all knew about the Holocaust when it was happening, and yet we did nothing about it... It was a large bloodstain, primary red color on everyone's radar, but no one did anything about it. And that is why I wanted to bring the color red in."

The only glimmer of hope for Mr. Spielberg was the slight use of color on the lighting of the Shabbes candles that open and close the film and provide the bookends of humanity to this extraordinary film about one of mankind's darkest and most horrifying times.

ONCE AGAIN, FATE & DESTINY:
In 1980, the writer Thomas Keneally was on his way to LAX to catch a flight back to Australia and by

chance stopped at a Beverly Hills luggage shop for a new briefcase. The owner of the shop happened to be one of the 1200 Jews that had been saved by Oskar Schindler and during his time at the luggage shop Mr. Keneally heard Mr. Leopold Pfefferberg's story, saw the back room, his cabinets filled with memorabilia and decided that he had just found the subject for his next book. That book would become the novel *Schindler's Ark* and eventually Mr. Spielberg's film, *Schindler's List.*

THE AWARDS:
Schindler's List, was nominated for twelve Academy Awards winning seven: Best Picture, Best Director, Best Adapted Screenplay, Best Cinematography, Best Film Editing and Best Original Score. It also won the Golden Globe Awards for Best Motion Picture (Drama) Best Director and Best Screenplay.

ONLINE RESOURCES:
Use Google Images & Google Videos for dozens of links...

Buy it on Amazon, Google Play, or iTunes.

THINKING OUTSIDE THE BOX:
Class Exercises:

1. While the film is still fresh, each student should write an essay about what worked best for them in the film and what worked least, what they liked and did not like and why.

2. Mr. Spielberg made this film without many of his usual filmmaking comforts: color film, the crane, zoom lenes, the Steadicam and storyboards. Each student should write an essay describing how this choice either helped or hindered him in the making of the film.

3. The use of the little girl in Red, the only color in the film was placed there as an indictment of the American, British and Russian governments, who knew about the Holocaust and did nothing. Each student should write an essay giving their opinions about why these powerful countries did not act in the face of such atrocities.

4. I can recall growing up after World War II and seeing my grandmother's books containing documentary photographs of the Holocaust and the piles of Jewish bodies found in various concentration camps. Each student should write an essay describing why they believe that there are people who deny that this genocide happened.

5. The students should team up and produce a short Digital or HD film in the semi-documentary style used in this film and about an important problem that needs to be addressed.

Chapter 36

1998
Saving Private Ryan

Steven Spielberg
The Price Of War

SPOILER ALERT:
Saving Private Ryan is a film about your grandfather's war, but it is not your grandfather's war film. It contains the most graphic depictions of the carnage and violence of battle ever to come out of Hollywood and the strongest ever put on the screen, with the exception of actual documentaries from the front lines. Of course this was the second major World War II film from Steven Spielberg; the first, *Schindler's List,* is dedicated to the Holocaust suffered by over six million Jews, this one to the bravery, suffering and sacrifice of Allied soldiers during the Normandy invasion, that led to the end of Nazi Germany.

The film's content is very graphic and may not be for everyone. It received an "R" rating for strong language and graphic violence, but Mr. Spielberg refused to cut it even for its release to India, which at first refused it without certain elements edited out. Mr. Spielberg instead decided not to have the film released in India, but finally the Home Minister screened it for himself and decreed that it should be released "uncut." Mr. Spielberg realized the importance and power of this film and has stated that even if it received an "NC17" rating that he would still have released it uncut.

THE CREATIVE TEAM:
Writer: Robert Rodat
Director: Steven Spielberg
Cinematographer: Janusz Kaminski
Editor: Michael Kahn

THE BASICS:
Steven Spielberg has always been interested in World War II. He grew up hearing stories about it from his father Arnold who served in Burma and his first 8mm films were always about WWII. He also covered it in many of his Hollywood films: *1941, Empire Of The Sun,* and the *Indiana Jones* productions. Of course it could be argued that one of these was a comedy and

that the *Indiana Jones* films were more or less comic book action adventures and escapist entertainment.

Mr. Spielberg has stated that, "...World War II is the most significant event of the last 100 years..." and during the 1990's with his productions of *Shindler's List* and *Saving Private Ryan*, he finally came of age as a serious filmmaker, and I believe that with these two productions, he made two of the most significant war movies in the history of motion pictures.

The writer, Robert Rodat was inspired by a monument he saw, that was erected in the memory of four brothers who had served and died in the Civil War. He was moved by their sacrifice and decided to tell a similar story but to place it in World War II. After eleven drafts, the script was finally accepted by producer Mark Gordon, who gave it to Tom Hanks, who gave it to Steven Spielberg. When it happens like that you can call it Luck, Timing, Good Fortune or simply Fate & Destiny.

THE PRODUCTION:
Nearly the first half hour of the film is spent along side the troops, storming the beaches of Normandy. The production began on June 27, 1997 on location at Ballinesker Beach in Ireland, with the assistance of over a thousand members of the Irish Reserve Army

acting as extras. Mr. Spielberg did not use storyboards, but like a documentary filmmaker, let the action dictate where he would place his cameras. This scene alone took two months to film and cost over 11 million dollars.

He also used amputees wearing prosthetic arms and legs to depict various soldiers having their bodies blown apart in battle and in the tradition of the Italian Neo Realist and French New Wave filmmakers, he shot mainly with hand held cameras, on natural locations and with only available light.

Of course since it was a big Hollywood production, Mr. Spielberg and his Cinematographer, Janusz Kaminski, could afford to bring in a huge crane to hold up a gigantic silk, that along with the added smoke, kept the light from the sun even during the weeks of shooting. Mr. Kaminski made some radical choices in photographing this film. First had the coating removed from the lenses in order that the images captured would be closer to the look of WWII, then he set the shutter from 180 degrees to 90 or 45 to make the movement more staccato and the explosions more vivid. He even used an ordinary drill attached to the camera to provide a more jarring movement during the explosions.

The director and cinematographer both agreed to the artistic choice of de-saturating the color for all of the final release prints. However, to show you that you do not always get to have things your way even if you are Steven Spielberg, when the film was shown on Cable TV, there were so many complaints from the viewing customers that the stations finally had to turn the color saturation back up to normal.

Edward Norton was offered the part of Private Ryan, but turned it down and Michael Madson was offered the part of Sergeant Horvath but declined and suggested his pal, Tom Sizemore for the part. Mel Gibson and Harrison Ford were both in the running for the part of Captain Miller that eventually went to Tom Hanks... Personally I felt that this performance by Mr. Hanks was his very best of all time and I said after my first screening of the film that this has to be Academy Award number three for Mr. Hanks... Well I've never claimed to be right all the time.

Another of the actors, Edward Burns had already Written and Directed, the independent feature, *The Brothers McMullen*. However, he has stated that seeing a Director of Mr. Spielberg's prominence, shooing ...Private Ryan on natural locations and often in available light, inspired him to use this same approach when continuing to make his independent films.

THE AWARDS:
Saving Private Ryan was nominated for eleven Academy Awards, winning five. Best Director, Best Cinematography, Best Film Editing, Best Sound Editing and Best Sound. It also won the Golden Globe Awards for Best Picture and Best Director, The Director's Guild Award and the Producers Guild Golden Laurel Award, among many more.

ONLINE RESOURCES:
Use Google Images & Google Videos for dozens of links...

Buy it on Amazon, Google Play, or iTunes.

THINKING OUTSIDE THE BOX:
Class Exercises:

1. While the film is still fresh each student should write an essay about what worked best for them in the film and what worked least, also what they liked or didn't like and why.

2. Mr. Spielberg has stated that World War II was the "most significant event of the last 100 years." Each

student should write an essay about what event, of the past 100 years, they think was the most significant and why.

3. Even though the films are very different in subject matter, tone and style, *Shindler's List* and *Saving Private Ryan* were both directed by Steven Spielberg. Each student should write an essay comparing and contrasting both films.

4. Much has been written and discussed about the first half hour of the film depicting the horrific violence, graphic warfare and human toll of the Normandy Invasion. Each student should write an essay about the positive or negative effect that these scenes had on them and why.

5. The students should team up, choose a subject and make a short Digital or HD film using some of the stylistic techniques used in Saving Private Ryan.

XIV. An Entirely New Paradigm

Chapter 37:

1999
THE BLAIR WITCH PROJECT

Daniel Myrick & Eduardo Sanchez
No Director No Crew

SPOILER ALERT!
Be afraid... Be very afraid, especially if you are someone who slavishly clings to the old, traditional style of filmmaking. This is the production that was thinking so far outside of the box, it created an entirely new box!

Exterior - Woods - Day.

The actors, Heather, Josh and Mike are improvising a scene portraying three documentary filmmakers who are trekking through the wood in search of the legend of the Blair Witch... Wait, where's the crew? Where's the Director? Where's the DP and Camera Operator? Where's the Sound and Boom Man? Where's the Script Supervisor? Where's Make-up, Props, Wardrobe, Craft Service? And especially, where's the bathroom and where's LUNCH?

Welcome to an entirely New Paradigm in filmmaking, where the one and only rule is: There Are No Rules!

THE CREATIVE TEAM:
Writers: Daniel Myrick / Eduardo Sanchez
Directors: Daniel Myrick / Eduardo Sanchez
Cinematographer: Neil Fredricks
Editors: Daniel Myrick / Eduardo Sanchez

WHY IS THIS FILM VISIONARY:
In 1999 with these ominous words:

"...In October of 1994 three student filmmakers disappeared in the woods near Burkittsville Maryland while shooting a documentary... A year later their footage was found..."

The young filmmakers Daniel Myrick and Eduardo

Sanchez swept aside all of the old methods of film production and let the cinematic world know that as of now, there was an entirely new paradigm. A new way of capturing, advertising and releasing a film and by the way: There Are No Rules!

Yes, this small film presented an entirely new paradigm, a new model by which a film could be shot, captured, advertised and presented and its effect is still being felt today not only with the overabundance of "reality television" programs that are flooding the world's cable channels, but also in the wide spread use of the Internet and Websites to publicize any film, large or small in an attempt to gain a mass audience.

This small film's effect has also spread to the plush offices of Hollywood, with the release of *Cloverfield*. The first Big Studio, Big Budget, Big CGI, Big Sci-Fi monster movie modeled on and captured in the same style as The Blair Witch Project.

THE BASICS:
This very small, guerrilla project became "the little movie that could." Even though its originators, Misters Myrick and Sanchez, much like Robert Rodriguez, were just hoping that their film might someday play on Cable TV, but instead it astounded everyone by causing an international sensation. It

began as a simple 35-page outline that was going to be improvised and ended up going into production pretty much the same way.

The three inexperienced actors were all cast for their improvisational skills and they also believed that the "legend of the Blair Witch" was real during the time that they were making the film.

Later after filming, the production was one of the first to utilize the Internet where their Website began to fuel the controversy as to whether or not the film was an actual documentary that was utilizing "found footage."

Even though over the years, all of the filmmakers have been interviewed many times about how it was actually done, there are still those diehard fans who believe that the footage that was supposedly "found" in the forest near Burkittsville is actually "real."

I honestly believe that the most groundbreaking and astounding choice that the two novice Directors, Mr. Myrick and Mr. Sanchez made, was their decision: **Not To Direct!** To my knowledge that is an All Time First in filmmaking history! Has anyone prior to this ever gone into filmmaking NOT to supervise or take part in the filming? Not to control the performances, the lighting or the framing of their film? Instead, they allowed the cast to decide what the "mise en scene" was going to be. It was totally unheard of for the cast to decide where and when and what was going to be discussed, performed, framed and shot each day! It's hard to believe, but the cast shot nearly all of the material for the film entirely on their-own in only eight days!

The unbelievable choice of removing of the director, cinematographer and supporting crew from all of the daily supervision, influence or participation in the process of making this film, is what gives this unique production the feeling that it was a real occurrence that was actually happening to these three people, because essentially it was.

THE PRODUCTION:
The production began in October of 1997 and during the eight days of shooting, (I will reiterate; this groundbreaking film was shot in only eight days!) food, clues as to the locations and individual instructions for the scenes to be done, were left each day in empty milk crates which the performers located with GPS devices. Also, the food for the cast was progressively, decreased as the days went by to heighten their fear, their discomfort with the situation and their frustration with each other.

Apparently, one of Mr. Myrick and Mr. Sanchez's associates, Greg Hale, had told them about the effects of "Hell Week" during military training, where his combat team was pushed hard during the day, harassed during the night and gradually deprived of their food. The directors liked the idea and put it to good use in the production of their film.

The frustrated actors ended up shooting most of the day, every day and captured about 19 hours of usable footage. The two directors then edited all the material down to 86 minutes over a period of nearly eight months.

This was one of the first DIY (Do It Yourself) low-to-no-budget, independent "guerrilla films" in the truest sense of those words. They used unknown actors, who were improvising their "reality show" everyday, on natural locations and in available light. They had very little money and used inexpensive equipment.

The production was so frugal that they actually bought a video camera to capture some of the footage and then promptly returned it for a refund once they had wrapped principal photography.

The total original cost to the filmmakers was around

$35,000, although they probably raised more to complete the 35mm blowup for festival screenings. After the film caused a sensation at the Sundance Film Festival it was quickly purchased by Artisan Entertainment for $1,100,000.

When Artisan got onboard they mounted an unprecedented multimillion-dollar distribution campaign utilizing the Internet, further hyping the, "is it real found footage or not" controversy, which developed an immense fan base for the film long before it opened.

The release was also inventively done, first by making the film a "must see" attraction and then by opening it in only a few limited theaters. The film sold out everywhere and the venues literally had to turn customers away before there was finally a 1500-screen summer release. Theatrically, The Blair Witch Project was a smashing success and became THE film to see that year. Eventually, "little film that could" ended up grossing over $160,000,000 in the US and over $240,000,000 worldwide.

According the Guinness Book of Records, after the film's grosses were made, when you compare the dollars invested to the revenues received, that made *The Blair Witch Project*, at the time, the most successful film in the history of the Cinema.

THE AWARDS:
After the film caused a sensation at The Sundance Film Festival, it was nominated for several awards and went on to win the Independent Spirit Award and the Cannes Film Festival Award of the Youth.

ONLINE RESOURCES:
Use Google Images & Google Videos for dozens of links...

Buy it on Amazon, Google Play, or iTunes.

Trailer Video URL
http://www.imdb.com/video/screenplay/vi9044249/

THINKING OUTSIDE THE BOX:
Class Exercises:

1. First, while the film is fresh in your mind, each student should write an essay about their thoughts, feelings, likes, dislikes, pros and cons.

2. *The Blair Witch Project* broke so many filmmaking rules, that it's utterly astounding. Each student should write an essay listing all of the production items that

this film did without, and theorize on how the filmmakers arrived at utilizing all of these "outside of the box" methods.

3. In 1999, this small production made a big impression. Ten years later in 2009 we had the release of *Paranormal Activity*. Each student should view that film and then write an essay comparing and contrasting these two films, and theorizing about why Hollywood never seems to learn how NOT to spend untold millions of dollars on only two hours of entertainment.

4. Many viewers seemed to have trouble with the "amateur, shaky" camera work that for many seemed to heighten the "reality" factor. Each student should write an essay about their thoughts, feeling, pros and cons of this type of cinematography and how they feel that it contributed to the success of the film.

5. This is the film that began what I call The New Paradigm. Each student should write an essay about the new paradigm and all of the fresh outside of the box elements that it offers to filmmakers today.

Chapter 38:

2000
TIMECODE

Mike Figgis
No Film No Editing

SPOILER ALERT!
Today we can say that the last century was the century of 35mm film, the photochemical process, the film lab and the 1000 ft. film magazine. This is the new millennium and there is an entirely new game in town. To quote Mr. Figgis: "...let's compare it to two things. One is the music industry with the advent of the port-o-studio and garage music. In other words, the idea of being able to have your own world class recording studio. I have one in my office in London... I have one really superb microphone and ProTools. I did the *Timecode* soundtrack in my front room. It can only be liberating. I mean to be honest the only thing standing in the way of the creative process of

filmmaking is the studios and the crews... Filmmaking is an art form... Some of the best things that have ever happened in the world have been as a result of art as opposed to the army or big business."

THE CREATIVE TEAM:
Writer: Mike Figgis
Director: Mike Figgis
Cinematographer: Patrick Alexander Stewart
Editor: ?

WHY IS THIS FILM VISIONARY:
It was the year 2000, the new millennium was being ushered in and along with it many new concepts and methods of film production. *The Blair Witch Project* had just removed their Directors, DP and Crew from the actual process of capturing the filmed or taped material, and with the advent of *Timecode,* the Script, the use of Film, a traditional Shooting Schedule and the Editor would also be set aside... The New Paradigm was definitely gaining momentum!

Mike Figgis is an artist, a jazz musician and a filmmaker, who used his knowledge of music to seriously test the boundaries and push the envelope of film production. Personally, I am not a fan of "split screen" material, so I initially took little interest in *Timecode* after I saw that the film was being told on a screen sectioned into four quarters. However, when I finally caught up to this groundbreaking film I was astounded by the production's audacity, bravado and style.

THE BASICS:
The film might not have been anything more than an underground project in London, but once again as Fate would have it the director happened to have lunch with a studio executive in Los Angeles. Mr. Figgis mentioned to him this small experimental production that he was thinking of doing and the executive asked if he would consider doing it in Los Angles. *Timecode* had just found its new home in Beverly Hills.

Being a musician, Mr. Figgis basically took the complexities of film production and treated them like a jazz quartet rehearsing and doing a live performance. He assembled his cast of fearless actors including, Salma Hayek, Stellan Skarsgard, Holly Hunter, Danny Huston, Jeanne Tripplehorn, Julian Sands and Kyle MacLachlan. They were each part of the four stories that were going to be told and captured simultaneously by four different camera teams in a never before attempted, real time, no cuts, one shot, 90 minute take.

The last time that happened was back in the 1950's during the golden days of live television when young directors like Sidney Lumet and John Frankenheimer were directing actors like Paul Newman, and Rod Steiger in 90 minute live television dramas on Playhouse 90... Of course back then there were breaks and interruptions for commercials... So *Timecode* was still breaking entirely new ground.

THE SCRIPT:
On top of that, there was no traditional script, instead Mr. Figgis plotted out the four stories beat by beat, minute-by-minute on the paper designed to be used for writing a <u>Musical Score</u>! That's right - the script was a stack of sheet music! Then Mr. Figgis had the actors over the period of a week, flesh out the characters with a series of improvisations. The actors were also responsible for their own make up and wardrobe and were instructed to wear something different each day that the team captured a performance, so that there would be no temptation to do any "editing" between one days performance and another.

THE PRODUCTION:
The film was shot, improvised and captured 15 different times over a two-week period during November of 1999 and *Timecode* was in the theaters

by March of 2000. Each take was screened, critiqued and reviewed by the cast as well as the production and camera teams so that adjustments could be made. Finally, Mr. Figgis selected the best version for the films theatrical release; it was the one captured on November 19, 1999 starting at 3 pm... By 4:30 that same afternoon, the take and the entire film was in the can. Not only had a film been completed in one day, it had actually been completed in 90 minutes in a one shot take!

To say the least, this was a bold and audacious way of producing a film, basically it was done in the same way as performing a jazz concert that would be shaped and polished during the rehearsal process and then performed at one sitting. I'm sure that you noticed at the beginning of this chapter where I usually credit the Writer, Director, Cinematographer and Editor; that the Editor's name is missing...? Because this film was Not Edited!

2020 HINDSIGHT:
From the perspective of 20/20 hindsight, I believe that "not editing" is the only misstep in this courageous, venturesome and outside the box, project: Instead, Mr. Figgis chose to present all four stories and performances in split screen at the same time. Finally, he added an improvised jazz score and

then did the sound mix "on the fly" as the film was screened at its premier at the Nu Art Theater in West Los Angeles.

The DVD actually contains the first 90 minute take captured by the four camera teams, as well as the one that was chosen for theatrical release and also offers the viewer the option of doing their own "sound mix" by deciding which story they would like to listen to as they watch the DVD.

Bold and courageous yes, but I believe that *Timecode* would have been an even better final film if ALL of the material captured had then been edited to present the best version of each story. Also, similar to a jazz quartet's performance where each instrument has the chance to perform a solo; it might have also made for a better film, if each story had been on the full screen part of the time (a solo) instead of always being relegated to ¼ of the viewing screen.

THE CASSAVETES CONNECTION:
Like John Cassavetes film, *Shadows* that was made over forty years before it, *Timecode* is not a great film, but nevertheless it is an extremely important film that deserves to be studied by every serious student of filmmaking. Most especially the "Director's Video Diary" documentary that is presented on the DVD!

Both *Shadows* and *Timecode* contain the similar elements of improvisation and Jazz while also providing outstanding and innovative templates for filmmakers to follow for creating future productions.

THE AWARDS:
Timecode did not win any awards, but its triumph was not only to show the world that a film could be captured in a day, but also that it could be captured in 90 minutes in a one shot take, a fact that the feature, *The Russian Ark* used to its advantage two years later.

This daring innovation alone served notice that, with the advent of Non Linear Editing, Video Tape and soon HD, the Red Camera, The Genesis, DSLRs and beyond, there was a New Paradigm happening in the world of film production and that the future may indeed belong to those filmmakers who were willing to adapt, be bold, adventuresome and joyfully embrace it.

ONLINE RESOURCES:
Use Google Images & Google Videos for dozens of links...

Buy it on Amazon, Google Play, or iTunes.

Trailer Video URL:
http://www.imdb.com/video/screenplay/vi1493041433/

THINKING OUTSIDE THE BOX:
Class Exercises:

1. First, while this unique film is fresh in your mind, each student should write an essay about their thoughts, feelings, likes, dislikes, pros and cons.

2. Mike Figgis is a musician. Each student should write an essay about how music influenced the innovations used in this film.

3. *Timecode* and *Shadows* have a lot in common. Each student should write an essay comparing and contrasting these two groundbreaking indie films.

4. Each student should write an essay or a treatment describing how they would create a totally "outside the box" film production.

5. Each student should use their home digital or HD camera and work with other students in making a short film in the style of TimeCode, captured in a one shot take.

Chapter 39:

2003
28 Days Later

Danny Boyle
Big Budget Home Video

SPOILER ALERT!
THIS FILM WAS SHOT ON HOME VIDEO! As I have already mentioned, I believe that the only noteworthy film to come out of the self-serving "Dogma 95" movement was the 1998 film by Thomas Vinterberg, *The Celebration*. That film was also photographed on natural locations, in available light and on Sony Hi-8 home video by the renowned, English/Danish Cinematographer Anthony Dod Mantle.

The Academy Award winning director Steven Soderberg had also used a home video camera, the Cannon XL1 for his 2002 film, *Full Frontal*. While it was not an important film, however, what was important was the fact that a Hollywood director of Mr. Soderberg's stature would have the bravado to shoot a feature film starring Julia Roberts and David Duchovny using a home video camera. Who would be next? Danny Boyle answered that question quite forcefully, with *28 Days Later.*

THE CREATIVE TEAM:
Writer: Alex Garland
Director: Danny Boyle
Cinematographer: Anthony Dod Mantle
Editor: Chris Gill

WHY IS THIS FILM VISIONARY:
The home video precedents were in already in place, when Danny Boyle and Anthony Dod Mantle teamed up for *28 Days Later.* They quickly discovered all of the nightmares involved in attempting to shut down traffic in order to shoot the scenes described in the script as: "Ext – London / Deserted - Day"

Realizing that they would often have only minutes to shoot and get all of the coverage for their scenes, they arrived at the conclusion that the only way it could be accomplished would be by using digital home video cameras, namely the trusty Cannon XL1's.

However, this was not a small 1960's George Romero

"zombie movie." It boasted a nearly ten million-dollar budget, hundreds of technicians and a host of horrific and bloody special effects. Its "must see" status was attained by having a number of scenes set in the highly trafficked parts of London, such as Oxford Street, Piccadilly Circus, Westminster Bridge and Horse Guards Parade that were totally abandoned and devoid of any human or vehicular traffic.

THE BASICS:
All of these "abandoned London" scenes were only able to be accomplished by blocking traffic for a very few minutes, quickly setting up 6 to 12 Cannon XL1 cameras and shooting. As the Producer Andrew Macdonald explained in the films production notes. "The police and the local authorities were quite happy to assist us because we could set up a scene so quickly. We could literally be ready to shoot with a six-camera set-up within minutes – something we would not realistically have been able to do if shooting under the restrictions of 35mm which takes a good deal more time to set up (for even) a single shot."

For the scene on the M1 motorway, the traffic was slowed between the hours of 7 to 9 am on a Sunday morning and the production utilized 10 Cannon XL1 cameras to capture the necessary footage in that brief amount of time. For the scene of the overturned double-decker bus, the bus was placed on its side, the scene was shot and the bus was removed all within only 20 minutes.

PANDEMIC RAGE:
Although the film has been categorized as a "horror film" or a "post apocalyptic zombie movie" it is actually set in the science fact environment of an unstoppable pandemic. The filmmakers used the recent examples of anthrax and bioterrorism in London as well as the spread of mad cow and hoof and mouth disease in that country, as a jumping off point for their horrific story.

Today of course, we have the examples of the spread of SARS and the recent possibility of the swine flu pandemic. Also, the "rage" suffered by the victims of the virus in 28 Days Later took the film another step away from the "brain-eating zombies" of the traditional horror movie and into the more psychological arena of today's road rage or the phenomenon of someone finally getting so stressed out that they "go postal." Before you rise up indignantly and say "... it's only a horror movie..." kindly remember, that so was the sensational little film entitled: *Psycho*.

ACCLAIM:
Finally, this film was very well received critically and at the box office. It won several British and European film awards for Danny Boyle and Anthony Dod Mantle and took in over 80 million dollars world wide.

Note: Within five years of making *28 Days Later* Danny Boyle and Anthony Dod Mantle would team up once again, this time on an international co-production. Much of it would be captured on a new, revolutionary HD camera that might help to change the face of filmmaking for many years to come... What is that film? Hint: "It is written."

ONLINE RESOURCES:
Use Google Images & Google Video for dozens of links...

Buy it on Amazon, Google Play, or iTunes.

Trailer Video URL:
http://www.imdb.com/video/screenplay/vi4071817497/

THINKING OUTSIDE THE BOX:
Class Exercises:

1. While the viewing of the film is still fresh, each

student should write an essay about their thoughts, feelings, pros and cons, likes and dislikes of the film.

2. Shooting an 8 - 10 million-dollar feature on Home Video seems highly improbable, so each student should write an essay discussing what the thought process may have been, to arrive at this conclusion.

3. Since *28 Days Later* was shot on home video and made upwards of 80 million dollars at the box office, each student should write an essay about how the tastes of the public has changed and what might have contributed to that change.

4. Whether you had seen *28 Days Later* before or if this is your first time, each student should write an essay describing how learning about its being shot on home video affected your appreciation of it, or your enjoyment of watching the film.

5. With the groundbreaking productions of, *The Blair Witch Project, Timecode* and *28 Days Later* we have been discussing the New Paradigm. Each student should write an essay describing new cutting edge, ideas and technologies that are now available for film production.

Chapter 40:

2003
Zero Day

Ben Coccio
No Budget Home Video

SPOILER ALERT!
This film should be the absolute be all and end all of DIY (Do It Yourself) productions, the Poster Child for low-to-no-budget Guerrilla Filmmaking, and an audacious underground sensation, but somehow it managed to stay well under nearly everyone's radar.

I discovered this film by accident by perusing the titles being offered on the very best source for anyone who is serious about studying films and filmmaking, namely: Netflix. I was curious, I ordered it and when it arrived, I watched it...

Seeing *Zero Day* for the first time was both a mesmerizing and troubling experience, similar to watching the jet planes hit the World Trade Center. Even though I knew the film had been "scripted," and was being "acted" it has the look and feel of actual "found" home videos and as such it becomes hyper-real and me as the viewer and felt as though I was experiencing the "documenting" of this event as it was happening. I found the emotional impact of the film to be much more devastating and profound than most of the "meaningful" films turned out by "professional filmmakers." This film is disturbing, upsetting and distressful. By all means... Watch it!

THE CREATIVE TEAM:
Writer: Ben Coccio, Christopher Coccio
Director: Ben Coccio
Cinematographer: Ben Coccio
Editor: Ben Coccio, David Shuff

WHY IS THIS FILM VISIONARY:
Way back in the last century, when the specter of home video first began to loom up on the horizon, no less a cinematic personage than Francis Ford Coppola is reported to have said something like, "...some day in the not too distant future, a gifted child in Kansas will pick up a video camera and become the next Mozart of filmmaking..."

In my estimation, Ben Coccio was that gifted child and his magnum opus was *Zero Day.* Unfortunately like many artists he has gone mostly unrecognized, unheralded and unappreciated during his lifetime. However, I trust that he has the insight to take those facts as a sign of his true artistic merit.

THE BASICS:
Mr. Coccio was profoundly affected by the Columbine High School killings in 1999 and set out to write a film about that subject. By 2001 he had a script and apparently did what has become known in guerrilla filmmaking circles as a "Rodriguez List." Which means that he utilized whatever was handy, free or obtainable in order to make his ultra low budget production, which is reported to have cost $20,000.00. (My estimate is much lower at around $5,000.00 - $10,000.00)

The film uses the best elements from the Italian Neo Realists, French New Wave and the American Independents: No Money, Inexpensive Equipment, Natural Locations, Available light, Non Actors, An Organic, Episodic Script, in other words he made the film with blood, sweat and passion. He cast his friends and their families as the characters in the film and shot the film entirely on the Canon XL1, which is basically a glorified home video camera.

THE PRODUCTION:
The Video Diary style that Mr. Coccio used for the film was apparently taken from the fact that the original Columbine killers made basement tapes about their planned shootings and it is this choice that makes the film so compelling and effective. Through these rough homemade videos you get to know these two young, troubled guys, you meet their unsuspecting families, understand their motives and feel devastated that you cannot alter their self made choices toward the abyss of violence, destruction and death.

Mr. Coccio's choice of viewing the final killings of the high school students and the two perpetrators on the schools surveillance cameras makes the ending of this extraordinary film that much more real and tragic. To show you the impact of these final scenes many viewers actually thought that what they were watching was footage from the original Columbine Massacre.

Even though the film was completed in 2001 it was delayed due to the tragedy of September 11th and was not released until nearly two years later in 2003. As a tribute to this small film's enormous impact as one reviewer stated online when comparing the film to the similarly themed and larger budgeted film *Elephant* "...it's much more painfully realistic... Overall this film is emotionally gripping and very haunting and much better than Elephant." It was also called "The one great Columbine film." by the author of a book on the subject and Journalist, Dave Cullen.

THE AWARDS:
In 2003, *Zero Day* won Awards at the Atlanta Film Festival, the Boston Underground Film Festival, the Florida Film Festival, the Had To Be Made Film Festival, the Slamdunk Film Festival and was nominated for an Independent Spirit Award.

ONLINE RESOURCES:
Use Google Images & Videos for dozens of links...

Buy it on Amazon, Google Play, or iTunes.

THINKING OUTSIDE THE BOX
Class Exercises:

1. While the film is still fresh, each student should write an essay about what worked best in the film and what did not work and what they liked and did not like and why.

2. Even though this is an important and exceptional film, it was not a successful one: each student should write an essay about how they feel about this fact and why do they think that it was not widely successful.

3. This is a film that was made with passion and not money; each student should write an essay about the merits of having to choose between either passion or money to work with, which one would they choose and why.

4. Each student should write an essay comparing and contrasting *Zero Day* with *The Blair Witch Project.*

5. The students should team up and make a small digital film in the style of *Zero Day* about another troubling subject.

XV. Big Films, Bold Visions

Chapter 41:

2003
CHICAGO

Rob Marshall
Redefining Mise-en-scène

SPOILER ALERT!
Very few film directors, when confronted with the overwhelming task of transforming musical numbers from the stage to film, have had the insight, imagination or determination to do much more than have the action pause while the star performers sing the lyrics of the various hit songs.

Often even great directors like Milos Forman have fallen victim to this syndrome, as he did when he directed the Musical, *Hair.* The wonderful director Norman Jewison, after making the inventive and groundbreaking musical, *Jesus Christ Superstar*, amazingly followed it up, with a stagy, backward-looking, theatrical version of *Fiddler On The Roof.*

While there have been some outstanding and creative Musicals over the years, like An *American in Paris 1951, Singin' In The Rain 1952* and *South Pacific* 1958, there have only been a few that were truly cinematic: *West Side Story 1961, Cabaret 1971, Jesus Christ Superstar 1972* and *All That Jazz 1979*. However, I recently had to expand my list of cinematic Musicals to include a new entry after several viewings of the remarkable Rob Marshall Film, *Chicago.*

THE CREATIVE TEAM:
Writers: Bill Condon / Bob Fosse / Fred Ebb
Director: Rob Marshall
Cinematographer: Dion Beebe
Editor: Martin Walsh

WHY IS THIS FILM VISIONARY:
I'm a huge fan of Bob Fosse and I've seen his film *All That Jazz* well over a dozen times. I always loved the world-weary cynicism and showbiz savvy that infused all of his work and no one has ever been able to equal his ability to cinematically imagine, stage and

shoot a musical number. Apparently Rob Marshal is also a Bob Fosse fan, because along with his own groundbreaking achievements, he does an amazing homage to Mr. Fosse in the film *Chicago,* which includes giving him a special "Thank You" in the closing credits.

The effort that it takes to film a musical number well is so complex that it is seldom undertaken: Taking the music, the lyrics, the lighting, the performances and the choreography, breaking them all down into their component parts, down finally to each musical beat and then laboriously planning and filming that material: shot by shot, move by move, light by light, set up by set up, line by line, emotion by emotion, beat by beat and finally editing it all together to the music, cut by cut...

That technique is a totally cinematic process, that when applied, infuses each musical number with an unmistakable power! Mr. Marshall has infused the musical numbers in *Chicago* with that power and it is the power of, in the words of Mr. Hitchcock: "Pure Cinema."

THE BASICS:
This modern approach to doing a Musical, more or less began with Robert Wise, (Who, as we know,

started his career as the Film Editor on Citizen Kane!) in his production of *West Side Story* and was carried much further along by Bob Fosse in *Cabaret,* Norman Jewison in *Jesus Christ Superstar* and reached its pinnacle with Mr. Fosse again in *All That Jazz.* Rob Marshal has obviously learned from all of these masters and has stood on their shoulders, in taking this cinematic technique to even newer heights in his production of *Chicago.*

Which brings us to the term, "mise-en-scène." What is it exactly? There appear to be several definitions. Basically, it is a French term from the world of theater, which means "to put onto the stage" or "to put into the scene." Originally it meant how the theatrical director visualized, blocked and presented everything that was in a scene on the stage. However, I believe that it has come to encompass much more as a cinematic term. Some feel that it only means the elements incorporated by a film director to create a long moving camera shot. I beg to differ.

Since a film director is involved with making decisions in so many areas of pre-production, production and post production: the script, the casting, the locations, the crew, the production design, the costumes, the colors, the framing, the lighting, the blocking, the performances and on into the editing, music, sound effects, titles, CGI's, ADR, final mix, color timing, digital master and even the advertising and promotion... For me, the term, "mise-en-scène" when applied to the Cinema, has come to mean: Everything that the Director utilizes to visualize each scene as well as to orchestrate the entire production!

THE PRODUCTION:
Chicago was produced in Toronto Canada in 2001 and two prominent members of the cast were not known for their musical abilities, namely Rene Zellweger and Richard Gere. They both received extensive coaching for their singing and dancing, which they eventually managed to bring off with award winning style.

Once again, it's amazing how Fate and Destiny played a part in the production process. At various times, Madonna, Nocole Kidman, Uma Thurman and Charlize Theron all were up for the role of "Roxie Hart." John Travolta, Hugh Jackman and Dustin Hoffman were all considered for "Billy Flynn." While Liza Minnilli, Angelina Jolie and Michelle Pheiffer were all in the running for "Velma Kelly." Then after all the dust had settle, and we saw the finished film... we all exclaimed that the casting was absolutely perfect and that all of the performers were, "born to play those parts!"

The film *Chicago* is one of the best examples of a director's, "mise-en-scène," and it can certainly be seen in all of the cinematically imagined musical numbers, but most especially in *"Cell Block Tango."* This showstopper actually begins with the sounds of a dripping water tap and footsteps. Followed by the photographing and editing of close ups of the dripping water along with the footsteps of a prison guard, then an ECU (Extreme Close Up) of a female prisoner's hand drumming her fingers…

Those sounds, and shots starts off the cadence and then the beats of the music take over… What follows, is a show stopping cinematic collage of precise compositions, actual and staged locations, textures, lines, lyrics, performances, dance moves, camera moves, lighting cues and beats that have all been carefully, planned, story boarded, rehearsed, framed, lit, sung, danced, photographed and most importantly: Directed and Edited To The Beats Of The Music.

It is an outstanding example and possibly a redefining of the term, "mise-en-scène" as we realize that all of these disparate elements have been overseen, conducted and most expertly Directed by Mr. Marshall, who has managed to take a piece that began as a staged musical theater number and transform it into a dazzling piece of bravura and totally cinematic filmmaking. His dedication was so thorough that he actually worked himself into a state of collapse, by even going onto the set on the weekends to supervise the nearly fifty lighting cues that make up this outstanding show stopping number.

MR. FOSSE:
Chicago was going to be the next project for Bob Fosse who had co-written, directed and choreographed the original 1975 Broadway production; but he "shuffled off this mortal coil..." to The Big Production Number In The Sky... before that could happen. Personally, I've always believed that he made the film, *All That Jazz,* which happens to be named after the opening number in *Chicago,* simply because he was unable to get that show, which was his personal favorite, into production.

THE AWARDS:
Among its many awards, *Chicago* won the DGA Award and The National Board of Review Award for Best Debut Director, it was nominated for 13 Academy Awards, winning six and was also nominated for eight Golden Globe Awards, winning three.

ONLINE RESOURCES:

Use Google Images & Google Videos for dozens of links...

Buy it on Amazon, Google Play, or iTunes.

Trailer Video URL:
http://www.imdb.com/video/screenplay/vi683540761/

THINKING OUTSIDE THE BOX:
Class Exercises:

1. While the film is still fresh, each student should write an essay describing their thoughts, feelings, pros and cons, likes and dislikes of the film.

2. Making a film is the most collaborative of art forms, however, after our discussion regarding "mise en scene" each student should write an essay about why a film director should be permitted to claim the title: "A Film By."

3. Go back through *Chicago* and choose your favorite moves from, *Cell Block Tango* or another musical number. Then each student should prepare storyboards for filming just that part of the scene.

4. There have been dozens of old-fashioned stagey

musicals. Each student should research them on the Internet, pick a song from one and after viewing it, write an essay or do a detailed set of storyboards showing how you could change that particular number into a piece of "Pure Cinema."

5. First, turn off the sound track and watch your favorite musical number in *Chicago*, silent. Then each student should write an essay detailing all of the careful, planning, rehearsing, shooting that it took just to do that one musical number and edit it to the music.

Chapter 42:

2004
The Bourne Supremacy

Paul Greengrass
State-Of-The-Art Action

SPOILER ALERT!
This film was an action film game changer. In fact the entire Jason Bourne Trilogy had everyone commenting that these films were much more exciting than the old, tired, campy James Bond series; that these films were in fact, the new James Bond for the new millennium. This was so widespread, that the producers in charge of the James Bond franchise took notice, and totally re-cast, re-imagined and revived their antiquated productions to be more in line with the action, pacing and sensibilities of the Bourne films.

Casino Royale has much more in common with the

tone of the Bourne series than with any of the previous films in the Bond franchise. If you look closely enough at the car chase that opens the next Bond film, *A Quantum of Solace*, you will find that its editing and camera work are nearly cloned from the style set during, *The Bourne Supremacy* car chase.

Paul Greengrass had come up with a new visceral look and everyone in the international action adventure business had to take notice in order to be able to keep current and deliver something close to his phenomenal style of state-of-the-art action.

THE CREATIVE TEAM:
Writer: Tony Gilroy, Robert Ludlum
Director: Paul Greengrass
Cinematographer: Oliver Wood
Editor: Richard Pearson, Christopher Rouse

WHY IS THIS FILM VISIONARY:
Director Paul Greengrass and his Cinematographer Oliver Wood have commented that they basically had to "retrain" their camera operators, on both first and second unit, NOT to give them precise, well composed images. The cameras were nearly always hand-held and contributed to the energetic style of the film, which seemed as though they were just barely able to keep up with the frenetic pace being set by the highly

skilled and elusive Jason Bourne.

Mr. Greengrass also insisted that most of the frenetic action in the film be done live on camera instead of being accomplished by using the latest in CGI technology. This was a fairly amazing choice given all of the astounding possibilities that are available to a director in today's overblown CGI super hero action films.

When it came to the pace of the editing this was also amped-up and in the final analysis the average length of each shot is only 1.9 seconds or 46 frames of 35mm film. Remember that's the "average" length, meaning that in all of the action, fight and car chase scenes many shots were much shorter, so short in fact, that many of them were nearly subliminal.

THE BASICS:
Jason Bourne never smiles, Jason Bourne only uses every day devices that could easily be purchased by anyone. His martial arts are derived from Escrima or Kali an old Philippine form of defense, which today is taught by using objects from everyday life.

Jason Bourne is an everyman, an anti-hero, anti-James Bond type character, who has renounced the "black ops" world of conspiracies and is seeking answers from a system and a government that has been lying him and to everyone. Basically, like all of us, except he has been highly trained, but he is still ordinary man in extraordinary circumstances, which is probably why this character resonated so well with movie going audiences around the world.

THE PRODUCTION:
Like most films, *The Bourne Supremacy* was shot out of continuity and what we see on the screen was actually shot in reverse order: The Moscow, Russia scenes first and the Goa, India scenes last.

After you screen the DVD, kindly watch all of the amazing behind the scenes extras. Especially the one that shows off the extraordinary stunt car called the "Go-Mobile" that was used in the famous Moscow car chase. This outstanding invention attaches to any vehicle and can safely strap in whatever star is on camera, putting them directly into the middle of all the action while the vehicle is being safely controlled by a highly skilled stunt driver. Matt Damon admits ruining takes several times because of laughing out loud at all the fun he was having in the midst of what appeared to be horrific and life threatening action.

There have, in my humble opinion, only been three serious car chases in cinematic history that have been awe-inspiring showstoppers. The first was *Bullit,* directed by Peter Yates. The second was *The French Connection*, directed by William Friedkin. And the third one is the film directed by Paul Greengrass, *The Bourne Supremacy.*

Many of the fight scenes were not choreographed in the usual manner using several cameras to cover a well-staged fight and allowing the audience to see all of the punches and kicks... Here much of the action is captured in only a blur of motion as you hear the hits and then see the result of whoever made the mistake of confronting Jason Bourne, lying on the floor unconscious.

THE AWARDS:
The film was nominated for numerous awards and won the World Stunt Awards for stunt coordinator Dan Bradley, and the Empire Awards UK for Best Actor Matt Damon as well as Best Film.

ONLINE RESOURCES:
Use Google Images & Google Videos for dozens of links...

Buy it on Amazon, Google Play, or iTunes.

View the Trailer or various scenes at:

www.imdb.com
www.youtube.com

THINKING OUTSIDE THE BOX:
Class Exercises:

1. Each student should write an essay about their feelings after seeing the film, what were their pros and cons.

2. Each student should write an essay about the visual style of the film, did they like it or not, was it effective and compelling or distracting and upsetting.

3. Each student should write an essay comparing and contrasting *The Bourne Supremacy* with any of the old and the new films from the James Bond franchise.

4. This film is just an action/adventure, however it touches on important subjects, like government lies and the employing of covert, black ops hit men. Each student should write an essay describing other major films that have touched on important subjects.

5. Each student should write an essay or treatment in which they use sensitive or meaningful subjects as the backdrop for a thrilling action/adventure.

Chapter 43:

2004
COLLATERAL

Michael Mann
The HD Revolution

SPOILER ALERT!
By 2004, filmmakers were in the midst of a serious revolution when it came to the capture and delivery of a motion picture on either Film or HD, and Michael Mann happened to be one of the leaders in siding with HD. During the later part of the last century and early part of the new millennium many filmmakers began to utilize the new groundbreaking technology that was beginning to appear.

First by adapting to non-linear editing then later, to the new digital and HD cameras, these filmmakers enabled the process of filmmaking to become much more streamlined, efficient and have even helped lead to its democratization.

As Mike Figgis pointed out, the music industry led the way with the breakthrough of "garage bands" during the 1990's and today with the help of inexpensive cameras and editing systems, there are now "garage filmmakers." However, it must be pointed out that the real breakthrough for mainstream filmmakers has been accomplished by several big names embracing the latest in High Def technology like: George Lucas, Michael Mann, David Fincher, Mel Gibson and of course, the indie mavens, Steven Soderbergh and Robert Rodriguez.

THE CREATIVE TEAM:
Writers: Stuart Beattie
Director: Michael Mann
Cinematographers: Paul Cameron & Dion Beebe
Editor: Jim Miller & Paul Rubell

WHY IS THIS FILM VISIONARY:
In 2004 Mr. Mann joined other brave souls by becoming part of the HD revolution. He directed one of the first major studio, major star production since the *Star Wars* sequels that was captured primarily on HD, and was the first to use the Viper FilmStream HD Camera.

His feature film *Collateral* was no small indie or experimental production by any stretch of the imagination. It was distributed by Dreamworks SKG in the USA Paramount Pictures in the rest of the world and starred Tom Cruise, Jamie Foxx and Jada Pinkett-Smith. This was a big $65,000,000.00 Major Studio film, yet Mr. Mann dared to go into new and uncharted territory and captured much of it on High Def.

THE BASICS:
The Cinematographer Paul Cameron did all of the initial HD and low light testing during pre-production and shot the first three weeks of principal photography. He then left the film citing, "creative differences" with Mr. Mann who brought in the DP from the film *Chicago*, Dion Beebe. It was widely known at the time, that Mr. Cameron was not pleased with the Viper's ergonomics, color bandwidth and lens support systems. This information later proved helpful to Panavision in the development of their HD Camera system, known as the Genesis.

THE PRODUCTION:
Collateral was very revolutionary in its lighting style, since Mr. Mann had wanted to take advantage of the natural light and the look of the streets of Los Angeles at night. The mock up of the taxi that was inhabited

by Tom Cruise and Jamie Foxx was primarily lit with small nearly cardboard thin portable lighting units that were designed by Novatech. These units were literally attached by Velcro to the back of the front seat and the ceiling of the vehicle's interior to provide a daringly small amount of ambient light.

Also, if you look closely at the dark interior office where Tom Cruise's character is stalking Jada Pinket-Smith's character during the climax of the film, you will see that the light used on the actors and Mr. Cruise in particular, is actually very little and is balanced to let the lights from outside, from the skyline of Los Angeles, to actually be brighter than the light on the stars, often silhouetting them against the exterior lights of the city. *This Was A Very Bold, Ballsy And Edgy Technique To Use In A Major Motion Picture And On A Major Star Like Tom Cruise!*

I can clearly remember seeing this outstanding film for the first time and when the scene of Jamie Fox running 180 degrees down the deserted Main Streets of downtown Los Angeles, at 3 am, in available light happened on the big screen, I could already see the headlines heralding the passing of Motion Picture Film. I also immediately realized that filmmakers all over the planet who had an HD camera were now able to capture the same quality as a big Hollywood movie. Whether they were on the streets of Stockholm, Singapore, Shanghai or Seattle. And I realized at that moment, that the handwriting was already on the wall for the demise of film and the photochemical process. The capture and delivery of a motion picture was about to go HD and by doing so become more streamlined, cost saving and accessible.

Michael Mann is known for being meticulous in his preparation. For *Collateral,* Mr. Mann and the writer, Stuart Beattie collaborated in constructing all of the background details of the main characters even including, family back stories and photos from their imagined hometowns. During pre-production, Mr. Mann also had Tom Cruise delivering Fedex packages in downtown Los Angeles as part of an exercise to emphasizing that his character always blended in and was able to get in and out without being seen or remembered.

FINALLY:
Collateral opened number one at the box office in August of 2004 and stayed in the theaters for over three months. It found a large worldwide audience that eventually drove its gross earnings up to nearly $220,000,000.00. This innovative Big Star, Big Studio film helped to underscore the fact that the last century was the century for film and the

photochemical process and that this new millennium was fast becoming the century for capturing in HD, the Viper, Genesis, Red Camera and far beyond.

At one time or another, Russell Crow, Collin Farrell and Edward Norton were all being considered for the part of "Vincent" while Cuba Gooding Jr. and Adam Sandler were both considered for the part of "Max but as we know the casting of Tom Cruise and Jamie Foxx turned out to be "perfect," and the stars chosen were "born to play those parts!"

THE AWARDS:
Collateral was also a critical success, winning the ASCAP Top Box Office Award, the BAFTA (British Academy of Film and Television Arts) Best Cinematography Award and the Black Reel Award for Best Supporting Actor for Jamie Foxx. It was also nominated for two Academy Awards, a Golden Globe Award and five additional BAFTA Awards.

ONLINE RESOURCES:
Use Google Images & Google Videos for dozens of links...

Buy it on Amazon, Google Play, or iTunes.

Trailer Video URL:

http://www.imdb.com/video/screenplay/vi431948057/

THINKING OUTSIDE THE BOX:
Class Exercises:

1. While the film is still fresh, each student should write an essay about their thoughts, feelings, pros and cons about it and if by the filmmakers using HD, they noticed anything different about the film or their enjoyment of it.

2. The term, "creative differences" came up it this chapter, each student should research it on the Internet and write an essay about the use of the term, citing examples and defining exactly what it means.

3. Unlike many Hollywood studio films, this production used a lot of "available light" or very "low light" levels to follow the action and the performances. Each student should write an essay describing how this might have affected the overall efficiency of the production.

4. Using this film as an example, each student should use their own digital or HD cameras to experiment with exactly how little light that they actually need to light an actor for a scene.

5. We have spent a good deal of time discussing the "New Paradigm." Each student should write an essay describing what exactly it means and what elements and areas of film production it has already changed and may change in the future.

Chapter 44:

2005
King Kong

Peter Jackson
The CGI Revolution

SPOILER ALERT!
Yes, the bottom line is, that this is an overlong and heavily CGI'd movie about a giant gorilla. However, it is hands down, the Very Best overlong and heavily CGI'd movie about a giant gorilla ever made! This film is so visually stunning and mesmerizing, that when I was out shopping and saw that *King Kong* was starting to be shown as a demonstration for a large-screen TV at Circuit City, I sat down in a nearby chair intending to only watch a few minutes. Three hours later, I was a satiated and grateful fan of some of the most extraordinary visual effects ever put up on the screen.

The film's depth and breadth of achievement is staggering, especially in the overall visual detail and most especially in the motion capture of Andy Serkis's portrayal of *King Kong*. You can literally see every emotion and hair on the ape's face down to the smallest nuance and detail. There are many show stopping set pieces of action in this film, that are unparalleled in their ability to deliver jaw-dropping, big-screen thrills. I'm only going to mention three of them.

Get a big bag of popcorn or two... relax and enjoy!

THE CREATIVE TEAM:
Writer: Merian C. Cooper, Edgar Wallace, Fran Walsh, Philippa Boyens, Peter Jackson
Director: Peter Jackson
Cinematographer: Andrew Lesnie
Editor: Jamie Selkirk

WHY IS THIS FILM VISIONARY:
Like *Jurassic Park* and the famous *Lord of The Rings Trilogy*, this film showed off possibly better than its predecessors, the amazing potential of Computer Generated Images (CGI's) to take the movie viewer on a stunning visual and emotional trip that only the mind and imagination of an extraordinary artist could achieve. The digitally produced New York of 1933 is

so detailed that there were literally over 90,000 separate buildings created!

With the recent release and success of *Avatar* in 3D and the overwhelming willingness of the worldwide movie-going audience to respond to this experience, it is being reported that Mr. Jackson is considering "re-mastering" *King Kong* in 3D. Personally, I'll be the first in line to buy a ticket if he does.

THE BASICS:
As a child in New Zealand, Peter Jackson saw the original 1933 King Kong at the age of nine and was so moved by it that he simply had to make his own version. But that was going to take him a very long time to achieve. If you look at his early films they are literally bloodbaths of poor taste, but Mr. Jackson had a vision and he had to start somewhere. That somewhere was in New Zealand, where he produced his early, often stomach churning work.

However, by 1994, after the artistic success of Heavenly Creatures he had the vision to join with fellow New Zealanders, Richard Taylor and Tania Rodgers, to create the Wetta Workshop which would, several years later, produce the 20 minute Show Reel of CGI effects that convinced New Line Cinema to give Mr. Jackson literally the hundreds of millions of dollars that he needed to direct the *Lord of The Rings Trilogy*. Finally, after the stunning success of those films, Mr. Jackson was paid the most money ever paid to a director prior to making a film. Universal Pictures paid him, $20,000,000 to be able to realize his childhood dream of re-making the film about the "eighth wonder of the world" *King Kong*.

THE PRODUCTION:
Because of his extraordinary work as Gollum, in the Lord of The Rings Trilogy, Andy Serkis was chosen to portray the leading character of the gorilla in *King Kong*. Painstakingly researching the part took him around the world, from watching apes in the London Zoo all the way to Rwanda to observe the great apes in the wild. Such attention to detail also went into every aspect of the production, including all of the other creatures as well as the flora and fauna of the infamous Skull Island. Many of their various descriptions can be found in the book: *The World of Kong: A Natural History of Skull Island*.

Mr. Jackson actually approached the original star, Fay Wray to do the final line in the film, "... it was beauty killed the beast." But unfortunately she died before that could happen. Mr. Jackson was so indebted and enthralled with the original 1933 production that there are props, lines, sounds and other homages to it throughout his version of the film, especially the line uttered by Jack Black after capturing Kong, "... In a few months, his name will be up in lights on Broadway! Kong, The Eighth Wonder Of The World!"

As I mentioned, there are many show stopping, thrilling action packed set pieces in this film but the three that I believe stand out as being unequaled are First: The Stampede Of The Dinosaurs. Second: King Kong Fighting the Raptors and the last of course: The Finale On Top Of The Empire State Building. Sit up close, turn up the sound and let yourself be transported into the world of pure mind, imagination and CGI effects where anything and everything is possible...

Where humans and dinosaurs can run and tumble and careen down a narrow gorge narrowly escaping certain death. Where a giant ape can battle vicious raptors and not only win, but can do so while deftly and safely cradling a beautiful damsel in distress with both his hands and feet. Where a tragedy of epic proportions can play out its climax atop the tallest building in the world and the beast can silently fall, lifeless to his death and the realization that "... it was beauty killed the beast."

Of course, a film of this size is not without it's sizable problems, the budget expanded from around $150 million to over $200 million, it's length from over two hours to over three and it's original composer, Howard Shore, was replaced with James Newton Howard a scarce seven weeks before it's release. But in spite of being beset with all of these difficulties, the film made it into the theaters on time and did over $50 million dollars on its opening weekend.

Although it did not perform as well as expected, the production sill managed to rack up nearly $220 million dollars domestically and over $330 million worldwide. It also did an astounding DVD business, selling over 7.5 million units and taking in over $140 million in US sales.

THE AWARDS:
The film received many favorable critical reviews and was nominated for four Academy Awards, winning for: Best Visual Effects, Best Sound Mixing and Best Sound Editing.

ONLINE RESOURCES:
Use Google Images & Google Videos for dozens of links...

Buy it on Amazon, Google Play, or iTunes.

THINKING OUTSIDE THE BOX:
Class Exercises:

1. While the film is fresh each student should write an essay about what worked for them and what did not work, as well as what they liked best and least about the film and why.

2. Each student should write an essay comparing and contrasting the original 1933 production with this one, also discussing what has been gained or lost with all of our CGI technology.

3. With the detailed and moving portrayal of King Kong, Andy Serkis could have been nominated for an Acting Academy Award as the rendering of Brad Pitts head for Benjamin Button was; each student should write an essay discussing their opinions regarding this fast approaching reality.

4. CGI's have given the audiences the experience of *Star Wars, Jurassic Park, The Terminator, Lord of The Rings*, as well as countless other less impressive films and video games; each student should write an essay discussing how they feel about the world of Computer Generated Images.

5. The Students should team up and make a short film on their computers using only Computer Generated Images.

XVI. Today's Studio: Anywhere...

Chapter 45:

2005
Grizzly Man

Werner Herzog
Home Video: Alaska

SPOILER ALERT!
This is a profound and a profoundly disturbing film. Timothy Treadwell spent 13 seasons shooting over 100 hours of documentary footage, observing and "protecting" the bears in Katmai National Park and Preserve in Alaska. Unfortunately, he and his girl friend Amy Huguenard both died in 2003 when they were mauled and partially eaten by a bear.

Werner Herzog took Timothy's documentary footage and used it as the basis for his documentary entitled *Grizzly Man.* He shot additional interviews with Treadwell's family and friends as well as some of the people whom Treadwell had come in contact with in Alaska, who did not approve of what he was doing.

The main reason I'm including this film as one of the Milestones... is because of the overpowering effect of its simplicity: Mr. Treadwell setting up his video camera in the wilderness near the Grizzlies and then played out his role as the "gentle warrior" in front of both the wild animals and his camera.

THE CREATIVE TEAM:
Writer: Werner Herzog
Director: Werner Herzog
Cinematographer: Timothy Treadwell, Peter Zeitlinger
Editor: Joe Bini

WHY IS THIS FILM VISIONARY:
Timothy Treadwell was a failed actor, who admittedly became addicted to alcohol and drugs after loosing out on the part that Woody Harrelson got for the TV Series, *Cheers.* He was well on his way to becoming just another Hollywood wannabe along the boulevard of broken dreams.

Fortunately, a trip to Alaska became the catalyst that he needed to turn his life around. He somehow identified with the plight of the Grizzlies, cleaned up his addictions, acquired camping gear, a video camera and became "the voice of one crying in the wilderness" over the neglected situation of the bears. Out of sheer will and audacity, Mr. Treadwell finally became someone, finally was the first at something, finally got his moment, his recognition, and his more than 15 minutes of fame.

When I say that he was he was "the first" I'm referring to the current Cable shows, *Man vs. Wild*, *Survivorman*, and others, none of which would exist, without Timothy Treadwell and his video camera first doing their tour of duty in Alaska.

THE BASICS
Jewel Palovak was Mr. Treadwell's former girlfriend and co-founder with him of Grizzly People a grassroots organization that fought for the concerns of Grizzlies. After his death, the 100 hours of his documentary footage was left under her control and she gave her approval for Mr. Herzog to use the material and proceed with his documentary. Mr. Treadwell had often told her that if anything happened to him to make sure that she "told his

story."

THE PRODUCTION:

Werner Herzog and his editor not only dug through the 100 hours of Mr. Treadwell's footage, Mr. Herzog also shot on camera interviews both pro and con about Timothy and did the narration for the film.

During one of Mr. Treadwell's rants against the Park Service, Mr. Herzog says on the narration track, "... I have seen this before on film sets... It's almost like an actor confronting a director..." Given the numerous temperamental outbursts that Mr. Herzog had to endure at the hands of the mercurial Klaus Kinski, I'm sure that he was able to recognize an actor's tantrum when he saw one.

Which leaves us to ponder... was Timothy Treadwell simply a failed actor seeking a part to play in front of the camera? I certainly hope not, because if that were true, this may be the only time in film history when an actor spent many of his adult years starring in a film, then paid for with his life: The ultimate price for the ultimate part.

As part of the film, when interviewing Jewel Palovak, Mr. Herzog actually listened on headphones to the sound recorded by Mr. Treadwell's camera of his death. Profoundly shaken by it, he warned her never to listen to this tape and in fact told her to immediately destroy it.

THE AWARDS:
Grizzly Man won numerous awards including; the Directors Guild of America Award for Outstanding Documentary Achievement, The Independent Spirit Award, The Los Angeles Film Critics Association Award, The National Society of Film Critics Award and The New York Film Critics Circle Award for Best Documentary as well as The Sundance Film Festival, Feature Film Prize.

ONLINE RESOURCES:
Use Google Images & Google Videos for dozens of links...

Buy it on Amazon, Google Play, or iTunes.

Look for it on Netflix.

Screen the Trailer & Various Scenes at:
www.youtube.com

THINKING OUTSIDE THE BOX:
Class Exercises:

1. Each student should write an essay about how they felt after screening this film, what were their pros and cons.

2. Each student should write an essay about what they liked most in the film and what they liked least and why.

3. Each student should write an essay about the kind of commitment and determination that it took to spend thirteen summers in the Alaskan wilderness capturing 100 hours of documentary video footage.

4. Each student should write an essay about how impossibly cumbersome and costly it would have been if this documentary had been attempted on film. (Calculate the weight of packing and carrying as well as the cost of developing and printing and telecineing 100 hours of 16mm film.)

5. Each student should do a home video in the same simple, straightforward style that Mr. Treadwell used, to inform the public about a cause that is important to them.

Chapter 46:

2007
Once

John Carney
Digital Film: Ireland

SPOILER ALERT!
You'll laugh, you'll cry, you'll cheer and if you are a prospective filmmaker and are not finally inspired by this small digital film from Dublin to make your own film, you may not have a heartbeat. This is a production that did not even have the smallest of chances of succeeding. This episodic slice of a street musicians life was shot with two non-actors, on natural locations and in available light in Ireland, in less than three weeks and for the cost of $60,000.

How far down in the pecking order of successful filmmaking formulas can you possibly go? But apparently, what this little film did have was heart, "miles and miles and miles of heart…" And to continue that quote from old Mr. Blue Eyes himself, "…when the odds are sayin' you'll never win, that's when the grin should start… You gotta have heart."

Oh yes, one other item, this was a musical! And it was going to be judged alongside of the other mega budget Hollywood musicals, like *Hairspray*, *Across The Universe* and *Sweeny Todd*.

THE CREATIVE TEAM:
Writer: John Carney
Director: John Carney
Cinematographer: Tim Fleming
Editor: Paul Mullen

WHY IS THIS FILM VISIONARY:
John Carney Directed *Once* on Digital, in the streets of Dublin without permits so that nobody knew that he was making a film or when he was shooting. This also enabled him to capture his two non-actors' performances with long lenses, on real streets among real people, so that they would act naturally and not be intimidated by the cameras or the small crew.

The actors wore wireless microphones and often Mr. Carney and his skeleton crew would roll the cameras and slate the scene several minutes before the two actors would meet up on the street and begin their dialogue. This way he also had free, and totally authentic backgrounds, traffic and extras that added to the reality of the scene and the believability of the two non-actors' performances.

This is an extremely effective technique, as long as you are shooting digital or HD and not film. It is a brilliant, innovative and effective template that filmmakers worldwide can use to their benefit. As we have seen before, filmmaking often boils down to, not the amount of money or the size of the crew that you have, but the amount of innovation, bravado, tenacity and especially heart that you are able to bring to the production.

THE BASICS:
Mr. Carney had tried to make this film for several years with a much higher budget and with a professional actor in the lead. When that actor finally left and took the producers and the financial interests with him, Mr. Carney was forced to rethink, re-cast and re-structure his entire production.

He cast his friend, former band member and the film's musical consultant, Glen Hansard as the lead and agreed to make the film under the radar, for what the Irish Film Board was willing to invest which was less than 45,000 British Pounds or roughly $60,000 US Dollars.

THE PRODUCTION:
The two leads are listed in the credits as "Guy" and "Girl," but during the production, Mr. Carney often referred to them as his "Bogart and Bacall," and since he could see their mutual attraction first hand, he envisioned a future romance. Yes, Glen Hansard and Marketa Irglova fell in love, and after the production lived together for some time. Now, however they have both moved on but still remain good friends.

The production skimped and saved wherever possible even using Mr. Hansard's own house as a location for a necessary party scene and many of his musician friends and his family to act as the partygoers.

When you view the DVD, be sure to look at the behind the scenes documentary on the making of the film. You are certain to be inspired by the under the radar, freewheeling, Digital, available light, production values, that surround the capturing of this unique, unpredictable and inspiring film.

FINALLY:
The musical maestro himself, Bob Dylan, was so taken

by the performances of Mr. Hansard and Ms. Irglova in the film, that he arranged for them open for him as part of his world tour. And no less a movie maestro than Steven Spielberg, said of the film, "A little movie called *Once* gave me enough inspiration to last the rest of the year."

Oh yes, and as a final grace note, the film did beat out all of the Big Hollywood Musicals in 2008, to take home the Academy Award for Best Original Song "Falling Slowly."

You Gotta Have Heart!

THE AWARDS:
Once won a host of Awards including: The Independent Spirit Award for Best Foreign Film, The Sundance Film Festival Audience Award and most especially the Academy Award for The Best Original Song.

ONLINE RESOURCES:
Use Google Images & Google Videos for dozens of links...

Buy it on Amazon, Google Play, or iTunes.

View the Trailer and various scenes at:

www.youtube.com

THINKING OUTSIDE THE BOX:
Class Exercises:

1. Each student should write an essay about their reactions to first seeing the film, what they liked best and least about it and what were their pros and cons.

2. Each student should write an essay about Mr. Carney's decision to go ahead and make the film despite not having the name lead, or the original budget that he felt was necessary.

3. Each student should write an essay about the technique of using long lenses and wireless microphones to assist in being able to capture realistic performances from non-actors or from professional actors.

4. Each student should write an essay about the audacity of Mr. Carney attempting to do a musical for $60,000.00. Was this a smart or a reckless decision?

5. Each student should make a small HD or home digital film that captures a musical performance in one take, as they often did in this film.

Chapter 47

2007
The Diving Bell & The Butterfly

Julian Schnabel
35mm POV: France

SPOILER ALERT!
This is an Art Film made by an Artist. Julian Schnabel is both an established Artist in the world of Art as well as a Film Artist. With his production, *The Diving Bell and The Butterfly*, he underscores his profound abilities as both.

The script is about the tragic life of the French publisher of Elle Magazine, Jean-Dominique Bauby. Mr. Bauby suffered a devastating stroke and was treated at a hospital in the French county-side, where he was diagnosed as having the rare, "locked-in syndrome." His active mind and imagination were completely intact while imprisoned within his own completely paralyzed body.

After Mr. Schnabel visited the hospital and met the doctors and staff that had treated "Jean-Do he held out to make the film in France, in French and with an entirely French cast. He even learned the French language himself in order to be true to the spirit of the memoir, by Mr. Bauby, that had inspired the script and the production.

THE CREATIVE TEAM:
Writers: Ronald Harwood, Jean-Dominique Bauby
Director: Julian Schnabel
Cinematographer: Janusz Kaminski
Editor: Juliette Welfling

WHY IS THIS FILM VISIONARY:
The Diving Bell & The Butterfly, is an Art Film by an Artist, that concerns one mans afflicted vision and it was directed with unique creative style by the visionary Artist, Julian Schnabel. Mr. Schnabel's Art has been both praised and reviled but his singular and undeniable ability to surprise and to astound the viewer has brought him world-renowned fame, fortune and his share of notoriety.

This is a film that is also astoundingly photographed by the Academy Award winning Director of Photography, Janusz Kaminski. He and Mr. Schnabel virtually reinvented the language of filmmaking for this project, which should have won the Academy Award for best Cinematography hands down. Instead the Award went to the well acted but highly overrated: *There Will Be Blood.*

THE BASICS:
The Diving Bell & The Butterfly is truly a groundbreaking film and happily it was also a critical and box office success. The script about Jean-Dominique Bauby was based on the book in French that he dictated letter by letter, while in his locked in state. The script was written in English and had been given to Johnny Dep as a staring vehicle by Kathleen Kennedy of the famous Kennedy/Marshall Company. Mr. Dep brought in his friend Julian Schnabel as the director but Mr. Dep eventually had to drop out of the film due to his commitments on one of the mega blockbuster, *Pirates of The Caribbean* movies.

STRONG ADVICE:
While reading up on Mr. Schnabel, I was immediately taken by something he stated in an interview, which to paraphrase was, "...older artists will often attempt to give younger artists advice, but they cannot and

should not take it, because it is the younger artists responsibility, if not their duty, to destroy all of the standards that the older artists have spent their lives establishing..." I really like that in-your-face attitude... But, then again, so much for mentoring!

Ideally, this advice from Mr. Schnabel would be the credo for artists of every description all over the world, whether they're novelists, poets, musicians, singers, song writers, chefs, dancers, standup comedians, painters, sculptors, architects, street performers, still photographers or filmmakers. (Did I leave anyone out?)

While the overthrowing of the establishment has often taken place in many of the other artistic disciplines, it is a much more uncommon occurrence in the world of commercial filmmaking. However, it is not so uncommon in the world of the Independent Cinema that Mr. Schnabel inhabits and in many of the films that we have been studying as our Milestones...

THE POV:
I saw a screening of Mr. Schnabel's film at the renowned Saul Zaentz Film Center in Berkeley, CA and felt that both he and Mr. Kaminski had truly reinvented the grammar of film with their extraordinary collaboration on the cinematography

of this production. Much of this remarkable film takes place from the POV of Mr. Bauby's one good eye and that in itself is an amazing feat and one that literally forces the viewer to "walk a mile" in Mr. Bauby's shoes.

Detail after detail from the actual event of this tragedy, have been accurately utilized: The actual hospital, the actual nurse and the actual physical therapist. There has also been a lot of after the production, "she said/she said" chatter as to whether it was actually Mr. Bauby's wife or his mistress who was utterly loyal to Jean-Do during his hospitalization.

Let's not let any of that ego-driven, tabloid style, infighting, diminish the stunning visual and emotional achievements of this film. Only those who were there and who actually participated in Jean-Do's life will ever actually know the truth about that particular situation.

THE AWARDS:
The Diving Bell and The Butterfly, was nominated for four Academy Awards and more than thirty others, including The DGA and ASC Awards and Mr. Schnabel won the Cannes Festival for Best Director.

Despite being a script that is about a hugely depressing subject, the experience of the film is ultimately one of exhilaration and a newfound appreciation for the little things in life that we all so often take for granted.

ONLINE RESOURCES:
Use Google Images & Google Videos for dozens of links...

Buy it on Amazon, Google Play, or iTunes.

Trailer Video URL:
http://www.imdb.com/video/imdb/vi4122018073/

THINKING OUTSIDE THE BOX:
Class Exercises:

1. While the film is still fresh, each student should write an essay about their thoughts, feelings, likes, dislikes, pros and cons.

2. We used the term, "re-invented the language of cinema..." concerning what Mr. Schnabel and Mr. Kaminski contributed to the film. Each student should write an essay comparing and contrasting "normal" film language, with what was used for this unique and outstanding production.

3. Can you begin to imagine the difficulty of writing an entire book, through another person, "one letter at a time." Each student should attempt to write only the first sentence of their essay using a friend to assist them letter-by-letter. Then finish the essay and describe what the process of writing his book might have been for "Jean-Do."

4. Each student should use their own digital or HD camera to shoot a POV of an unknown character, who will only be revealed in the last shot of their scene.

5. Also each student should write an essay or a treatment describing the film that they might like to do utilizing this above mentioned character and style.

Chapter 48

2008
Slumdog Millionaire

Danny Boyle
HD Home Run: India

SPOILER ALERT!
Once again we meet the extraordinary team of the outstanding Director, Danny Boyle and his astounding DP, Anthony Dod Mantle. We first spotted Mr. Dod Mantle shooting with a small Sony Hi-8 home video camera for the Danish Dogma film, *The Celebration* and again when he teamed up with Mr. Boyle for the first time, using the Canon XL1 home video cameras to capture the frightening, *28 Days Later.*

On *Slumdog Millionaire,* they had the very difficult task of capturing a lot of Mumbai's slum and street life while having to maintain a very low profile. They decided on a light, portable, HD camera from Silicon Imaging, even though it was a prototype that was not quite ready for the rigors of India. Silicon Imaging did their best to overcome the technical difficulties that they knew would occur, by supplying the production with several technicians who were always on the set to deal with their camera's many glitches.

They also used 35mm film for certain scenes, especially for the TV studio portion of the film, but all of the street and slum scenes utilized the Silicon Imaging HD cameras. It's been reported that for capturing several scenes in the train station, the production even used a DSLR. This is the Digital HD version of a normal still photography camera and one of its best uses is, when you do not want to draw any attention to the fact that you are making a film.

THE CREATIVE TEAM:
Writer: Simon Beaufoy, Vikas Swarup
Director: Danny Boyle
Cinematographer: Anthony Dod Mantle
 Editor: Chris Dickens

WHY IS THIS FILM VISIONARY:
While the script of *Slumdog Millionaire* is basically a blending of the old-fashioned themes of a love story and a rags to riches story, however the script's

extraordinary element of taking the audience into the slums, streets and lives of the urchin children of Mumbai elevated this film into the winner's circle with audiences around the world.

Using their experience of utilizing home video to capture the "deserted London" sequences and then the entire production of *28 Days Later,* enabled Mr. Boyle and Mr. Dod Mantle to understand the necessity of using a small HD camera for the extraordinary slum and street scenes done in Mumbai.

They chose the prototype Silicon Imaging HD camera, because the body could be carried separately in a backpack while the capturing lens could fit in the palm of Mr. Dod Mantle's hand. What they were able to capture for the audience was an exhilarating peek through the lens of the HD camera as it followed the street children through the actual slums, streets, rivers, garbage dumps, markets, alleys, and rooftops, teeming with local color, poverty, traffic and littered with years of aging, trash, refuse and neglect. This was breathtaking, in-your-face filmmaking.

THE BASICS:
Danny Boyle nearly didn't make this film, because the title suggested a TV program that anyone could watch

every week, but after reading the script by the talented Simon Beaufoy he was hooked. Then they actually scouted Mumbai to see if the production was even going to be feasible there and discovered that when it came to crew, equipment and filmmaking savvy, Bollywood was actually better than Hollywood!

This enabled the production to be done very economically by not having to take a large English or European crew to India, which would have included paying for their airfares, hotel rooms and per diem. Instead they only took several key personnel and then utilized an entirely indigenous Indian cast, crew and technicians.

Mr. Boyle also discovered that India could not really be controlled, not in the manner that a Film Director wants and needs to control things. He knew that he would have to more or less "wing it," and "go with the flow" when it came to capturing all the scenes with the children and in the streets, alleys and slums of Mumbai.

THE PRODUCTION:
The film began shooting on November 5th 2007 and it was a production that seemed to be infused and surrounded by Destiny. In interviews Mr. Boyle has

said that the only way that many of the people in India can accept their life, amidst such massive poverty and with no possible way out, is to believe that it is simply their Destiny.

Destiny plays a large part in many Eastern philosophies as well as for many in the West who have taken the time to examine Eastern thought and wisdom. *Slumdog Millionaire* is finally about Destiny. Not the Destiny of simply accepting your lot and station in life, but of using your knowledge of the past to carve out a new Destiny and a new life and a new future for yourself.

Loveleen Tandan is listed as a Co-Director for India and I can tell you from my experience in that part of the world that this was probably a co-production requirement. I directed two martial arts films in Indonesia in the early 1990's and we used basically the same template *as Slumdog Millionaire.* We only brought the two lead actors and myself to Indonesia, all of the rest of the cast, crew and technicians were from Jakarta and I was also required to have an Indonesia co-director.

Of course these were very small, under a million dollar productions that were not easy to pull off with a semi-professional crew. When I first saw Danny

Boyle's amazing film I immediately recognized what they were doing and I applauded and respected all of their efforts and the fact that they were able to accomplish it with such tremendous style and professionalism.

Finally, *Slumdog Millionaire* is a new film in the new millennium made in one of the oldest of countries, India. It has new young stars that are still seeking the oldest of emotions, Love. It is a modern look at a very old story that is captured with the latest cutting edge technology, HD. Most importantly, in a time of uncertainty, corruption, greed, war, injustice and cynicism, it is about what the world needs most... Hope and Love!

THE AWARDS:
It won among many, The Directors Guild Award, The American Society of Cinematographers Award, The American Cinema Editors Award, The Screen Actors Guild Award, Cinema Writers Guild Award, National Society of Film Critics, National Board of Review, The New York Film Critics Circle, the London Critics Circle, Los Angeles Film Critics Association, MTV Movie Awards, on and on and on... Including Four Golden Globes and Eight Academy Awards including Best Picture, Best Directing, Best Cinematography, Best Editing, and Best Screenplay!

Right... "It is written!"

PS:
Anthony Dod Mantle and Slumdog Millionaire became the first Cinematographer and Film to be honored with a best Cinematography Academy Award for a production that was captured primarily on HD!

Welcome to the new millennium & Viva la Revolution!

ONLINE RESOURCES:
Use Google Images & Google Videos for dozens of links...

Buy it on Amazon, Google Play, or iTunes.

View the Trailer, Interviews & Scenes at:
www.youtube.com

THINKING OUTSIDE THE BOX:
Class Exercises:

1. Each student should write an essay about how they felt after viewing the film, what were their likes or dislikes, their pros and cons.

2. Each student should write an essay about the

advantages of doing an international feature film using this template: going on location, taking only a few key crew & cast and totally utilizing the indigenous talent where ever you happen to be.

3. Each student should write an essay about the disadvantages of doing an international feature using this template.

4. Each student should write an essay about the emotional cord that this film struck with audiences around the world and why.

5. Each student should attempt to make a small Digital film using a cast and crew who do not speak English and doing all of the work through a translator. Then you will begin to understand how very difficult that process was...

XVII. Microcosm & Macrocosm

Chapter 49:

2009
Paranormal Activity

Oren Peli
Right Film Right Place Right Time

SPOILER ALERT!
If you do not like films that cause you to scream, jump in your seat and grab at your date or significant other, films about unexplained or paranormal events, films about demonic possessions, or unseen and unnatural forces that create havoc in your home, then this may not be the film for you.

Like *The Blair Witch Project*, exactly ten years earlier, *Paranormal Activity* is an extremely small, handmade, no budget, no name, non-Hollywood, totally independent guerrilla film that literally held its audience by the throat and would not let go. They had to see it, they wanted to see it, they demanded to see it. That same audience managed to see this miniscule $15,000 production enough to bring its worldwide grosses to nearly $200,000,000 and like *The Blair Witch Project'* make it one of the most successful small films of all time.

THE CREATIVE TEAM:
Writer: Oren Peli
Director: Oren Peli
Cinematographer: Oren Peli
Editor: Oren Peli

WHY IS THIS FILM VISIONARY:
This film is extraordinary as well as being visionary simply because of Oren Peli's hutzpah! Read The Creative Team: Again! It is nearly unimaginable and certainly unequaled that someone with absolutely no filmmaking credentials or experience, none: Someone who had done a smattering of work in video gaming and post production, would have the brass balls to even attempt to do an entire feature film, shot on home video, with no budget, in less than ten days

with two unknown actors in his own house in San Diego!

Talk about being at the right place at the right time! Even before it reached the theaters, this miniscule homemade production won a Horror Film Festival and got Mr. Peli a contract with CAA, and his film eventually picked up by Paramount and DreamWorks, where it then sat in limbo...

THE BASICS:
Oren Peli, the singular driving force behind Paranormal Activity, was very influenced by *The Blair Witch Project* another very small film that was literally hand made by its cast and was one of the first to utilize home video cameras. What had impressed Mr. Peli most was the "first person" way the film had been captured, the non-scripted feeling of the scenes and the "found footage" aspects of the production, all of which seemed to heighten the sense of reality and believability.

Also, that the filmmakers had been ballsy and audacious enough to simply buy a video camera, hire some inexperienced actors and turn them loose to make the film. Mr. Peli eventually stopped one day, looked in the mirror and said to himself, "Hey, I can do that..." And so he did!

THE PRODUCTION:

It's been reported that Mr. Peli spent a year of his spare time getting his home ready for the production by painting the walls, laying down carpeting and adding a railing to the stairs. He then began his casting sessions by first putting an ad on Craig's List! Then he auditioned a couple of hundred people until he came up with the chemistry that he was looking for between the two unknowns, Katie Featherston and Micah Sloat.

Mr. Peli decided to shoot the production on home video not only to add the film's plausibility but to also eliminate the need for any kind of a professional production crew. The dialogue would be natural because there was no script the actor's were simply given an outline of what to cover in the scene and then asked to improvise.

In a final attempt to save both time and money Mr. Peli gave himself only seven days to complete the film. By imposing a seven-day shooting schedule he actually finished a day under the schedule that was reported for *The Blair Witch Project.*

The rest, as they like to say, is history. The film was screened at the Screemfest Horror Film Festival in

2007 where it won the Trophy and also impressed representatives at the Creative Artists Agency (CAA) enough to sign Mr. Peli to a contract. With CAA championing the project it was eventually purchased by DreamWorks and Paramount where it sat in limbo for a year, because the executives thought the film should be remade with a "name" cast. Mr. Peli agreed but with the stipulation that first there would be a "test screening" of the original film.

Mr. Peli was right and the test screening was huge hit and totally off the charts! With the success of the test screening and eventually with Mr. Spielberg's blessing, the film gained a huge fan base on the Internet and they began to "demand" to see the film.

Finally the Paramount executives got onboard and stated that if the film got 1,000,000 demands online at www.eventful.com it would have a nationwide release... Of course it did and the film sold out screening after screening eventually racking up domestic grosses of over $107,000,000 and worldwide of over $193,000,000!

THE AWARDS:
The film was nominated for the MTV Awards, The Independent Spirit Awards, The People's Choice Awards and Won the ScreamFest Festival Trophy.

ONLINE RESOURCES:
Use Google Images & Google Videos for dozens of links...

Buy it on Amazon, Google Play, or iTunes.

THINKING OUTSIDE THE BOX:
Class Exercises:

1. While the film is still fresh each student should write an essay about what worked best and what worked least, what they liked and did not like about the film and why.

2. Like other independent films that we have discussed, namely *Shadows* and *Sweet Sweetback's BaadAsss Song*, it may not be a great film; however, it is an important one that demonstrates the democratization of film production and provides a format for future productions. Each student should write an essay discussing why this film is important.

3. Each student should write an essay comparing and contrasting *Paranormal Activity* with both *Zero Day* and *The Blair Witch Project.*

4. A seven day shooting schedule, a ten to fifteen thousand dollar budget, a home video camera and two unknown actors, each student should write an essay about how they think that Oren Peli was able to get so much recognition out of so little production value.

5. The students should team up and make a short digital film in the style of Paranormal Activity.

Chapter 50:

2009
Avatar

James Cameron
The Global Game Changer

SPOILER ALERT!

2009 was an astounding year for the Cinema, from *Paranormal Activity* to *Avatar*, from the smallest of the small budgets to the largest of the large budgets, from a few simple special effects to wall-to-wall Imax, CGI's and 3D, from invisible demons in San Diego to the blue Na'vi on Pandora. To put it simply, we went from the microcosm to the macrocosm in films and film production and the bottom line is that the audience made them both hugely successful.

However they apparently enjoyed *Avatar* more... Everyone on the planet saw *Avatar*, many saw it several times and witnessed again and again the stunning and staggering other world of Pandora that James Cameron and his team of production specialists created. My wife and I along with our son visiting from college got up on December 25th 2009 and went to the first show presented in Imax 3D at the AMC theaters in Emeryville CA. When it was over we all sat there, dazzled and awestruck by what we had seen. Then my wife quietly asked if we could stay and see it again! Thanks to Mr. Cameron, we all had a very Merry Christmas.

THE CREATIVE TEAM:
Writer: James Cameron
Director: James Cameron
Cinematographer: Mauro Fiore
Editor: James Cameron, John Refoua, Steven Rivkin

WHY IS THIS FILM VISIONARY:
Because it was a global game changer, a film that took the gimmick of 3D and turned it overnight into an art form that made *Avatar* a must-see, cinematic experience. As well as being a mega blockbuster, it was also a film with a message and that message was that all living things are connected. Whether on Panadora or Planet Earth, all things have history, meaning and value and the films theme is that much of that value is being wasted or destroyed by over

ambitious militarism and our Corporation's outright greed. Bravo Mr. Cameron for telling it like it is!

THE BASICS:
Mr. Cameron conceived and wrote the original draft of the screenplay in the early 1995. He attempted to make the film happen at that time, but discovered that the technology was not really there and that the overall cost would have been in the $400 million dollar range, which no studio would approve. His Plan B was to make the film *Titanic*, which turned out to be the most successful film in history and sent Mr. Cameron on a decade long hiatus locating the wreck of the Titanic as well as developing a deep sea diving apparatus, outfitted with 3D camera systems.

By 2005, after seeing THE LORD OF THE RINGS films, especially the character of Gollum, Mr. Cameron realized that the technology had advanced to the point where he felt, that by pushing it, he could achieve his vision of *Avatar* and Pandora. He dug through his files and dusted off the script that he had written over ten years prior and decided to bring it to the big screen in 3D.

THE PRODUCTION:
By 2007 the production began capturing the performances and other world CGI special effects that

would astound audiences all over the planet. Everyone on this groundbreaking film realized that they were going beyond where the technology was, that the production was going to push it out beyond the limit and into the unknown, the uncharted territory that Mr. Cameron seems quite at home with.

Since he was dealing with creating an entire world, Mr. Cameron enlisted a team of world-renowned artists to visualize, construct and capture the vast array of plant and animal life as well as a host of space age military hard and software that were all conceived and realized down to their smallest detail. A linguist was also brought onboard to develop the language of the Na'vi, which contained over 1000 words.

Much of the production technology was being created and used for the very first time: Mr. Cameron had a viewing screen that he could watch as the actors were performing against a green screen, that would show him the actual CGI backgrounds and virtual locations that would be added later in post production. In this way he was better able to see how the performances would play and fit into their various environments.

Yet despite all of this film's advanced technology, staggering size, eye popping CGI's and jaw dropping

3D images, the most important and eloquent element in the film is the 100% capture of the actor's performances and the molding of those performances into fully realized CGI characters. First, the actor's bodies were motion captured so that a skeleton based on them would be at the core of the CGI characters that were going to be created.

Most importantly, a special helmet was constructed with a small camera attached in order to capture every minute detail, all of the varied emotions of each actor's performance. Mr. Cameron's overriding concern with getting the emotions right as well as the technology, is what ultimately sets this epic, 3D, blockbuster, worldwide-event-film, apart from all of the rest.

To help understand exactly how very much time and effort went into this production, it has been estimated that for the CGI effects alone, it took over 47 man-hours to complete <u>each and every frame of film</u>!

THE AWARDS:
Avatar was nominated for nine Academy Awards and won three, for Best Cinematography, Best Special Effects and Best Art Direction. As well as a host of other awards including the Golden Globe Awards for Best Director and Best Motion Picture Drama. It also

became the most successful film of all time and the only film to ever make over 2 billion dollars. And yes, it has been reported that not only a sequel, but a trilogy are already in the planning stages.

Trust me, I'll be the first in line…

ONLINE RESOURCES:
Use Google Images or Google Videos for dozens of links…

Buy it on Amazon, Google Play, or iTunes.

THINKING OUTSIDE THE BOX:
Class Exercises:

1. While the film is still fresh, each student should write an essay about what they liked most and what they liked least about the film, what worked for them and what did not?

2. After seeing the film in 3D on the big screen, view it again normally then compare and contrast the two screenings; which did you like best and why?

3. Mr. Cameron has stated, "…on Pandora or the planet Earth, all living things are connected…" Each student should write an essay describing what he

meant by this and how should it affect our lives on this planet.

4. This section of the book is called "Microcosm and Macrocosm." In keeping with that theme, each student should write an essay comparing and contrasting *Paranormal Activity & Avatar.*

5. Since Mr. Cameron has described the technology of Avatar as being only the "first step" each student should write an essay describing where they imagine filmmaking technology is going and what is going to be possible for filmmakers to accomplish in the future.

XVIII. Epilogue...

SUMMING UP & The Times They Are A-Changin'

Film is an amazing, beautiful and wonderful medium and many of our Milestones In Cinema were captured on film and utilized the photochemical process. In fact, every significant film in history, up to and including much of the 1990's was captured on Film and we need to remember its importance as we move forward.

Today, our new methods of capture and delivery should not come down to arguments of Film versus HD. In fact when comparing the quality of Film to the quality of HD if the HD has been captured 4:4:4, or with 4K or 8K quality and a 14 or 15 stop dynamic range, then Film is going to be left far behind.

Several years ago I attended a RED Camera seminar and we viewed a 4K projection on a 40-foot screen of a scene captured by David Fincher on the RED's new Mysterium X Sensor at ASA 2000. It was Leonardo DiCaprio on a totally dark set lighting his cigar and key lighting himself, with his own match!

A recent Sony A7s could achieve a staggering ASA or

ISO or over 400,000! And the professional Cannon C300 & C500 that were introduced to the film community several years ago by no less a Filmmaker than Martin Scorsese, could capture at ASA 10,000 & ASA 20,000 right out of the box!

The difference between Film and HD simply comes down to one word "Progress".

 There is nothing wrong with film, except for the fact that Progress, in the new millennium, has taken us and will continue to take us far beyond its capabilities. Progress has rendered Film and the photochemical process obsolete.

Remember electric typewriters? Where are they now? Right, either in storage or nonexistent simply because everyone is using Microsoft Word or something similar. Unfortunately, the medium of Film has become the electric typewriter of this century. Sorry for the "duh" but it's simply time get over it and move on.

When you have Directors as different in age, tone, style and sensibility as the late Maestro, Sidney Lumet and Troublemaker Studios own Robert Rodriguez both telling you that, "Film Is Dead trust me, you need to listen, and guess what - They're right! Get over it, climb aboard the New Paradigm Express or it will run you over and leave you in its wake.

I also believe that today's audience no longer really cares how their entertainment is captured or delivered they only care about one thing: Whether or not it's compelling and there for them whenever and wherever they want it. We live in a time when anyone can sit at home with their remote, flip between the hundreds of cable channels and view: The letter-box version of Lawrence of Arabia, A "Best of the Best Barbeque" cooking show, American Idol, The latest disaster on CNN, The Olympics from Anywhere on the Planet, The World Series, The Super Bowl, European Soccer, Mixed Martial Arts, The Worlds Wildest Police Videos or HBO, Cinemax or dozens of other Films, TV Series and entertainments. Not to mention the endless Websites, Movies, Web Series or Webcams offered on the Internet and the next step is home 3-D or something we cannot even imagine.

As I mentioned, in the chapter about Collateral, I was thrilled when I saw the available light HD shots of Jamie Foxx running 180 degrees down the deserted streets of Downtown Los Angeles at 3 am. And I immediately asked myself: How are these HD image any different from the ones that could be captured by young filmmakers with their own HD cameras shooting on the streets of Seattle, or Stockholm or Singapore or Saigon, or Shanghai? The answer is, that there would be no difference. The quality of their HD would be exactly the same. Making movies has become totally democratized!

The Language of Cinema has been evolving ever since the days of D.W. Griffith in the early 1900's and it is still evolving today in our new millennium. The main difference now, is that during a large part of the last century, becoming a filmmaker was an extremely exclusive and expensive undertaking, that only a very small percentage of the world's population could ever hope or dream of accomplishing.

That is no longer the case. Nearly anyone who desires to put in the time and effort can access information on the Internet, buy DVD's to study or simply rent them on Netflix, rent or purchase a HD camera and a non-linear editing system like Final Cut Pro and produce a small film like *Zero Day* or *Paranormal Activity*. It is no longer the impossible dream, which was proven by the Sundance Film Festival winner in 2015 *Tangerine* that was totally captured on two iPhone5's!

New techniques of capture and new high concept

genre sub-categories are being created every day. Not only in the offices and sound stages of the big studios, but also in the basements, garages and back yards of the world. Perhaps the vast majority of those creations will be mindless drivel. However, there are bound to be a handful that will cause a stir, rise to the top of the Cinematic World and impact us all.

As we look forward toward the horizon, we need to keep our minds and our hearts open, as these ever-evolving new paradigms, new technologies and new techniques of storytelling, capture and distribution continue to emerge.

I like to point out to my film students that it took Motion Picture Film nearly 100 years to develop a sensitivity to light from ASA 5 to ASA 800: from the early 1900's through the 1990's. Yet in only the first 15 years of this century the sensitivity of HD Camera Sensors in DSLRs like the Sony A7s has gone from ISO 1000 to over ISO 400,000! And the latest surveillance camera from Canon can shoot by starlight at ISO 4,000,000!

We all need to pause and take a deep breath, then smile, move on from the technology of the last century and embrace the future. It is evolving exponentially and we each need to be prepared for the unimaginable technological and paradigm changes that are going to transpire during the rest of this century. Remember it is only 2016, exactly 100 years ago D.W. Griffith released *Intolerance.*

I trust that many of you will take what you have discovered from these visionary films and filmmakers and will now "stand on their shoulders," and expand the Language of Cinema with your own films. If you do I will be more than happy to include your work in any future versions of MILESTONES IN CINEMA... Perhaps I will need to expand it to 100 Visionary Films & Filmmakers.

In the words of the legendary Mr. Dylan... "The Times They Are A Changin'..." It was true then, back in the day and it is still true now...

View & Listen:
http://www.youtube.com/watch?v=ItPz7f-k-dE

Appendix:
Acknowledgements, Bibliography & Suggested Reading:

Among others:
www.imdb.com/
www.Bing.com/
www.google.com/
www.filmreference.com/
www.youtube.com/
Amazon Prime, Google Play, or on iTunes/

Intolerance:
Gish, Lillian: The Movies, Mr. Griffith, and Me: New York, 1969.

Griffith, D. W.: The Man Who Invented Hollywood: The Autobiography, edited by James Hart: Louisville, Kentucky, 1972.

Stern, Seymour: "D. W. Griffith's Intolerance: A Sun-Play of the Ages,": in The Essential Cinema: New York, 1975.

The Battleship Potemkin:
Leyda, Jay: "On Potemkin," in Kino: A History of the Russian and Soviet Film: London, 1960.

Leyda, Jay, and Zina Vignow: Eisenstein at Work: New York, 1982.

Mayer, David: Eisenstein's "Potemkin,": New York, 1972.

Napoleon:
Brownlow, Kevin: Napoléon: Abel Gance's Classic Film: London, 1983.

Kaplan, Nelly: Napoléon: London, 1994.

The Grapes of Wrath:
Bogdanovich, Peter: John Ford: Berkeley, 1968; revised edition, 1978.

Ford, Dan: Pappy: The Life of John Ford: Englewood Cliffs, New Jersey, 1979.

French, Warren,: Film guide to "The Grapes of Wrath,": Bloomington, Indiana, 1973.

Fantasia:
Culhane, John: Fantasia: Abrams, Harry N. Inc: 1999

Culhane, John, Disney, Roy: Fantasia 2000: Visions of Hope: Disney Editions, New York, 2000

IMDb: Fantasia (1940)

Citizen Kane:
Bogdanovich, Peter, and Orson Welles: This Is Orson Welles: New York, 1972.

Cowie, Peter: The Citizen Kane Book: Boston, 1971.

Tolan, Gregg: "Realism for Citizen Kane," in American Cinematographer: (Los Angeles), February, 1941.

The Bicycle Thief:
Armes, Roy,:Patterns of Realism: A Study of Italian Neo-Realist Cinema: New York, 1971.

Samuels, Charles Thomas: Encountering Directors: New York, 1972.

Rashomon:
Tyler, Parker: The Three Faces of Film: New York, 1960.

Richie, Donald: The Films of Akira Kurosawa: Los Angeles, 1965; revised edition, with Joan Mellen: Berkeley, 1984, 1996.

Hiroshima Mon Amour:

Armes, Roy: The Cinema of Alain Resnais: London, 1968.

Cowie, Peter: Antonioni, Bergman, Resnais: London, 1963.

MacDonald, Dwight: On Movies: Englewood Cliffs, New Jersey, 1969.

Shadows:
Alexander, Georg, and others: John Cassavetes: Munich, 1983.

Carney, Raymond: American Dreaming: The Films of John Cassavetes and the American Experience: Berkeley, 1985.

Gavron, Laurence, and Denis Lenoir: John Cassavetes: Paris, 1986.

IMDb: Shadows (1959)

Breathless:
Dixon, Wheeler W: The Films of Jean-Luc Godard: Albany, 1997.

Godard, Jean-Luc: Godard on Godard: Critical Writings, edited by Jean Narboni and Tom Milne: New

York, 1986.

Sterritt, David: Jean-Luc Godard; Interviews: Jackson, 1998.

Psycho:
Leigh, Janet: Psycho: Behind the Scenes of the Classic Thriller: New York, 1995.

Rebello, Stephen: Alfred Hitchcock and the Making of Psycho: New York, 1990, 1998.

Spoto, Donald: The Life of Alfred Hitchcock: The Dark Side of Genius: New York, 1982, London, 1983.

8 1/2:
Affron, Charles, Editor: 8 ½ Federico Fellini Director: Rutgers University Press, 1963

Miller, D.A: Film Classics 8 ½: Palgrave Macmillian, 2008

IMDb: 8½ (1963)

Dr. Strangelove or, How I Learned To Stop Worrying & Love The Bomb:
Kagan, Norman: The Cinema of Stanley Kubrick: New York, 1972.

Kubrick, Stanley: "How I Learned to Stop Worrying and Love the Cinema," in Films and Filming: (London), June 1963.

Walker, Alexander: Stanley Kubrick Directs: New York, 1972.

A Hard Days Night
Burke, John: The Beatles In A Hard Day's Night: Dell: Mass Market Paperback, 1964

IMDb: A Hard Day's Night (1964)

The War Game:
Watkins, Peter: The War Game: Avon Books, New York, 1967

IMDb: The War Game (1965)

Persona:
Bjorkman, Stig, and Torsten Maans, and Jonas Sima: Bergman on Bergman: Interviews with Ingmar Bergman: Cambridge, 1993.

Cohen, James: Through a Lens Darkly: New York, 1991.

Michaels, Lloyd, Editor: Ingmar Bergman's Persona: Cambridge, 1999.

The Battle Of Algiers:
Celli, Carlo: Gillo Pontecorvo: From Resistance To Terrorism: Scarecrow Press, 2005

Kauffman, Michael T: What Does The Pentagon See In Battle Of Algiers: New York Times, September 7, 2003

IMDb: The Battle of Algiers (1966)

2001, A Space Odyssey:
Geduld, Carolyn: Filmguide to 2001: A Space Odyssey: Bloomington, Indiana, 1973.

Phillips, Gene D: Stanley Kubrick: A Film Odyssey: New York, 1975.

Sweet Sweetback's Baadasssss Song:
Van Peebles, Melvin: The Making of Sweet Sweetback's Baadasssss Song... Collector's Edition: Neo Press, 1972

IMDb: Sweet Sweetback's Baadasssss Song (1971)

The Devils:
Crouse, Richard: Raising Hell: Ken Russell and the

Unmaking of the Devils: ECW Press, 2012

IMDb: The Devils (1971)

A Clockwork Orange:
LoBrutto, Vincen:, Stanley Kubrick: A Biography: New York, 1997.

Raphael, Frederic, Eyes Wide Open: A Memoir of Stanley Kubrick: New York, 1999.

Walker, Alexander: Stanley Kubrick: Director: New York, 1999.

The Conversation:
Murphy, Sean: Coppola's The Conversation, A Love Letter To The Process Of Making Art: POPMATTERS, September 7, 2011

Shorard, Catherine: My Favorite Cannes Winner: The Conversation: The Guardian, 2015

IMDb: The Conversation (1974)

Swept Away...
Ebert, Roger: Swept Away By An Unusual Destiny In The Blue Sea Of August: RogerEbert.com, February 20, 1976

IMDb: Swept Away (1974

And Now My Love:
Weiler, A.H: Toute un vie (And Now My Love): New York Times, 1974

And Now My Love, 1974: IMDb:

And Now My Love at Allmovie

Barry Lyndon:
Ciment, Michel. "Kubrick on Barry Lyndon". http://www.visual-memory.co.uk/amk/doc/interview.bl.html. Retrieved on 2007-05-31.

Robey, Tim, "Kubrick's Neglected Masterpiece in Telegraph Review (Saturday January 31, 2009)

Network:
Itzkoff, Dave: Mad As Hell, The Making Of Network...: Harry Holt & Co. LLC, New York, 2014

Parker, James: Madder Than Hell: How Network Anticipated Contemporary Media: The Atlantic, March, 2014

Stardust Memories:
Alan, Woody: Four Films of Woody Alan: Faber & Faber Ltd. 1983

IMDb: Stardust Memories (1980)

Raging Bull:
Allstar, Rex: 30 Knockout Raging Bull Facts: ShortList, 2014

Schickel, Richard: Brutal Attraction: The Making Of Raging Bull: Vanity Fair VFNEWS, February 22, 2010

IMDb: Raging Bull (1980)

Chariots of Fire:
IMDb: Chariots of Fire (1981)

Weatherby, William J: Chariots Of Fire: Harper Collins Publishers, 1983

JFK:
Crowdus, Gary: "History, Dramatic License, and Larger Historical Truths: An Interview with Oliver Stone," in Cineaste: (New York), vol. 22, no. 4, 1997.

Sharrett, Christophet: "Conspiracy Theory and Political Murder in America: Oliver Stone's JFK and the Facts of the Matter,": in Jon Lewis, editor: The New American Cinema: Durham, North Carolina, 1998.

El Mariachi:
Rodriguez, Robert: Rebel Without A Crew: Plume, Published by the Penguin Group, 1996

IMDb: El Mariachi (1981

In The Company Of Men:
Tobias, Scott: In The Company Of Men: The New Cult Cannon, November 12, 2009

IMDb: In The Company of Men (1997)

The Celebration:
Thomson C: Thomas Vinterbergs Festen (The Celebration): Nordic Film Classics Paperback, October 14, 2013

Thomson, Claire C: Thomas Vinterbergs Festen: University of Washington Press, 2015

IMDb: The Celebration (1998)

Schindler's List:
Nunez, Christian: Schindler's List: Movie Comarisons:

Thejewishhero.weebly.com, 2005

Raven, Greg: Schindler's List, A Review: The Journal Of Historical Review, May-June, 1994

IMDb: Schindler's List (1993)

Saving Private Ryan:
Spielberg, Steven, James, David: Saving Private Ryan: The Men, The Mission, The Move: Newmarket Press, 1999

IMDb: Saving Private Ryan (1998)

The Blair Witch Project:
Ascher-Walsh, Rebecca: "Rhymes with Rich," in Entertainment Weekly (New York), vol. 1, no. 496, 30 July 1999.

Travers, Peter: "The Blair Witch Project," in Rolling Stone (New York), no. 818, 5 August 1999.

Timecode:
Ebert, Roger: Timecode: Roger Ebert.com, April 28, 2000

IMDB: Timecode, 2000

28 Days Later:
28 Days Later: AMC.com, 2002

IMDb: 28 Days Later, 2002

Nelson, Michael Alan: 28 Days Later Omnibus: BOOM Studios, 2014

Zero Day
Mitchell, Elvis: Zero Day: Disaffected Teenagers And Looming Clamity: New York Times, September 3, 2003

IMDb: Zero Day (2003)

Chicago:
IMDB: Chicago,

Marshall, Rob, Richards, Martin, Condon, Bill: Chicago The Movie & Lyrics: Newmarket Press, 2003

The Bourne Supremacy:
Hollis, Kim: Book vs. Movie: The Bourne Supremacy: Box Office Prophets, 2006

IMDb: The Bourne Supremacy (2004)

Collateral:
Le0pard13: Mann's Nights Of Fates Intertwined: If It Rains... You Get Wet: February 20, 2012

IMDb: Collateral (2004)

King Kong:
Sidney, Brian: Peter Jackson: A Filmmakers Journey: Harper Collins, UK: November 1, 2006

Wake, Jenny: The Making of King Kong: Pocket. Paperback: December 3, 2005

IMDb: King Kong (2005)

Grizzly Man:
Jans, Nick: The Grizzly Maze: Timothy Treadwell's Fatal Obsession With The Alaskan Bears: Plume, January 31, 2006

IMDb: Grizzly Man (2005)

Once:
Cathy, 756 Books Blog: Once The Little Irish Film That Could: March 5, 2006

IMDb: Once (2006)

The Diving Bell & The Butterfly:
Bradshaw, Peter: The Diving Bell & The Butterfly: The Guardian, February 8, 2008

Ebert, Roger: The Diving Bell & The Butterfly: Roger Ebert.com: December 20, 2007

IMDb: The Diving Bell & The Butterfly (2007)

Slumdog Millionaire:
Ebert, Roger: Slumdog Millionaire: Roger Ebert.com: November 11, 2008

Hughes, Eric: Book vs. Movie: Slumdog Millionaire: Box Office Prophets: January 5, 2009

IMDb: Slumdog Millionaire (2008)

Paranormal Activity:
Nemiroff, Perry: Paranormal Activity: CinemaBlend: September 25, 2009

IMDb: Paranormal Activity (2007 – 2009)

Avatar:
Jessar, Jody Duncan, Fitzpatrick, Lisa: The Making Of Avatar: Harry N. Abrams, October 1, 2010

Pitesa, Nicole: James Cameron's Avatar: The Na'vi
Quest: Festival, November 4, 2009

IMDb: Avatar (2009)

Special Thanks To:

The host of Visionary Filmmakers from the last century to the present who have inspired this work and instilled in me the passion for films, filmmakers, and the entire filmmaking process.

Leslie Otis: My Long time filmmaking colleague and 1st Assistant Cameraman who has an amazing sense of humor, and as I have discovered, is also an outstanding English scholar and proofreader.

Dr. Arnold Chanin: My personal physician as well as exceptional writer and poet, who has always given me his advice and encouragement. I am honored to have his kind assistance in proofing this book.

David Paul Wertheimer II: My son and computer maven whose maturity is well beyond his years, and whose knowledge and insight have been invaluable in proofing my MA projects as well as this book.

About The Author:

David Worth has a resume of over forty feature films as a Director of Photography and Director and has worked with talents like Clint Eastwood, Jean-Claude Van Damme, Shelly Winters, Roy Scheider, Dennis Hopper, Sondra Locke and Bruce Campbell. He has taught filmmaking at Chapman University, USC, Chapman Singapore, UCLA and he is currently an adjunct film professor at The Academy of Art University in San Francisco. His textbooks including: *The Citizen Kane Crash Course In Cinematography...* And: *ZEN & The Art Of Independent Filmmaking...* are available at: www.amazon.com
Website: www.davidworthfilm.com